Innovative Methods of Teaching and Learning Chemistry in Higher Education

Edited by

Ingo Eilks
University of Bremen, Germany

and

Bill Byers
University of Ulster, United Kingdom

RSCPublishing

Table of Contents

Preface

ANTHONY K. SMITH
Lyon School of Chemistry, Physics and Electronics (CPE) Lyon, France and Co-ordinator of the European Chemistry Thematic Network (ECTN)

This book has been produced as part of the work carried out by the *European Chemistry Thematic Network* (ECTN). This is a network of over 150 institutions, mainly university chemistry departments but also some National Chemical Societies, from all Member States of the European Union, Norway, Iceland, Switzerland, and Turkey. There are also associate members from countries outside Europe.

The ECTN was founded in 1996 and is funded by the European Commission as part of the Erasmus programme. It is one of the 40 or so thematic networks established under this programme. They provide a forum for the analysis and study of the state of development of education and training in Europe in order to encourage and improve its quality on a European level. Their philosophy has always been to emphasise the teaching dimension of university activity. The two major tasks of the thematic networks have been: (i) The mapping, enhancing and disseminating of good practice in higher education throughout Europe, and (ii) facilitating European co-operation.

The first task has involved a number of activities such as:

· Describing, analysing and comparing existing teaching methods.
· Defining and experimenting with new teaching methods.
· Identifying existing teaching material and placing this at the disposal of the members of the network with the aid of databases.
· Producing or updating, translating and disseminating new teaching material.
· Activities in the field of quality assurance.

An Association, the ECTN Association, was established in 2003, as one of the outcomes of the first 7 years of activity of the ECTN.

In June 2004, the ECTN Association was admitted as the sixth partner in the *Alliance for Chemical Sciences and Technologies in Europe* (AllChemE), thus joining the *European Association for Chemical and Molecular Sciences* (EUCheMS), the *European Chemical Industry Council* (CEFIC), the *European Federation of Chemical Engineering* (EFCE), *European Cooperation in the field of Scientific and Technical Research: Technical Committee on Chemistry* (COST Chemistry), and the *Chairmen of the European Research Councils Chemistry Committees* (CERC3). This

I. Eilks and B. Byers (Eds.). Innovative Methods in Teaching and Learning Chemistry in Higher Education, pp. 1-4. © 2009 RSC Publishing

alliance provides a wide representation of chemistry and chemical engineering in Europe.

The ECTN has created numerous expert European groups working on a range of topics and producing reports with a real European dimension. In particular we can mention the work carried out on the Eurobachelor and Euromaster frameworks and the associated quality labels, and the internet-based tests in chemistry: *EChemTest*. Reports relating to the teaching of chemistry have been produced on such topics as: Developing Independent Learners; Postgraduate Education and Training; Chemistry Education using Multimedia; and Teaching and Learning: Practical Skills. These reports are available on the network website at www.ectn.net.

The many and varied activities of the *European Chemistry Thematic Network* (ECTN) and the *ECTN Association* are aimed at providing Europe with more and better trained chemists, and at meeting the challenges facing higher education institutions in the implementation of the Bologna process.

The current project, *ECTN4: Chemistry in the European Higher Education Area*, has been running from October 2006 and ends in September 2009. This latest project has brought together all actors in the chemistry sector to enhance the employability of graduate chemists; to enhance the professional/generic skills of doctoral level students; to identify best practices in the creation of study programmes combining chemistry and chemical technology; to create an internet-based test in biological chemistry; to enhance the public image of chemistry; to enhance the value of previous European projects involving chemistry; and to report on and evaluate innovative teaching methods. It is this last topic that has led to the production of this book. The next few paragraphs outline the reasons and the procedures adopted for this book.

The past decade has seen considerable expansion in Higher Education as we move from the elitist approach of the past towards the mass higher education system that will be needed to support the knowledge-based economy envisaged by the 'Lisbon Agenda'. Expansion has not however been accompanied by a similar increase in resources and it is becoming increasingly clear that traditional approaches to teaching are no longer appropriate to this new situation. At its plenary meeting in Vienna in April 2006 the ECTN therefore decided to form a new working group dedicated to "Innovative Methods in University Chemistry Teaching". The new working group received widespread support from the assembly; it was agreed that Ingo Eilks (University of Bremen, Germany) and Bill Byers (University of Ulster, United Kingdom) would act jointly as the working group leaders.

The aim of the working group was to survey good practice involving innovative teaching methods in university chemistry education at all levels across the EU. This includes many of the previous initiatives introduced by ECTN working groups and is therefore a logical extension of much of the on-going work of the network. It was decided that the working group should aim to produce a viable and tangible end-product and it was agreed that the production of a book to be printed and widely disseminated with ECTN support should form a major objective for the working group.

The group leaders met in Bremen, Germany, in December 2006 to agree on the best way forward. It was decided that the book should contain a number of chapters, each chapter dealing with a separate field of innovation for chemistry teaching and learning. Each chapter includes ideas, approaches and a pedagogical justification along with a review of the relevant literature and examples and experiences from within ECTN and beyond. Each chapter has been coordinated and edited by two or three members of the working group who have also acted as sub-group leaders. Consultants from within ECTN were asked to review each chapter.

An open meeting of the working group was held at the ECTN Plenary meeting in San Sebastian, Spain, in April 2007. This was very well attended and the meeting divided into sub-groups to consider and discuss each of the proposed chapters. Two to three members of each sub-group were identified as prospective chapter coordinators.

Work on organizing the chapters started following the San Sebastian, Spain, meeting, a further group meeting was held in Helsinki, Finland, in May 2008 and the writing of chapters continued throughout the year. A final meeting of the chapter coordinators was held during the 2009 ECTN Plenary Meeting in Poznan, Poland, to enable final arrangements for formatting and printing to be agreed.

The whole project would not have been possible without the support of the Erasmus-Socrates programme of the European Commission for which we are extremely grateful.

The book is published with financial support from the Societa Chimica Italiana. We are very grateful and thank the SCI for this support.

As the coordinator of the ECTN, I wish to express my thanks to all the contributors to this volume, and especially to the editors Ingo Eilks and Bill Byers. A special thank also goes to Rita Fofana (University of Bremen, Germany) who produced the format and layout of the book and the University of Bremen, Germany, which supported the process by providing financial support for these issues.

Education and Culture

Socrates

 Universität Bremen

I believe that this book, involving a truly European approach, will make a significant contribution to improving the teaching and learning of chemistry in higher education and thus to the quality of chemistry graduates throughout Europe.

4

The Need for Innovations in Higher Level Chemistry Education – A Pedagogical Justification

BILL BYERS
University of Ulster, United Kingdom

INGO EILKS
University of Bremen, Germany

Higher Education is currently experiencing a period of unprecedented change. In Europe the Bologna Process is necessitating changes to the duration and structure of many courses while the Lisbon Agenda, which seeks to develop a Knowledge-Based European Economy, is identifying the need for many more graduates in key areas including chemistry. It is clear that the traditional teaching methods will be inadequate and inappropriate to support the mass higher education system that is now emerging. This book has been written as a guide for all lecturers interested in developing their chemistry teaching in order to promote more effective student learning at Universities and other higher education institutions. This first chapter introduces readers to important aspects of modern learning theory, and from this starting point goes on to provide a pedagogical justification for the need for new and innovative methods to be applied in higher level chemistry education with the aim of promoting the meaningful learning required to educate future generations of chemistry graduates. The chapter therefore aims to motivate readers to develop their own teaching using pedagogically sound strategies.

Introduction

> *"Most people tire of a lecture in ten minutes; clever people can do it in five. Sensible people never go to lectures at all."*
> *Stephen Leacock: Discovery of England (1922)*

To teach well, it is surely necessary for a teacher to possess not only a good knowledge of the subject to be taught (*the what*), in our case chemistry, but also a well-developed understanding of how people learn (*the how*). This

---

Chapter consultants: Paul C. Yates, Keele University, United Kingdom, and Silvija Markic, University of Bremen, Germany

I. Eilks and B. Byers (Eds.). Innovative Methods in Teaching and Learning Chemistry in Higher Education, pp. 5-22. © 2009 RSC Publishing.

has long been appreciated in primary and secondary education where qualifications in both a discipline and pedagogy are considered as prerequisites even to apply for a job as a teacher (Eurydice, 2006).

University chemistry departments however, have traditionally adopted a very different approach. The selection of candidates for employment as lecturers has largely been determined by subject specific knowledge and skills and especially their achievements and potential in doing chemistry research (e.g. measured by the number of research papers, impact factors, or research grants) with little emphasis being placed on teaching skills as such. In fact until relatively recently virtually no university chemistry lecturer had even attended formal tuition on pedagogy or domain-specific didactics, an approach that could surely only be justified by the mistaken belief that anyone who knows a subject well enough themselves will be able to teach it well to others (Shulman, 1986).

Although universities have now, somewhat belatedly, started to realize that lecturers need to be trained on how to teach effectively (i.e. in domain specific aspects of pedagogy), training, where provided, tends to be offered only after employment as a teacher has commenced, and often appears to be regarded as a chore, or at best a distraction, by new lecturers under increasing pressure to rapidly develop creditable research profiles.

This introductory chapter seeks to provide university chemistry lecturers, the targeted audience for the book, with an overview of recent developments in educational theory that might help them to appreciate how general and domain-specific aspects of educational theory can help them to promote more effective student learning. We hope to motivate readers to think about how their students learn and thus how best to select and develop their teaching approaches, possibly along quite different lines to those they have been used to, so as to increase the effectiveness of their teaching.

And in the beginning was the lecture

The tradition of 'lecturing' derives from medieval times and dates back to the founding of Europe's earliest universities. The German word for lecture, 'Vorlesung', conveys these roots in its original meaning, the reading of a book in front of others. Tuition of course was not arranged in this way on pedagogical grounds but as a practical concession to the need for distributing information. At this time books were both rare and expensive, so many students were unable to obtain their own books. Rather students were asked to copy essential information from the books by listening to the reader and writing down the information given word for word.

Times have fortunately changed; books are now readily available at reasonable prices. All students, in Europe at least, should now be able to afford a small collection of their own books, be able to borrow copies of key texts from university or public libraries and be able to copy and paste a wealth of relevant information of more or less good quality from the Internet. Photocopying machines are available everywhere and the arrival of the internet and the digital age has meant that information is now both plentiful and readily available to those who know where to look for it. Today therefore, there should no longer be any need to make copies of books by listening and writing.

Nevertheless, even today, lecturing in its traditional form remains a major component of the vast majority of university chemistry teaching programmes and at its worst still amounts to little more than a lecturer reading a prepared transcript to the students. This does not necessarily mean that we should immediately drop all lectures from our programmes, but, rather that we need to start to rethink their role, structure, and methods of delivery.

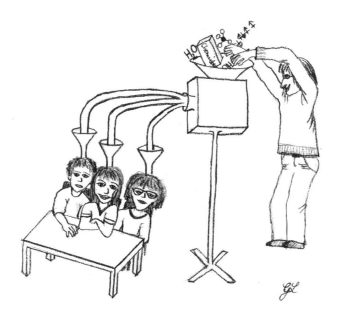

Figure 1. The 'Nuremberg Funnel' - An illustration of the belief that learning is simply transmissive.

The approach that dominated university chemistry teaching throughout the twentieth century involved little more than a simple process of information transfer or as we might call it the 'Passive Diffusion Model of Knowledge Transfer'. This was a teacher-centred paradigm that involved the lecturer showering knowledge over the students and all they were required to do was to absorb it (Figure 1). It is of course this teacher-centred approach that many of us bring into teaching with us, believing that we have knowledge to impart and that the better we teach the better our students will learn. Deficiencies in this approach are now, somewhat belatedly, being widely recognized and include the fact that we are not always able to explain everything fully or even comprehensibly to others, while our students in turn may often fail to listen and follow with sufficient care and attention, or even on occasion, lack the necessary cognitive ability or previous knowledge to permit the desired interpretation of newly acquired information to occur. The underlying problem however is surely that learning is much more complex than merely listening, memorizing and repeating words. It has been recognized for some time that most information obtained simply by listening is forgotten very quickly, with only a small percentage even reaching the long term memory (e.g. Peterson & Peterson, 1959).

Thus, unfortunately all too often, when we start to mark examination scripts we quickly discover that what we thought we had taught, and what our students had actually learned, are frequently very different. So of course we try to teach better; looking for that little bit of magic that will enable our knowledge to be transferred over to our students. Unfortunately, much though we might wish it otherwise, knowledge cannot be transferred intact from the mind of one person to the mind of another (Bodner, 1986). Information may be transferred but meaning and understanding can only be constructed in the mind of each individual learner (e. g. Wittrock, 1989) in line with the central idea of constructivist learning theory (e.g. Bodner, 1986; Taber, 2000; Coll & Taylor, 2001; Bailley & Garratt, 2002). We suggest an analogy with human digestion where, even for a cannibal, ingested proteins are not directly incorporated into body structures. They must first be broken down into their constituent amino acids which can then be reassembled into useful biomolecules within the body. Similarly, meaningful learning requires the integration of incoming information with knowledge already possessed by an individual. The subsequent interpretation placed on this new information will then depend heavily on what the learner already knows (Johnstone, 1997). What we often find, of course, is that the better we teach the better our students rate our teaching but not, alas, the better they learn. Clearly there is a need, not merely to teach better, but also to teach differently. This dichotomy of teaching and learning might well explain the different perceptions many chemistry lecturers have concerning the success of teaching and learning. An informal survey of chemistry lecturers at a number of education conferences suggested that while a significant majority of lecturers believed that university chemistry teaching had improved significantly over the past fifteen to twenty years, very few appeared to think that students' learning of chemistry had improved over this period. This of course should not surprise us as George Bodner told us, over twenty years ago that *'Teaching and learning are not synonymous; it is possible to teach and to teach well without having the students learn'* (Bodner, 1986, p. 873).

It should however concern us, as student learning will clearly depend to a large extent on the tuition received, although the relationship is far from being a simple one. The quality of teaching is usually assessed in terms of the effort being put in by the teacher, while the quantity and particularly the quality of learning is surely much more dependent on the effort being put in by the learner. All too often, when the teacher increases input to try to address learning difficulties being experienced by students, the students are merely encouraged to reduce their own efforts. Doing the wrong thing better is unlikely to succeed. Learning, like teaching, is an active process, so we need to focus less on what the teacher should do, and more on what the students should be expected to do, if we are to promote more effective learning.

Of course students' perceptions of their own learning progress may also be flawed. Many students having failed chemistry examinations, when asked what went wrong have replied that they had expected to do better, as they had understood it when it was covered in class (Byers, 2001). They hadn't of course; they had merely been able to follow it. Research by Katona in 1940 identified lecturers working examples on a blackboard as something that doesn't promote good learning (quoted by Herron, 1996, p. 99). This might suggest that where lectures become too user-friendly and students feel too comfortable with material being presented, they are less inclined to think about it and hence fail to develop the real understanding that will be needed for successful future application. Just like passengers in a car who see no difficulty with a journey because the driver knows the way, they may often, nevertheless be incapable of making the journey on their own at a future date.

It is important to realize that both teaching and learning are active processes and effort by the learner is therefore a necessary condition for learning to occur. It isn't of course sufficient, as this effort also needs to be well directed. If we as teachers therefore wish to support our students' learning, we must try to ensure that they are making well focused efforts to achieve the desired learning outcomes.

Belief in the efficacy of the information transfer method has been particularly resistant to change, probably because it actually appears to work. After all, it is the students who have been the most successful in spite of this approach who have tended to form the next generation of chemistry lecturers. Not surprisingly these students tend to believe that as the traditional teacher-centred approach has worked for them, it should also be the appropriate way for them to teach future students (Bandura, 1986). Such beliefs have remained hard to change in the absence of clear evidence supporting the efficacy of alternative models (Hewson, Tabachnik, Zeichner & Lemberger, 1999). Geddis and Roberts (1998) for example identified beliefs developed by student teachers, while exposed to traditional university lectures, as key to their subsequent adoption of a teacher-centred approach. Why should we not think that this will be the case for all science students? Exposure to the predominantly teacher-centred approach still experienced in most universities will surely influence students to adopt the same style of teaching, if later on they are employed by a university as a member of the teaching staff (Geddis & Roberts, 1998; Fischler, 1999). Based on the view that education should be active, demanding and cooperative Chickering and Gamson (1987) published a seminal paper asserting that good practice in undergraduate education:

(1) encourages student-faculty contact;
(2) encourages cooperation among students;
(3) encourages active learning;
(4) gives prompt feedback;
(5) emphasizes time on task;
(6) communicates high expectations;
(7) respects diverse talents and ways of learning.

The efficacy of these seven principles in supporting meaningful learning in undergraduate classes has been discussed (Sorcinelli, 1991). While, on occasion, didactic lectures can be inspirational they nonetheless demote the learner to a very passive role and clearly embrace none of the above principles. We would contend that a bad lecture, providing it is followed by outside reading or peer group discussions to try to make sense of the content, represents a much richer learning experience than a good lecture, whatever that may be, with little student follow-up.

Recent attempts to increase student interactivity in lectures, (Kogut, 1997; Byers, 2001; Smith, 2006) have enjoyed only partial success because of the difficulties of involving all students in large classes, and also on account of the reluctance of many students to become involved in case they humiliate themselves in front of their peers. However, the recent availability of efficient, reliable and easy to use electronic voting systems ('Clickers') now offers the promise of making lectures more interactive for all (Martyn, 2003; Banks, 2006; Bates & Howie, 2006). Today's undergraduates are very comfortable with the technology involved and appear to like and be motivated by the approach (MacArthur & Jones, 2008). The controlled use of electronic voting systems readily embraces at least four {(2), (3), (4) and (6)} of Chickering and Gamson's seven principles.

It has been argued that to be effective any educational change needs to be introduced relatively slowly, so as to enable students – as well as the teacher – to become accustomed to the demands associated with a novel approach (Orzechowski, 1995). 'Clickers' of course are not magic wands and care and thought will be needed if they are to be used effectively. This is of course only one example of how practice may be improved through small innovations. Subsequent chapters of this book will present and discuss many more.

Learning chemistry involves much more than merely learning the facts

Chemistry represents one of the most abstract and symbolic of disciplines and its study therefore places high cognitive demands on learners (Johnstone, 1991). Studies over the past thirty years have indicated that many entrants to chemistry courses are not able to think in the conceptual terms needed to understand the more theoretical aspects of the subject (Herron, 1978). Chemistry lecturers have therefore resorted to a range of algorithms to try to overcome this dilemma (Frank, Barker, & Herron, 1986; Cardulla, 1987). Alas, while algorithms represent excellent time-saving procedures for the expert, all too often, they merely remove the need for a novice to think (Schrader, 1986). Surely this is the last thing we wish to encourage, and it is also likely to result in the marks being awarded for assessment to overestimate the amount of real understanding that has taken place (Zoller, Lubezki, Nakhleh, Tessier, & Dori, 1995).

We also need to bear in mind that using algorithms to solve problems means to solve a problem where an established procedure is already available. If it is our intention to educate future chemists to undertake research and solve problems in new and developing fields, e.g. in nanotechnology or environmental protection, they will need to be able to look for new pathways to solve these currently unknown problems. A good knowledge base covering the body of facts and theories of chemistry will undoubtedly be necessary, but students will also need to develop other, more process oriented skills (Coll & Taylor, 2001; Bailley & Garratt, 2002). Such skills will include problem solving, project managing and aims negotiating, skills that cannot be developed simply through a knowledge dissemination approach to teaching and learning (Zoller, 1993). If our students are to develop such process orientated skills we will surely need to re-negotiate both our curricula with their objectives and our methods of teaching on the basis of good evidence-based practice. A quote from Pickering (1980, p. 80) illustrates how this may be approached in a laboratory environment:

> "*The job of lab courses is to provide the experience of doing science. While the potential is rarely achieved, the obstacles are organizational and not inherent in laboratory teaching itself. That is fortunate because reform is possible and reform is cheap. Massive amounts of money are not required to improve most programs; what is needed is more careful planning and precise thinking about educational objectives. By offering a genuine, unvarnished scientific experience, a lab course can make a student into a better observer, a more careful and precise thinker, and a more deliberative problem solver. And that is what education is all about.*"

If we are to support and encourage our students to learn better, we must first seek to understand how students learn, and then adapt our teaching to support this process. While there is little doubt that we can all become better teachers, there are no quick fixes. Learning to teach is a process that never ends. If we are to improve as teachers we must continually reflect on the effects of our teaching on our students' learning and keep amending our practice appropriately: '*Good teaching involves striving continually to learn about students' understanding and the effects of teaching on it*' (Ramsden, 2003, p. 8).

It is also important to realize that the learner is not a stationary target. As we make modifications to our teaching the learners are likely to modify their responses; in the worst-case scenario merely nullifying any learning benefits that we sought to introduce. This can be thought of as a behavioural version of Le Chatelier's Principle. It is not enough that our students are learning better; we must also seek to understand why this is so if improvements are to be maintained and built upon. An understanding of why something works is likely to be particularly important when we seek to disseminate and share good practice. It is equally important to try to understand why certain innovations haven't worked, so that appropriate modifications can be made. To enable readers to better understand the pedagogical background to their teaching the remainder of this chapter is given over to the consideration of a number of modern theories concerning how learning takes place. All subsequent chapters will contain brief pedagogical introductions describing the benefits of the approaches described to student learning.

Understanding knowledge growth: From behaviourism to constructivism

In Germany, the 'Nuremberg funnel' (see above, Figure 1) remains a frequently used metaphor for teaching and learning, and a casual observer of much of today's university chemistry teaching could easily be forgiven for believing that education remains little more, than the transmission of knowledge from the head of the teacher, or from within a book, directly into the head of the learner.

Such a belief however, is based on naïve ideas from classical theories of learning and instruction. The theory of Behaviourism, which dominated thinking about education during the first half of the last century, interpreted every human action (actions, thinking, feelings, etc.) in terms of 'behaviour' (Skinner, 1976; Mills, 2000). According to this theory, every action is considered simply as a response to a stimulus; if the correct stimulus is provided the required behaviour will inevitably follow. It is argued that you can train any animal, including a human, providing you can identify a stimulus necessary to promote the desired response. Thus if a teacher wishes a student to learn something, it becomes a matter of simply finding the right stimulus to achieve this, e.g. presenting the right pieces of information in the right sequence, at the right moment within the lecture hall.

Behaviourism, which developed from experimental studies on animals; the classic example of such experiments being provided by the response of Pavlov's dog (Pavlov, 1927); thus considers that learning is dependent on the teacher and places the learner in a very subordinate role. Behaviourism concentrates solely on observable behaviour, without considering any accompanying mental processes. Indeed, leading American Behaviourists in the last century, such as Watson and Skinner, considered cognitive studies as unscientific, as results and observations tended to be incapable of independent verification (Skinner, 1990).

Behaviourism undoubtedly builds on aspects of practice that are known to be effective, such as the importance of repetition to promote learning and the value of specifying clear, achievable and verifiable learning outcomes. In fact learning outcomes are a product of behaviourist thinking. Similarly computer based training, with its reliance on rote and drill, is based on behaviourist principles. Although the theory of Behaviourism is now quite complex, and has been developed (Mills, 2000) to account for a range of observations, it is often still interpreted in a very simplistic way, suggesting, for example that simply giving the correct information to a student, will enable that student to:

(a) Store this information in his/her memory.
(b) Assign the intended meaning to this information.
(c) Have this information readily available for future use.

Unfortunately, evidence from educational research suggests, that none of the above three expectations is justified. Peterson and Peterson (1959) showed that some 85% of the information entering the short time memory is no longer available to a learner a mere 15 seconds later, if it has not been connected to any constructed meaning, or if no any additional stimuli are given to support memorization in the meantime If you present the Gibbs-Helmholtz equation expressed as a formula on the chalkboard to a non-chemist, he or she might well be able to read, memorize and reproduce it. However if he or she is questioned about the equation again only a few minutes later, they will, most probably, no longer be able to answer, as the initial information was neither meaningful, nor understandable to the student. However, even when such information was meaningful to the students, only some 20% of the information given out in class was found to be still available a mere week later (McLeish, 1968).

While Behaviourism can certainly be helpful in understanding the simple issues associated with basic training processes, it has proved much less successful when it comes to understanding important issues of higher level learning, such as concept acquisition, problem solving and creativity. It is therefore not a model ideally suited to university level education, and few would now argue against the need to involve cognitive processes when attempting to understand how students learn.

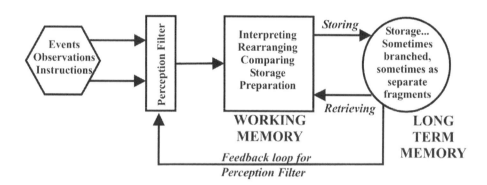

Figure 2. Johnstone's model of learning

Just as early studies of atomic structure a hundred years ago, relied heavily on the metaphor of the solar system, one of the earliest cognitive models, the information processing model uses the metaphor of a computer. Such a model has been developed and applied to science teaching by Alex Johnstone (Johnstone, 1997). Johnstone's simple model to look into the black box between teaching and learning identifies three distinct but inter-connected components, a filter, the working memory and the long term memory (the store), each of which can be the source of learning difficulties (see Figure 2).

The filter decides what will be allowed through from the vast range of stimuli we routinely encounter. If we concentrate on the wrong stimuli, the lecturer's jokes rather than the science, or how to ask the attractive person two rows ahead for a date rather than second order kinetics, learning will be inefficient. The working memory is where incoming information can be thought about and related to what is already known. This region fulfils a dual role, it both stores incoming information briefly, and enables us to work on it and try to relate it to what is already known. Unfortunately, it has very limited capacity 7 ± 2 working units (Miller, 1956). If we try to hold too much information we can't carry out any processing or add to it without forgetting some of it (Johnstone, 1984). Evidence to date suggests that we can't increase the size of our working memory but we can learn to use it more efficiently by a process known as chunking (Millar, 1956). In chunking the learner identifies a pattern or relationship between information units, which can then be combined to occupy less space in working memory. Thus while it is not possible to memorize a random number such as 1914149210661953, once one is aware that the number is actually composed of 4 dates of significance in British history, 1066, 1492, 1914 and 1953, it becomes manageable.

Overload of working memory is clearly a major cause of inefficient learning. In our lectures we are usually discussing material that seems very straightforward to us, as we already appreciate the implicit relationships and have successfully chunked the material. However, all too often, this is not the case with the students who are then overwhelmed by the amount of apparently unrelated information that they are expected to process.

The long term memory is a vast permanent store for our knowledge, facts, theories procedures, beliefs, biases etc. It is important to realize that learning is not just about adding more chunks of information, but also is involved with refining and improving the cognitive structures that are already there. We constantly modify this store by testing it against new information/experiences. If incoming information can't be related to anything in long term memory, no learning will occur. The filter is clearly connected to the long term memory, and David Ausubel suggested 40 years ago (Ausubel, 1968) that the most important thing in deciding what is learned is what the learner already knows. Learning thus involves the integration, linking and interpretation of incoming information with what is already known by an individual.

As we all have different stores of knowledge we may well interpret incoming information differently. An important factor is whether the learning can be embedded into a meaningful context (Greeno, 1998; Mandl & Kopp, 2006), as only knowledge which is situated in a meaningful framework can be efficiently stored in the long term memory and subsequently be available for recall (Whitehead, 1953). The affective domain can also be helpful in promoting situated linking of information in the long term memory. An example of this is where information is better stored in long term memory and subsequently recalled, because it can be related to important but independent events that were happening while the information was initially being processed. Most of us for example will still remember what we were doing when he heard about the 9/11 terrorist attacks in the United States. Similarly a student who learned something while listening to piece of music is likely to be reminded of this learning when hearing the music again.

It seems reasonable that where new information can be easily linked to and interpreted by pre-existing knowledge that is what is likely to happen. This is what Piaget referred to as assimilation (Wadsworth, 1996) and under low resolution it appears indistinguishable from passive diffusion. However this is frequently not the case, particularly during education and confusion/disequilibrium will occur whenever new information cannot easily be assimilated into our existing schemes. What happens now? Well the learner can just ignore it (close the filter) and it seems that this is exactly what many students are now choosing to do when something doesn't easily appear to make sense to them. Alternatively the learner might resort to rote memorising without any understanding of the significance of the new material. However, it is not enough of course to move information into storage, we must also be able to recall it when it needs to be applied. As with any filing system, for information to be readily retrievable it must be correctly stored and linked (cross-referenced) to other appropriate data. Recall will depend heavily on our understanding of what the information means. An example may illustrate this. A chemist hearing the word *water* is likely to recall that water is a chemical substance, consisting of two hydrogen atoms and one oxygen atom, with the formula H_2O and having characteristic properties. Saying water to a non chemist however may well lead to the question what kind of water do you mean: Sea water, river water, drinking water, or sparkling water? One can readily understand how communication between two such individuals could easily lead to misunderstandings. Thus it is possible that we might link and interpret new information incorrectly leading to misconceptions or, as they are often referred to alternative frameworks or alternative conceptions (e. g. Gilbert & Watts, 1983; Wandersee, Mintzes, & Novak, 1994). From a teacher's point of view of course these are all unsatisfactory outcomes.

However, there is a further possibility, the learner might modify/improve pre-existing schemes until discrepancies are able to be resolved and equilibrium restored. Piaget initially referred to this as accommodation, though we now tend to think of it in terms of conceptual change which is one of the central ideas of constructivist learning (Posner, Strike, Hewson, & Gertzog, 1982). Education surely involves learning not just more but learning better, and no effort should be spared to improve understanding by promoting such conceptual change. Unfortunately Dudley Herron has postulated that learning operates on a principle of minimum effort (Herron, 1996, p. 18). This suggests that whenever possible learners resist restructuring their cognitive schemes, preferring to ignore data that doesn't fit or to make false connections. Knowledge construction is an active process requiring effort from the learner. We do our students no favours by making things seem more straightforward than they really are. It is important to break through any sense of complacency and encourage our students to constantly challenge their ideas as new information is encountered. Learning outcomes depend primarily on the effort put in by the learner not that put in by the lecturer. Anything which produces active involvement of the learner is therefore likely to enhance the quantity and in particular the quality of learning. To promote learning the learner must become actively involved, but any effort to improve student involvement will demand time. Although not specifically considered in the information processing model discussed above, time is clearly a key variable in determining both the quantity and the quality of learning that can take place. Using the metaphor of a rate determining step (rds) in reaction mechanisms learning can be considered to involve the simple two-step process illustrated in Figure 3 (Byers, 2001).

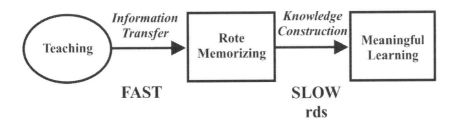

Figure 3. Model showing the effect of time on learning

It is surely much easier and therefore quicker merely to transfer information to the learner than for meaningful learning to occur. In fact getting information into the mind of a learner can be thought of as really the first step towards meaningful learning. This corresponds to what is usually called *rote memorising* or *surface learning*. Time and effort are then required to link, interpret, possibly correct and then accommodate this new information to produce meaningful learning. Far from being alternatives, memorising and meaningful learning can be considered as different stages within the learning process. The second step requires not only effort from the learner but time for understanding to develop. If new concepts are taught too quickly without time for reflection, meaningful learning can not occur. Teaching less, i.e. reducing the rate of information transfer may therefore actually lead to more learning taking place.

So what do we need to do so that learning environments promote student activity and constructivist learning? It seems obvious that learning environments that allow for and provoke activity are necessary. For example problem-based approaches which require consideration of a problem and the subject matter behind it and challenge students' understanding of subject matter can clearly promote active learning (Anderson, 2007). However, merely solving a problem may not always provide a rich learning experience. Deeper learning is likely to be promoted when students are required to work in a group to solve a meaningful problem. Here students will be encouraged to exchange suggestions for possible solutions to the problem, and as a result will tend to clarify their own thinking on the issues in question (Silver, Hanson, Strong, & Schwartz, 2003). The principles of learning through articulating one's own thoughts, and of being encultured into a scientific community by learning the language and style of scientific argumentation are central to the constructivist philosophy (Hodson & Hodson, 1998).

In practice

If we are to promote knowledge and understanding through classroom practise we must surely move the emphasis from teaching to learning (Barr & Tagg, 1995). The constructivist framework (e.g. Bodner, 1986; Taber, 2000; Coll & Taylor, 2001; Bailley & Garratt, 2002) currently represents the most commonly accepted theory of how the learning of science in either formal or informal settings can take place, and some basic ideas about how this approach can support the teaching and learning of chemistry are outlined below:

- Chemistry teaching should take account of the prior learning and background of students, as effective learning is most likely to occur when teaching starts with ideas that the learners already posses. Concepts, ideas, including misconceptions/alternative frameworks that students bring into class with them therefore need to be considered when learning processes are being planned, selected, structured and evaluated (e.g. Gilbert & Watts, 1983; Garnett, Garnett, & Hackling, 1995). Provoking cognitive conflicts, contradictions between previous ideas and new phenomena, and seeking resolution has high potential for promoting a change in student thinking from naïve preconceptions into valid scientific concepts (Posner et al., 1982).
- Learning is an active process and while it can undoubtedly be initiated by the teacher it can only be conducted by individual learners through actively testing their existing cognitive frameworks with new information. Student-centred approaches including peer-group work (Byers & Wilkins, 2005) and peer tutoring (Coe, McDougell, & McKeown, 1999) where meaning is developed through consensus in a supportive collaborative/cooperative setting have often proved to be very successful for learning science (Lazarowitz & Hertz-Lazarowitz, 1998).
- Cooperative learning environments (Lazarowitz & Hertz-Lazarowitz, 1998) provide students with opportunities for interacting and communicating which are essential for sustainable learning. Communication with others helps students develop a clearer understanding of both the subject matter and appropriate problem solving strategies. This approach also helps an individual to become encultured into the language and world of chemistry. Methods of instruction that seek to encourage learners to formulate, communicate and possibly defend their own ideas about the subject matter to be learned are necessary (Hodson & Hodson, 1998).
- Learning should take place in an environment that offers meaningful and supportive contexts (Greeno, 1998; Mandl & Kopp, 2006). Only where new information can be actively linked to and interpreted by previous knowledge can it be stored in the long term memory as meaningful and usable knowledge (Whitehead, 1953). Multiple representations of new information will often help to promote better conceptualisation of the content indicating the potential of multimedia to support learning in lecture hall and laboratory (e.g. Kozma & Russel, 2005).

- Sustainable learning of chemistry involves far more than merely memorizing as many facts as possible. Sustainable learning includes the learning of strategies to solve problems and is therefore dependent on process-oriented skills that cannot simply be learned from the blackboard (Coll & Taylor, 2001). This means that problem-based learning environments which challenge learners' to develop their own ideas and ways to solve authentic problems are necessary. It also suggests that there is a need to rethink the role of laboratory instruction as only where students are involved in actively planning as well as conducting experiments, and are required to critically evaluate any results obtained will the full potential of practical work to promote process-oriented skills and a deeper understanding of the nature of chemistry be achieved (Johnstone & Al-Shuaili, 2001; Nakleh, Polles, & Malina, 2002; Hofstein, 2004).

Reflecting on past experience to improve future performance

Although recent research into science education has undoubtedly contributed to our knowledge on how students learn, it appears to date to have had only limited impact on how chemistry is being taught at universities (Bucat, 2004). Shulman has suggested that this probably reflects the fact that pedagogical knowledge has tended to dominate over subject specific knowledge (Shulman, 1986). Useful though knowledge of general pedagogical theory may be, the teaching skills needed by a university lecturer are nonetheless likely to include much that is domain specific, and the teacher also needs to take into account the characteristic learning demands of the subject matter being taught. This need is now being mirrored in recent science educational research where one of the most rapidly developing fields has involved investigating the *Pedagogical Content Knowledge*' (PCK) of science teachers (Shulman, 1986).

PCK has been defined as *"the knowledge that a teacher uses to provide teaching situations that help learners make sense of particular science content."* (Loughran, 2001, p. 289). Thus, PCK refers to domain specific knowledge about how to teach science, its content, structure, models, methods, examples, etc. PCK can therefore be thought of as 'Craft Knowledge' (Van Driel, Verloop, & De Vos, 1998; Bond-Robinson, 2005), and for chemistry this relates to the ability of a teacher to transform an explanation of the way expert chemists currently think about a topic so as to make its significance accessible to students, with their more limited knowledge and previous experience. While struggling to make complex subject matter understandable to students it is of course important to avoid distortion and over-simplification (Barnett & Hodson, 2001). Shulman (1986) has described PCK as that special amalgam of content and pedagogy that is not learned in either pedagogy courses or science lectures. Nevertheless, it is clear that PCK is every bit as necessary as well-developed content and knowledge of pedagogy in creating a supportive and effective learning environment. As expressed by Geddis (1993, p. 675):

> *'The outstanding teacher is not simply a 'teacher', but rather a 'history teacher', a 'chemistry teacher', or an 'English teacher'. While in some sense there are generic teaching skills, many of the pedagogical skills of the outstanding teacher are content specific'.*

The teacher needs therefore to understand the teaching and learning demands of particular topics and to appreciate any difficulties and misconceptions likely to be experienced by students. Thus the ideal approach for the teaching of 'Group Chemistry' for example is likely to differ significantly from that taken to introduce 'Group Theory'. In general the better teachers are able to recognize learning difficulties and to deploy a range of models and representations to facilitate effective learning. On the other hand when teaching an unfamiliar topic, a teacher is likely to encounter difficulty in identifying suitable representations of the subject matter. PCK is therefore largely experiential and is likely to develop and mature with experience, particularly when this is accompanied by reflection on previous practice (Schön, 1983). It follows that dissemination of good practice on the teaching of specific topics by experienced teachers is likely to be of immense value to new staff.

The following chapters will provide more detailed justifications for innovative teaching and provide a broad range of ideas and examples of recent innovations. The authors hope that this information will help and encourage readers to innovate within their own chemistry courses as we look to provide education in chemistry to support a future 'Knowledge Based Economy', as envisioned by the Lisbon Agenda, at universities throughout Europe.

Resources

For further reading we recommend the papers of Bodner (1986), Taber (2000), Coll and Taylor (2001), and Bailley and Garrett (2002).

References

Anderson, R. D. (2007). Inquiry as an organizing theme for science curricula. In: S. K. Abell & N. G. Lederman (Eds.), *Handbook on research on science education* (pp. 807-830). Mahwah: Lawrence Erlbaum.

Ausubel, D. P. (1968). *Educational psychology: A cognitive view.* New York: Holt, Rinehart & Winston.

Bailley, P. D., & Garrett, J. (2002). Chemical education: Theory and practice. *University Chemistry Education, 6*, 39-57.

Bandura, A. (1986). *Social foundation of thought and action: A social cognitive theory.* Englewood: Prentice-Hall.

Banks, D. A. (2006). *Audience response systems in higher education.* Hershey: Information Sciences Publishing.

Barnett, J., & Hodson, D. (2001). Pedagogical Content Knowledge: Towards a fuller understanding of what good science teachers know. *Science Education, 85*, 426-453.

Barr, R. B., & Tagg, J. (1995). From teaching to learning - A new paradigm for undergraduate education. *Change*, November/December, 13-25.

Bates, S. P., & Howie, K. (2006). The use of electronic voting systems in large group lectures: Challenges and opportunities. *New Directions in the Teaching of Physical Sciences, 2*, 1-8.

Bodner, G. M. (1986). Constructivism: A theory of knowledge. *Journal of Chemical Education, 63*, 873-878.

Bond-Robinson, J. (2005). Identifying pedagogical content knowledge (PCK) in the chemistry laboratory. *Chemistry Education Research and Practice, 6*, 83-103.

Bucat, R. (2004). Pedagogical content knowledge as a way forward: Applied research in chemical education. *Chemistry Education Research and Practice, 5*, 215-228.

Byers, W. (2001). Using questions to promote active learning in lectures. *University Chemistry Education, 5*, 24-30.

Byers, W., & Wilkins, H. (2005). The Midwich Cuckoos revisited: Promoting learning through peer group work. *Proceedings of the Science Learning and Teaching Conference (University of Warwick, United Kingdom)*, 90-95.

Cardulla, F. (1987). Solving chemistry problems without the factor-label approach. *Journal of Chemical Education, 64*, 519-520.

Chickering, A. W., & Gamson, Z. F. (1987). Seven principles for good practice in undergraduate education. *AAHE Bulletin, 39*(7), 3-7.

Coe, E. M., McDougall, A. O., & McKeown, N. B. (1999). Is peer assisted learning of benefit to undergraduate chemists?. *University Chemistry Education, 3*(2), 72-75.

Coll, R. K., & Taylor, T. G. N. (2001). Using constructivism to inform tertiary chemistry pedagogy. *Chemistry Education Research and Practice, 2*, 215-226.

Eurydice (2006). *Science teaching in schools in Europe – Policies and research.* Brussels: Eurydice.

Fischler, H. (1999). The impact of teaching experiences on student-teachers' and beginning teachers' conceptions of teaching and learning science. In: J. Loughran (Ed.), *Researching teaching* (pp. 172-197). London: Falmer Press.

Frank, D. V., Baker, C. A., & Herron, J. D. (1987). Should students always use algorithms to solve problems?. *Journal of Chemical Education, 64*, 514-515.

Garnett, P. J., Garnett, P. J., & Hackling, M. W. (1995). Students alternative conceptions in chemistry: A review of research and implications for teaching and learning. *Studies in Science Education, 25*, 69-95.

Geddis, A. N., & Roberts, D. A. (1998). As science students become science teachers: A perspective on learning orientation. *Journal of Science Teacher Education, 9*, 271-292.

Gilbert, J. K., & Watts, D. S. (1983). Concepts, misconceptions and alternative conceptions: Changing perspectives in science education. *Studies in Science Education, 10*, 61-98.

Greeno, J. G. (1998). The situativity of knowing, learning, and research. *American Psychologist, 53*, 5-26.

Herron, D. (1975). Piaget for chemists. *Journal of Chemical Education, 52*, 146-150.

Herron, D. (1996). *The chemistry classroom.* Washington: American Chemical Society.

Hewson, P. W., Tabachnik, B. R., Zeichner, K. M., & Lemberger, J. (1999). Educating prospective teachers of biology: Findings, limitations and recommendations. *Science Education, 88*, 373-384.

Hodson, D., & Hodson, J. (1998). From constructivism to social constructivism: A Vygotskyan perspective on teaching and learning science. *School Science Review, 79* (289), 33-41.

Hofstein, A. (2004). The laboratory in chemistry education: Thirty years of experience with developments, implementation, and research. *Chemistry Education Research and Practice, 5*, 247-264.

Johnstone, A. H. (1984). New stars for the teacher to steer by?. *Journal of Chemical Education, 61*, 847-849.

Johnstone, A. H. (1991). Why is science difficult to learn? Things are seldom what they seem. *Journal of Computer Assisted Learning, 7*, 75-83.

Johnstone, A. H. (1997). Chemistry teaching - Science or alchemy?. *Journal of Chemical Education, 74*, 262-268.

Johnstone, A. H., & Al-Shuaili, A. (2001). Learning in the laboratory: Some thoughts from the literature. *University Chemistry Education, 5*(2), 42-51.

Kogut, L. S. (1997). Using cooperative learning to enhance performance in general chemistry. *Journal of Chemical Education, 74*, 720-722.

Kozma, R., & Russell, J. (2005). Multimedia learning of chemistry. In: R. Mayer (Ed.), *The Cambridge handbook of multimedia learning* (pp. 409–428). New York: Cambridge University Press.

Lazarowitz, R., & Hertz-Lazarowitz, R. (1998). Cooperative learning in the science curriculum. In: B. J. Fraser & K. G. Tobin (Eds.), *International Handbook of Science Education* (pp. 623-640). London: Kluwer.

Loughran, J., Millroy, P., Berrry, A., Gunstone, R., & Mulhall, P. (2001). Documenting science teachers' content knowledge through PaP-eRs. *Research in Science Education, 31*, 289-307.

MacArthur, J. R., &. Jones. L. L. (2008). A review of literature reports of clickers applicable to college chemistry classrooms. *Chemistry Education Research and Practice, 9*, 187-195.

Mandl, H., & Kopp, B. (2006). Situated learning - theories and models. In P. Nentwig & D. Waddington (Eds.), *Making it relevant: Context based learning of science* (pp. 15-34). Münster: Waxmann.

Martyn, M. (2007). Clickers in the classroom: An active learning approach. *Educause Quarterly, 2*, 71-74.

McLeish, J. (1968). *The lecture method*. Cambridge: Institute of Education.

Miller, G. A. (1956). The magical number seven, plus or minus two: Some limits on our capacity for processing information. *Psychological Review, 63*, 81-97.

Mills, J. A. (2000). *Control: A history of behavioral psychology*. New York: University Press.

Nakleh, M. B., Polles, J., & Malina, K. (2002). Learning chemistry in a laboratory environment. In: J. K. Gilbert, O. De Jong, R. Justi, D. Treagust, & J. H. Van Driel (Eds.), *Chemical Education: Towards research-based practice* (pp. 69-94). Dordrecht: Kluwer.

Orzechowski, R. F. (1995). Factors to consider before introducing active learning into a large, lecture-based course. *Journal of College Science Teaching*, Mar/Apr., 347-349.

Pavlow, I (1927). *Conditioned Reflexes*. Oxford: Oxford University Press.

Peterson, L. R., & Peterson, M. J. (1959). Short-term retention of individual verbal items. *Journal of Experimental Psychology, 58*, 193-198.

Pickering, M. (1980). Are lab courses a waste of time?. *The Chronicle of Higher Education, 19*, 80.

Posner, G. J., Strike, K. A., Hewson, P. W., & Gertzog, W. A. (1982). Accommodation of a scientific conception: Towards a theory of conceptual change. *Science Education, 66*, 211-227.

Ramsden, P. (2003). *Learning to teach in higher education* (2nd Ed.), London: Routledge-Farmer.

Schön, D. A. (1983). *The reflective practitioner: How professionals think in* action. New York: Basic Books.

Schrader, C. L. (1987). Using algorithms to teach problem solving. *Journal of Chemical Education, 64*, 518-519.

Shulman, L. S. (1986). Those who understand: Knowledge growth in teaching. *Educational Researcher, 15*, 4-14.

Silver, H. F., Hanson, J. R., Strong, R. W., & Schwartz, P. B. (1996). *Teaching styles & strategies*. Trenton: The Thoughtful Education Press.

Skinner, B. F. (1976). *About behavioursm*. New York: MacMillan.

Skinner, B. F. (1990). Can psychology be a science of mind?. *American Psychologist, 45*, 1206-1210.

Smith, D. K. (2006). Use of the mid-lecture break in chemistry teaching: A survey and some suggestions. *Journal of Chemical Education, 83*, 1621-1625.

Sorcinelli, M. D. (1991, Fall). Research findings on the seven principles. *New Directions in Teaching and Learning, No. 47* (pp. 13-25). San Francisco: Jossey Bass.

Taber, K. S. (2000). Chemistry lessons for universities?. A review of constructivist ideas. *University Chemistry Education, 4*(2), 26-35.

Van Driel, J. H., Verloop, N., & De Vos, W. (1998). Developing science teachers' pedagogical content knowledge. *Journal of Research in Science Teaching, 35*, 673-695.

Wadsworth, B. J. (1996). *Piaget's theory of cognitive and affective development.* White Plains: Longman.

Wandersee, J. H., Mintzes, J. J., & Novak, J. D. (1994). Research on alternative conceptions in science. In: D. Gabel (Ed.), *Handbook of Research on Science Teaching and Learning* (pp. 177-210). New York: MacMillan.

Whitehead, A. N. (1953). The aims of education and other essays. In: F.S.C. Northrop & M. W. Gros (Eds.), *Alfred North Whitehead.* New York: MacMillan.

Wittrock, M. C. (1989). Generative processes of comprehension. *Educational Psychologist, 24,* 325-344.

Zoller, U. (1993). Lecture and learning. Are they compatible?. Maybe for LOCS. Unlikely for HOCS. *Journal of Chemical Education, 70,* 195-197.

Zoller, U., Lubezki, A., Nakhleh, M., Tessier, B., & Dori, Y. J. (1995). Success on algorithmic and LOCS vs. conceptual chemistry exam questions. *Journal of Chemical Education, 72,* 987-989.

The Uniqueness of Teaching and Learning Chemistry

MICHELE A. FLORIANO
University of Palermo, Italy

CHRISTIANE S. REINERS
University of Cologne, Germany

SILVIJA MARKIC
University of Bremen, Germany

GUSTAVO AVITABILE
University of Naples Federico II, Italy

Unfortunately, the current perception of Chemistry held by many students and the general public alike appears to be in stark contrast to its true nature. Although chemistry is ubiquitous in all aspects of our daily lives it continues to be perceived as highly theoretical and of little relevance. A clearer understanding of the fundamental Nature of Chemistry will be needed if students are to recognize its true importance and character. It is not possible to fully understand, and as a consequence accept on an intuitive basis, the 'mystery' and fascinations arising from the transformation of matter, without first adopting a convincing sub-microscopic view, able to connect observed macroscopic properties to the behaviours of atoms and molecules. Insightful use of models and computer generated visualization techniques now offer a way forward, but only once the learning difficulties being encountered by students have been fully appreciated by their university lecturers.

Introduction

"It is not the strongest species that survive, nor the most intelligent, but the ones most responsive to change." (Charles Darwin)

Chapter consultants: Peter E. Childs, University of Limerick, Ireland, Bill Byers, University of Ulster, United Kingdom, and Ingo Eilks, University of Bremen, Germany.

I. Eilks and B. Byers (Eds.). Innovative Methods in Teaching and Learning Chemistry in Higher Education, pp. 23-42. © 2009 RSC Publishing.

In the past few years, different researchers have reexamined the perception, beliefs and opinions about chemistry (e.g. Price & Hill, 2004). The focus has switched from analyzing students' learning to students' beliefs, knowledge and attitudes (De Jong, 2007). Different studies show that chemistry is perceived as abstract, difficult and, above all, disconnected from relevant problems in everyday life (Black & Atkin, 1996).

One reason could be that students, even at the university level, often misunderstand and misrepresent the Nature of Chemistry, and indeed the Nature of Science[§] (Abell & Smith, 1992; Rubba & Harkness, 1993). Abd-El-Khalick, Bell, and Lederman (1998) stated that the Nature of Science "...*refers to the epistemology of science, science as a way of knowing, or the values and beliefs inherent to the development of scientific knowledge*" (p. 418). However, Johnson (1991) found that many teachers also have a naïve view on the Nature of Science and often think that theories are only tools to help explain a number of phenomena. They believe that scientific knowledge is stable and unproblematic and insist that information given to students should be "accurate". Pomeroy (1993) compared the beliefs about the Nature of Science of university professors, scientists, secondary science teachers, and elementary teachers. She concluded that beliefs become progressively more traditional as we move along the above sequence from elementary teachers to university professors.

Research into understanding of the Nature of Science (e.g. Lederman and colleagues, 1985; 1987; 1998; 2002) has identified several factors that can lead to a lack of appreciation of the true Nature of Science among science teachers and researchers. Prominent among these factors is a view that an understanding of the Nature of Science is of less significance than other instructional outcomes. A study by Murcia and Schibeci (1999) identified a number of concepts containing elements that clearly did not correspond with a developed understanding of the Nature of Science. The respondents displayed a naïve and unclear understanding of the scientific method and a poorly developed understanding of scientific theory in general. Aguirre, Haggerty, and Linder (1990) also showed that most pre-service teachers hold only a naïve view of the Nature of Science, believing that the function of science is simply to discover the Laws of Nature. In a study of 47 elementary school science teachers, Hammrich and Blouch (1996) concluded that teachers (before taking any courses) didn't consider themselves to be involved with science and viewed it simply as a set of facts or theories to be learned. This is not exclusively a phenomenon associated with trainee school science teachers. When investigating beliefs held about the image of science among 300 staff members and students from two Australian universities Rowell (1982) found a dominant belief that science

---

[§] Driver, Leach, Millar, and Scott (1996) defined students' perspective about the 'Nature of Science' as: "...*ideas which a student has about science, as distinct from their ideas about the natural world itself how the body of public knowledge called science has been established and is added to; what our grounds are from considering it reliable knowledge; from the agreement which characterizes much of science is maintained*" (p. 31).

was a hybrid of Popperian ideas (Popper, 1959) with earlier, more naïve views.

Scholars and philosophers have been discussing the character of science since the beginning of the 19th century. They have also been concerned with the history and development of science education and have repeatedly identified knowledge about the Nature of Science as a neglected and underdeveloped aspect of science teaching (e.g. McComas, 1998). In recent decades, science education research has continued to emphasize the importance of promoting the learning and understanding of topics related to the Nature of Science in order to allow students to develop a deeper understanding of science, and enable them to recognize that such knowledge can make a valuable contribution towards developing their personal scientific skills (e.g. McComas, 1998).

Driver et al. (1996) identified five important arguments to show why an understanding of the Nature of Science can make a valuable contribution to science education. These are outlined below:

·   A utilitarian argument (the necessity of making sense of science and managing technological objects and processes from everyday life).
·   A democratic argument (necessary for making sense of socio-scientific issues and for participating in a democratic decision-making process).
·   A cultural argument (the necessity of appreciating science as a major element of contemporary culture).
·   A moral argument (the necessity of helping develop awareness of the Nature of Science and, particularly, the norms of the scientific community embodying moral commitments which are of general value).
·   A science learning argument (necessary for supporting successful learning of science content).

Furthermore, Korpan, Bisanz, Bisanz, and Henderson (1997) argued that understanding the Nature of Science enhances one's ability to comprehend, interpret and evaluate information and conclusions based on scientific research. Lederman (1999) argues that an understanding of the Nature of Science should be an important worldwide educational objective. Additionally, he views such an understanding as a significant aspect of scientific literacy (Lederman, 1992). Thus, a clear and well-formed understanding of the Nature of Science will allows citizens to critically question media reports and advertising, allegedly based on scientific claims.

Many of the initial beliefs held by students prove themselves to be naïve, superficial and, in many cases, do not even mirror modern educational theory. Nevertheless, science education programmes frequently continue to neglect a thorough discussion and debate among students about their own beliefs, stereotypes and prejudices (Zeichner & Hoeft, 1996). Czerniak and Lumpe (1996) stress the importance of evaluating student preconceptions *"before planning classes, workshops, or seminars"* (p. 259).

We know from educational psychology, that the concepts (or beliefs) that teachers have will determine how they behave and what decisions they make while teaching (Pajares, 1992). In fact, Bandura (1986) concludes that beliefs are the best indicators of why a person behaves, handles information, and makes decisions in a certain way. This is true not only for the way in which an individual will act as a scientist but also for every action taken as a teacher in class. Incompletely developed concepts will act as a filter through which future learning must be filtered and this is why poorly elaborated concepts about the nature of science will influence the ways in which chemistry teachers and lecturers teach their classes. This suggests that courses on the history and philosophy of science should become an essential and integral part of the training required by the new generation of higher education chemistry lecturers as well as for secondary level teachers.

A study by Schwartz, Lederman, and Crawford (2004) found that students developed more sophisticated views about the Nature of Science following appropriate teaching interventions. Reflection, context and perspective were also identified as important factors in developing more mature views about the Nature of Science. In addition, Palmquist and Finley (1997) found that while only a minority of students at the beginning of a science teacher training programme held post-positivist beliefs about scientific knowledge and the role of the scientist, the number of post-positivist beliefs in the group had doubled and the number holding mixed beliefs decreased by more than half after completing the course, (also Schmidt & Kennedy, 1990).

From this point of view science teacher training programmes in higher education as well as those in secondary schools should place more emphasis on teaching and reflecting on the Nature of Science. Both future scientists and educated citizens in general need a reflective view about the strategies and limitations of the way in which science works and to be able to distinguish between scientific and non-evidence-based arguments. An overview of the state of the art of the research and ideas about teaching the Nature of Science has been given by McComas (1998) and a programmed approach towards developing understanding of the Nature of Science, with different activities for undergraduate chemistry education described by Warren (2001).

Problems of chemistry as an empirical science

Different levels of thinking

"...Chemistry was the **art** of making substances change, or watching their spontaneous transformations....Today chemistry is the **science** of molecules and their transformations." (Hoffmann & Torrence, 1993, p. 15) Though chemistry has changed over a period of a few hundred years, one feature remains constant: "Chemistry is about change, it always was, and always will be" (ibid). It is devoted to explaining the properties and transformations of substances at a particulate i.e. sub-microscopic level.

The development from an art to a science was accompanied by the development of the scientific method. This was first stated explicitly by Galileo Galilei in the 17th century and was later incorporated into general thinking, especially by Kant (1787). In the foreword of his *Critique on Pure*

Reason Kant mentioned the two central constituents of the scientific method: Experiment and Theory.

When considering any experiment the question of evidence is fundamental. Assuming that evidence includes anything that gives reason for believing something, a closer look at the ways in which experimental chemistry research is carried out becomes necessary.

While chemistry involves change and the properties of substances before and after change has occurred can be observed, the process itself can still only be explained by using models and theories. Consequently scientific knowledge relies heavily, though not entirely, on observation and experimental evidence (McComas, 1998), and most of our so-called 'knowledge' about the structure of matter remains indirect (Hoffmann & Torrence, 1993)

One theory that has proved to be extremely successful in chemistry is the atomic theory of matter, which operates in different ways. On the one hand it can enable scientists to design molecules exhibiting certain specific desired properties (synthesis), while on the other hand synthesized products can be analyzed, in order to confirm that the intended product has indeed been obtained (analysis). This is done using a range of methods such as IR, Mass and NMR spectroscopies and X-ray diffractometry which have also in fact been developed on the basis of atomic theory. Consequently theory works in two different directions. On the one hand it explains properties and on the other hand it predicts properties. Taking into account synthesis and analysis together this leads to a circuit of argumentation (Figure 1):

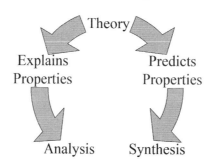

Figure 1. Circuit of Argumentation

This means that a theory has validity only within a certain framework, in which macroscopic properties and changes are related to sub-microscopic processes (Johnstone, 1991; Gilbert & Treagust, 2009b). Outside such a framework the theory loses both meaning and its powers of prediction and explanation.

Atomic theory is an unusual and non-intuitive concept that requires a shift from the 'continuous' thinking that typifies our experience of everyday-life to the 'discontinuous' thinking that is needed to understand the fundamentals of chemistry. This includes a shift from thinking about substances (everyday-life) to thinking about relationships (chemistry) (Reiners, 1996). Such shifts contribute to the uniqueness of chemistry but are also the source of many of the learning difficulties encountered by its students.

In addition, chemistry does not only deal with the transformation of substances but with a transformation of (chemical) language as well (Jacob, 2001). *"On the one hand, chemists analyze and synthesize new compounds in the laboratory; on the other, they make analytical and synthetic statements about these compounds in research articles."*

How should evidence be dealt with?

Many projects dealing with the Nature of Science have attempted to answer this very question. It is a myth that carefully accumulated evidence can ever result in certain knowledge (McComas, 1998), for there is of course no absolute evidence. The power of any theory is supported on the one hand by its ability to explain our observations and on the other hand by its ability to predict future results. However, in principle all scientific knowledge is subject to change as new evidence becomes available, so nothing can be regarded as certain (McComas, 1998). Consequently it should be stressed, that science is a blend of logic and imagination (AAAS, 1990). The use of logic and the close examination of evidence are necessary, but not usually sufficient, for the advancement of science. They must also be accompanied by creativity.

How can experimental results be interpreted in terms of their power and limitation?

It is all too easy for simple dualistic thinking, based on "either/or decisions", to be used to design experiments, but it is surely important to encourage future teachers and chemists alike to develop a more creative approach to experimentation based on "as-well-as considerations" (e.g. Tobin, 1990; Kipnis & Hofstein, 2007). Such an approach is intended to widen students' horizons and to support them on the way from experimental results to experimental processes in which the experimenter plays a crucial role. It should also help to eliminate once and for all, the popular but naïve notion that scientific knowledge has a final, objective form independent of the person conducting scientific experiments. Consequently, there is a need for students to be exposed to experiments that provide open-ended situations, i.e that cannot be predicted without reference to the prevailing conditions. Such open-ended experimental situations should help students to progress beyond the simplistic thinking associated with typical cook-book type laboratory experiments (e.g. Tobin, 1990; Domin, 1999; Abd-El-Khalick et al., 1998).

One of the characteristics of scientific knowledge is its reliance on certain conditions, including a dependence on the experimenters who set or choose these conditions (Warren, 1991). Although every experimental result depends on certain conditions there are some where the "if-then-conclusion", and with it, the influence of the experimenter is rather obvious as for example when working with amphoteric systems (Reiners, 1998). Such systems are therefore well suited to provide opportunities for real scientific investigations rather than mere laboratory exercises (Nott & Wellington, 1996). Students are able to get involved in practical work which is open-ended and does not merely consist of an effort to obtain the one right answer, i.e. they are able to experience science in the making rather than ready-made science (e.g. Tobin, 1990; Kipnis & Hofstein, 2007). Therefore investigations on amphoteric systems can be used as a stimulus to initiate reflection on the generation of scientific knowledge, on its degree of certainty and on its limitations, in order to use scientific knowledge adequately within and beyond scientific contexts.

Innovative ways to teach about the power and limitations of evidence

A number of different approaches can be taken to help both school and university students to appreciate the power and limitations of empirical evidence. One suggestion to break new grounds in laboratory work is to open the experimental tasks (Tobin, 1990) by introducing inquiry-type experiments (Kipnis & Hofstein, 2007), in which students are involved in an inquiry process that includes all relevant skills such as identifying problems, formulating hypotheses, designing experiments, gathering and analyzing data, and drawing conclusions about scientific problems and phenomena. All these activities should contribute to helping students gain a better understanding of the Nature of Science.

Another suggestion proposed by Derkse (1981) deploys Popper's epistemology as a didactic principle by claiming "Let them make more 'mistakes'":

> *"When setting up laboratory experiments in which Popper's criterion of falsification forms the epistemological background, one can choose between two alternatives. Either the students must perform experiments with an explicit falsification purpose or do practical work with a falsifying aim 'built in', in which falsification is contained implicitly"* (Derkse 1981, p. 566)

Apart from implicit approaches, explicit approaches are also possible and it seems in general that a combination of explicit and implicit factors is likely to be most effective (Lederman, 2007).

In their review about the laboratory in science education, Hofstein and Lunetta (2003) summarized methodologies for research on laboratory work which has been developed in the last 20 years and they concluded: "*To many students, 'a lab' means manipulating equipment but not manipulating ideas.*" In order to get rid of these problems they suggested empowering professional teachers to support and assess science laboratories and to realize that the chemistry laboratory offers a unique mode of learning, instruction and assessment (Hofstein, 2004).

Arguments against such innovative approaches are generally along the lines that there is not enough time. However following the principle of AAAS that "Less is more", advantages and disadvantages should be weighed. A clear advantage of introducing such innovative methods is that students will be able to develop a better understanding of both the Nature of Science and the uniqueness of Chemistry. Warren (1991) has suggested a number of activities to encourage students to reflect on aspects of practical work such as accuracy, relevance and the reliability of measurements taken in the lab.

Chemistry is unique: Explaining observations with atomic-scale effects

From what has been said, it would appear that, in order to gain a "natural" and instinctive perception about the essence of chemistry, it is necessary to fully adopt a sub-microscopic perspective. This has never been easy and the conceptual hurdles to be overcome probably still persist even when students enter higher education.

From a historical perspective, the origin of Chemistry as a branch of modern science can be closely linked to Antoine Lavoisier (1743-1794), who introduced quantitative methods into experimental chemistry. Lavoisier systematically adopted a quantitative approach by performing very careful and reproducible experiments. The idea that all substances are composed of a small number of constituent elements had been around since Greek times, but the ability to perform chemical reactions in a controlled way produced a radical revision of the notion of element. As we will see later, the properties of compounds are not the simple sum of the properties of their constituent elements but are usually completely new and unpredictable.

Furthermore, the quantitative study of reactions soon yielded exciting fruits. It became clear that elements combine in fixed ratios to form compounds, and in addition, when different compounds contain the same elements, their amounts are correlated in simple ratios. Such laws, indicating a lack of continuity in the composition of matter, could only be explained by a revolutionary theory, which accepted the discontinuous nature of matter. The atomic theory, formulated by John Dalton in the early 1800's, is no doubt chemistry's greatest contribution to science. The theory states that matter is not indefinitely divisible into smaller and smaller parts, but is in fact composed of elementary particles called atoms (the word, from Greek ατομος (ΰλη) *átomos (hýle)*, means non-divisible), that are not divisible further. Dalton had little idea of the size of his atoms, except that they were so small that they couldn't be perceived by our senses.

We now know the mass of atoms with great precision; we know that atoms are not truly indivisible and that they have a complex structure (incidentally, this structure is the real key to understanding their chemical behaviour); even atoms of the same element are not always identical (isotopes) and some atoms can be transformed into other ones by nuclear reactions. In addition, sophisticated experiments using, for example, Atomic Force Microscopy (AFM), suggest that atoms and molecules can now actually be "seen". However, the basic intuition is still valid; chemical reactions are due to the rearrangement of atoms and to the forming and breaking of bonds between atoms, but the atoms themselves are conserved.

A unique feature of the nature of chemistry emerged following the introduction of Dalton's atomic theory. In order to explain experimental, macroscopic data (like combination ratios) we need theories based on non-visible objects and behaviours (atoms and their bonds). Chemistry therefore requires a sub-microscopic approach and this presents a major difficulty for the learning and teaching of chemistry (Johnstone, 1991).

The turn of the 20th century was marked by major developments in physics, with the advent of relativity and quantum mechanics and investigations into the structure of atoms. Different discrete atomic models were proposed following the discovery of the electron, but subatomic particles do not behave according to the rules of classical mechanics. A major breakthrough for our understanding of atoms and their chemical behaviour came with development of quantum mechanics. Unfortunately this in turn resulted in a new set of problems for university students trying to learn chemistry (e.g. Tsaparlis, 1997)

Although the new model proved extremely successful in explaining the behaviour of elementary particles, it also introduced new problems in understanding. Many concepts in classical mechanics are intuitive, that is they can be related to everyday experience. Force is connected to physical effort by muscles and position to the operation of finding a hidden object. In quantum mechanics, we must abandon such analogies, and rely only on mathematical descriptions, that are quite satisfactory, but lack the comfort of recognizing familiar facts (Stefani & Tsaparlis, 2009).

Quantum mechanics has now reached a stage where its premises are clearly stated and powerful calculation methods can be developed. It requires a radical revision of classical mechanics, starting from its fundamentals, i.e. the concept of 'a body' and the way of measuring its state. The debate about its theoretical basis is still on-going and its conclusions far from widely accepted.

Several formulations of the principles of quantum mechanics have been proposed, each with its own advantages and pitfalls. The form most useful for chemical applications, and therefore the one generally adopted, is based on Schrödinger's equation and the wave function. According to this approach, a system is fully described by its wave function ψ. The wave function is the solution of Schrödinger's differential equation, whose form is similar to the equation for a wave in classical mechanics. All measurable properties of the system can be calculated simply by applying proper operators to ψ.

This rather complex approach, though far from intuitive, is non-the-less able to account for all the properties that we observe in electrons and other particles, including energy quantization, electron shells, electron diffraction, and so on. It is admittedly not possible to explain why the fundamental laws of wave mechanics work this way but it is equally impossible to explain "why" the laws of classical mechanics work in the macroscopic world.

Is quantum mechanics the "true" mechanics? Probably it is simply just a more advanced model than classical mechanics that works well at the sub-microscopic level also. We certainly cannot exclude the possibility that further experiments in the future will prove incompatible with quantum mechanics. Up to now, however, it provides an effective framework for the observations and experiments that have been performed.

It might be argued that, as chemical properties are determined by the behavior of electrons, and electrons obey Schrödinger's equation, any chemical problem should be solvable by writing the appropriate equation for the system and finding the solution. This is unfortunately not the case. The mathematics of quantum-mechanics is so complex that no exact solution can be worked out even for relatively simple systems involving few electrons. Students must therefore learn how to apply quantum-mechanical principles in qualitative or semi-quantitative ways, in order to make problems treatable and obtain hints as to what may actually happen in the laboratory. So, electron distributions can be described using point charges and local dipoles; ring stability can be interpreted through the concept of aromatic delocalization and many molecular shapes can be explained in terms of a framework of four tetrahedral orbitals around a central atom.

The real challenge for the teacher is how to introduce such concepts while making it clear that they are neither absolute nor mysterious. However, the solution to this problem is not to hide from it and try to ignore the complexity of how nature seems to be working. Teaching strategies for introducing quantum mechanical thinking in a well reflected manner have been described e.g. in Kalkanis, Hadzidaki, and Stavrou (2003) or Hadzidaki (2008) and a thorough review of relevant literature on the teaching and learning of quantum mechanics has been published by Tsaparlis (2007).

Chemical bonds and *emergent* properties

A very relevant feature of chemistry that is currently raising new questions and new perspectives about the "adaptive" (Lehn, 2007, p. 151) behavior of large supramolecular aggregates is related to interactions among the constituent atoms, that is "bonding". Interacting entities of various kinds, such as individuals in a population, stocks and shares in the market, musicians playing different instruments in an orchestra or atoms in molecules, can give rise to properties or phenomena that are not present in the individual components, and that furthermore, are not predictable from observing the individual entities. Such *complex* behavior (Müller, Dress & Vögtle, 1995) is characteristic of chemistry as the properties of a compound are not simply the sum of the properties of the constituent atoms, but rather depend mainly on how these atoms are linked or bonded together. It follows that the concept of bonding is central to the teaching and learning of chemistry and, once again, a sub-microscopic view is indispensable.

We are accustomed to recognize the properties of the constituents in composite objects. Consider a house for example. We can easily recognize the strength and sturdy features of bricks, the warmth and flammability of wood panels and the transparency of windows because they are made of glass. Properties of the constituents may also be identified even when the constituents themselves are not visible. One can for example make a cake sweeter by adding sugar, or salty by adding salt, or denser by adding more flour. In each case, the properties of the product resemble, or are a weighted average, of the properties of the constituents.

Now consider a chemical compound such as water, for example. Water is made up of hydrogen and oxygen, in the fixed ratio of 2:1 in atoms and 1:8

in mass. Compare a sample of water with a mixture of elementary hydrogen and oxygen, in the same ratio. They are completely different. Water is liquid, whereas H_2 and O_2, and their mixtures, are gases. As a consequence, water has a much higher density. Water is a good solvent for ionic compounds, whereas hydrogen and oxygen are not. Water has a high dielectric constant, and in general the properties of a polar substance, contrary to its constituent elements. Clearly, the properties of the compound here are not the simple sum of the properties of elements from which it is composed, but are mainly due to the nature of chemical bonds (in the case of water, two highly polar bonds) and non-bonded electron pairs.

As a further example consider ammonia, NH_3. Ammonia contains different elements than water (nitrogen rather than oxygen), but its properties resemble those of water much more closely than those of a mixture of hydrogen and nitrogen. Though ammonia is gaseous under normal conditions, it can be liquefied at relatively high temperatures, and certainly very much higher than is the case for H_2, O_2 or N_2. Ammonia is a polar substance and in the liquid state, it will dissolve ionic substances, and is similar to water in many ways. This clearly suggests that it is the nature of the bonding (polar bonds in an asymmetric molecule) that makes the most significant contribution to the resulting molecular properties.

The importance of chemical bonds in determining the nature of substances is also demonstrated by isomers. Isomers are substances that have the same elemental composition, but their atoms are linked together in different ways, giving rise to properties that can be very different. Let us compare, for example, the two isomers ethanol C_2H_5-OH and dimethyl ether CH_3-O-CH_3. Ethanol is an alcohol, it is able to undergo esterification reactions, it is strongly polar and so is less volatile than the ether. Such properties and many more, are clearly due to the O-H bond that is present in ethanol but not in ethers.

In isomers not only the nature of bonds is important, but also their sequence. Compare n-octane $CH_3-(CH_2)_6-CH_3$ and 2,2,4-trimethylpentane $(CH_3)_3C-CH_2-CH(CH_3)_2$. Both isomers contain only saturated C-C and C-H bonds, so their properties are not so different. They are, however, two distinct compounds, and one important difference lies in their combustion properties, as a result of which they contribute very differently to the so-called octane number of petrols.

The nature of chemical bonds is therefore central to the discipline of Chemistry, and many topics such as acids and bases, redox reactions, coordination chemistry, organic analysis and synthesis should constantly make reference to it. Teaching should also stress the variety of chemical bonding and this should not merely be restricted to referring to ionic, covalent and metallic bonds but should also include consideration of weaker bonds, such as hydrogen bonds and polar and non-polar interactions, thus allowing an appreciation of the difference between aqueous and fatty environments. This is especially important in Biology, for example, when considering the structure and function of cell membranes and the roles of many enzymes. Aspects of research on understanding 'bonding' are discussed e.g. by Van Hoeve-Brower and De Vos (1994) or Taber and Coll (2002).

The use of models in experimental science

The above discussion suggests, that in order to make chemistry understandable, and therefore, acceptable at an intuitive level, we need to explain it in terms of objects that cannot be seen, and that furthermore, may behave in very strange ways. In our chemistry teaching therefore, we often introduce objects and effects that are not true phenomena but, are rather pictorial images of a reality that is too complex to be treated rigorously. Such images invariably involve approximations but are non-the-less very useful for building representations of chemical features that can now be handled not only mathematically, but also by the pictorial abilities of our minds. To facilitate this process we often try to relate developing ideas to classical concepts by analogy.

We generally adopt the Born-Oppenheimer approximation which involves the separation of nuclear and electronic motions. In this approximation, wave functions are considered for systems with fixed nuclei, taking into account just the motion of electrons. The nuclei are of course in motion, but their velocities tend to be several orders of magnitude lower than those of electrons. Nuclear motion is then treated as if the nuclei are moving in an energy field provided by electronic energy calculated at each static nuclear position, and such motions are subject to the laws of quantum mechanics.

The next simplification generally introduces the concept of orbitals (e.g. Albright & Burdett, 1992). The basic idea involves decomposing the total wave function into a set of one-electron wave functions. Each wave function produced then describes a single electron moving in the averaged field of all other electrons and nuclei and is referred to as an orbital (actually each orbital is able to accommodate two such electrons, with opposite spins, but this is only a minor complication). Using these orbitals, we can then think of the energies, shapes, displacements and so on associated with specific electrons.

Note that it is only possible to calculate an exact value of orbital energies for very simple systems, in practice only for the hydrogen atom and hydrogen-like (one-electron) ions. We then transfer this information to many-electrons atoms, assuming that individual electrons can be described by the orbitals calculated for the one-electron models, after making appropriate corrections. This requires the concept of empty or available orbitals that can describe an electron if it is subsequently added to a system, without appreciably perturbing the other components. While such a concept has no physical meaning, it can be very useful in practice in allowing us to build a reasonable approximation of the state of a many-electron system. Orbitals provide a rationalization for the arrangement of elements in the Periodic Table, a theoretical foundation for the description of chemical bonds and an explanation for observed molecular geometries.

In summary, macroscopic behaviour is explained in terms of sub-microscopic effects, but this explanation is mediated through the use of appropriate models. This is undoubtedly a source of great difficulty for many students, who are not accustomed to thinking in terms of invisible objects or of different mechanical behaviour (Albright & Burdett, 1992; Tsaparlis, 1997).

A major challenge for any chemistry teacher therefore, is to strike the right balance between the experimental evidence that forms the basis for all science including chemistry, and the rigorous but difficult descriptions that are needed to explain it. This often requires many trade-offs and it is important, for example, to stress what approximations are being made and to emphasize the heuristic power of the techniques being adopted.

Modern science is based on experiments, but it must go further and produce coherent pictures to give heuristic power to experimental evidence. This is achieved firstly by adopting a quantitative approach whenever this is possible. It is important to know not only what happens, but also to what extent it happens. The established and consolidated experimental evidence must then be elaborated to produce hypotheses and theories. The ill-defined differences between such terms can be circumvented by using the generic term "model". But, what is a model? A model is a theoretical construct used to explain chemical phenomena. Such models can never provide an exhaustive description of a physical reality, but rather can be thought of as a bet made on the probability of explaining a given phenomenon on the basis of a few, well defined, generally mathematical rules by a researcher, and open for future change (e.g. Gilbert & Boulter, 1998; Van Driel & Verloop, 1999).

Demonstrations are possible with models but not in the real world. In order to make a demonstration work, premises are required that are taken for granted. No such premises can exist in the physical world, but a model is a mathematical structure, and its premises are unequivocally stated. So, models can be elaborated and consequences and possibilities can be predicted. No result can be demonstrated to be true in the physical sense; it can only be shown to be consistent with the model. This gives a model great heuristic power. Predictions from a model can be compared with real experimental data, which can lead either to reinforce or to amend and improve the model (e.g. Van Driel & Verloop, 1999; Justi & Gilbert, 2002).

Experimental data can help identify generalizations which can then be formulated into laws, such as the ideal gas law, which allows us to describe the behaviour of gases. Although ideal gases do not actually exist, real gases can behave like ideal gases under certain conditions of temperature and pressure. In order to explain the relationship $PV = nRT$, which can be derived from experimental data, i.e. from observation, it is necessary to construct a model for an ideal gas, which is now no longer empirical but rather a mental construct able to predict and explain the behaviours of real gases.

For a concise discussion of the nature of models and their use in science education see e.g. Gilbert and Boulter (1998), Van Driel and Verloop (1999) or Justi and Gilbert (2002). A discussion about the teaching of orbital theory in higher education can be found in Albright and Burdett (1992).

Molecular models and visualization tools

Molecular models can be very useful learning tools. They may be real objects that can be manipulated in the material sense, or they may be generated by computers, yielding images that can be viewed and manipulated, in the virtual sense. The former have been around for many years and are still widely available in the marketplace and in use in many classrooms.

Unfortunately most students encounter a range of problems whenever they are required to "think in models" (e.g. Gilbert & Boulter, 1998; Saborowski, 2000; Justi & Gilbert, 2002; Taber, 2008). Many scholars in the past, e.g. Johnstone (1991), Grosslight, Jay, Unger, and Smith (1991) or Gilbert and Treagust (2009b), have attributed the difficulties encountered to the need for thinking on more than one level, which is required to relate the models to real world problems. Probably as a result of some of the pedagogic issues outlined in Byers and Eilks (in this book) and the problems associated with the need to contextualise information as discussed in detail in Overton, Byers, and Seery (in this book), students do not easily appreciate the discontinuous structure of matter, i.e. they try to transfer macroscopic properties to sub-microscopic particles. In addition, they have difficulty in differentiating between models and real things and consequently do not develop an adequate understanding of the methodological role of models (Grosslight et al., 1991).

The use of concrete models in chemistry education might have something to do with this. Concrete models are supposed to make the abstract nature of sub-microscopic entities more tangible. However, since they can "touch" them, students tend to look upon these concrete models as a reproduction of reality and not as constructed images. This arises from the different effects 'models' can have on the processes of learning and construction of meaning (e.g. Justi & Gilbert, 2002; Taber, 2008). The diagram in Figure 2 represents the epistemological and learning process including the elements "subject", "object" and "model" and clarifies that a concrete model belongs to the same area as the epistemological or learning object and is directly accessible by the subject, so that learners may confuse an object with its concrete model.

Computer visualizations (see Lagana et al. in this book, or the discussion in Gilbert 2005; Gilbert, Reiner, & Nakleh, 2008) now offer an interesting possible alternative. Virtual models can be handled like real (concrete) models without being or ever seeming real (like the object). They are vivid but not so close to the subject as is often the case with concrete models. This may help students to avoid confusing these models with the object. Computers can offer new possibilities for visualization that go well beyond anything that can be offered by concrete (material) models, thus enriching the potential of computer models to promote understanding. Last, but by no means least, computer visualizations can allow the use of a number of different models, side-by-side, thus offering enormous interactive potential to foster the notion of models as mental constructs.

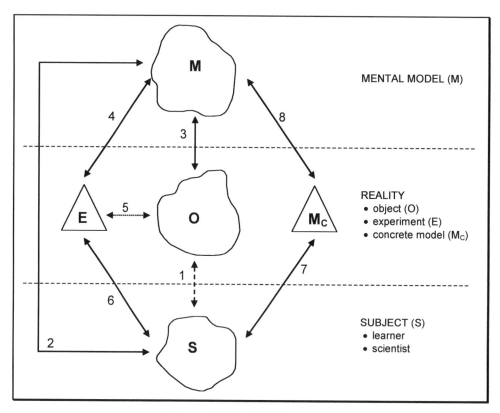

Figure 2. M-O-S-Diagram

Models are often designed to evidence certain aspects of molecular geometry, but they may of course hide others that are of equal importance. A sticks-and-balls model of ethanol (Figure 3) clearly shows atoms and their bonds. The overall occupied space however is better shown using a so-called space-filling model (Figure 4), although as can be seen the bonds are now much less visible. Such static models do not of course take into account thermal motions which may be important in some cases. These can be precisely determined, using X-ray diffraction and represented by ellipsoid models (Figure 5).

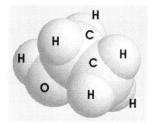

Figure 3. Sticks and balls model of the ethanol molecule   *Figure 4. Space filling model of the ethanol molecule*

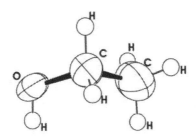

Figure 5. Structure and thermal motion of an ethanol molecule as determined by X-rays in an inclusion compound (courtesy of R. Centore and A. Tuzi)

In conclusion, the constant need to build relationships between the macroscopic and sub-microscopic worlds (Johnstone, 1991) defines a distinctive feature of chemistry, though there are other levels in-between which can also be important for chemical thinking (see discussions in Gilbert & Treagust, 2009a, i.e. Meijer, Bulte, & Pilot, 2009). Experiments belong to the macroscopic stage, and include reactivity, physical and biological properties, and trends in properties from one substance to another. The molecular interpretations of the behaviour of substances however, belong to the sub-micro world. Thus, one of the most important skills that we can help our students to develop is an ability to systematically relate what is observed to its underlying sub-microscopic interpretation.

Being able to discuss observed phenomena at the particulate level makes sound interpretations possible. The reverse can also be true: Starting from considerations at the molecular level one can predict macroscopic behaviour, and design molecules and substances with desired properties. This is well illustrated by the targeted syntheses of biomolecules (drugs, analogues of bioactive substances) and of materials for use in electronics or as polymers and so on.

For a discussion about models and visualization in science education the reader is referred to Gilbert and Boulter (1998), Gilbert (2005) and Gilbert et al. (2008). An activity to probe students' mental models of a substance or reaction at the molecular level before showing animations portraying the phenomenon is describe in the *VisChem Learning Design* by Tasker and Dalton (2006).

Resources

For further reading on the Nature of Science see McComas (1998), Warren (2001), or the Springer journal *Science & Education*, on models and visualization Gilbert (2005), Gilbert et al. (2008), or Gilbert and Treagust (2009a), and on working in the laboratory Johnstone and Al-Shuaili (2001), Hofstein (2004), or Hofstein and Mamlok-Naaman (2007).

References

American Association for the Advancement of Science [AAAS] (1990). *Science for all Americans*. New York: Oxford University Press.

Abd-El-Khalick, F., Bell, R. L., & Lederman, N. G. (1998). The nature of science and instructional practice: Making the unnatural nature. *Science Education, 82*, 417- 437.

Abell, S. K., & Smith, D. C. (1992). What is science?. Perspective elementary teachers` conceptions of the nature of science. In: S. Hills (Ed.), *The History and Philosophy of Science in Science Education, (Vol. 1)* (pp. 11-22). Kingston: Queen`s University.

Aguirre, J. M., Haggarty, S. M., & Linder, C. J. (1990). Student-teachers` conceptions of science, teaching and learning: A case study in preservice teacher education. *International Journal of Science Education, 12*, 381-390.

Albright, T. A., & Burdett, J. K. (1992). *Problems in molecular orbital theory*. Oxford: Oxford University Press.

Bandura A. (1986). *Social foundation of thought and action: A social cognitive theory*. Englewood: Prentice-Hall.

Black, P., & Atkin, J. M. (Eds.) (1996). *Changing the subject: Innovations in science, mathematics and technology education*. London: Routledge.

Chalmers, A. F. (1976). *What is this thing called science?*. Queensland: University Press.

Czerniak, C. M., & Lumpe, A. T. (1996). Relationship between teacher beliefs and science education reform. *Journal of Science Teacher Education, 7*, 247-266.

De Jong, O. (2007). Trends in western science curricula and science education research: A bird's eye view. *Journal of Baltic Science Education, 6*, 15-22.

Derkse, W. (1981). Popper's epistemology as a pedagogic and didactic principle, or let them make more 'mistakes'. *Journal of Chemical Education, 58*, 565-566.

Domin, D. S. (1999). A content analysis of general chemistry laboratory manuals for evidence of high-order cognitive tasks. *Journal of Chemical Education, 76*, 109-111.

Driver, R., Leach, J., Miller, R., & Scott, P. (1996). *Young people`s images of science*. Buckingham: Open University Press.

Gilbert, J. K. (2005). *Visualization in science education*. Boston: Kluwer.

Gilbert, J. K., & Boulter, C. J. (1998). Learning science through models and modelling. In: B. J. Fraser & K. G. Tobin (Eds.), *International Handbook of Science Education* (pp. 53-66). Dordrecht: Kluwer.

Gilbert, J. K., Reiner, M., & Nakleh, M. B. (Eds.) (2008). *Visualization: Theory and practice in science education*. Boston: Springer.

Gilbert, J. K., & Treagust, D. F. (Eds.) (2009a). *Multile respresentations in chemical education*. Dordrecht: Springer.

Gilbert, J. K., & Treagust, D. F. (2009b). Towards a coherent model for macro, submicro and symbolic representations in chemical education. In: J. K. Gilbert & D. F. Treagust (Eds.), *Multile respresentations in chemical education* (pp. 333-350). Dordrecht: Springer.

Grosslight, L., Unger, S., Jay, E., & Smith, C. L. (1991). Understanding models and their use in science: Conceptions of middle and high school students and experts. *Journal of Research in Science Teaching, 28*, 799-822

Hadzidaki, P. (2008). 'Quantum Mechanics' and 'Scientific Explanation' an explanatory strategy aiming at providing understanding. *Science & Education, 17*, 49-73.

Hammrich, P. L., & Blouch, K. K. (1996). Elementary teacher candidates` conceptions of the Nature of Science and science teaching. *Paper presented at the Annual Meeting of the National Science Teacher Association. St. Louis, USA.*

Hoffmann, R., & Torrence, V. (1993). *Chemistry imagined. Reflections on science*. Washington: Smithsonian.

Hofstein, A. (2004). The laboratory in chemistry education: Thirty years of experience with developments, implementation and evaluation. *Chemistry Education Research and Practice, 5*, 247-265.

Hofstein, A., & Lunetta, V. N. (2003). The laboratory in science education: Foundations for the twenty-first century. *Science Education, 88*, 28-54.

Hofstein, A., & Mamlok-Naaman, R. (2007). Experiments and the laboratory in chemistry education (Theme issue). *Chemistry Education Research and Practice, 8*, no. 2.

Jacob, C. (2001). Analysis and synthesis. Interdependent operations in chemical language and practice. *HYLE, 7*, 31-50.

Johnson, K. (1991). High school science teachers` conceptualisations of teaching and learning: Theory and practice. *European Journal of Teacher Education, 14*, 65-78.

Johnstone, A. H. (1991). Why is science difficult to learn?. Things are seldom what they seem. *Journal of Computer Assisted Learning, 7*, 75-83

Johnstone, A.H., & Al-Shuaili, A. (2001). Learning in the laboratory: Some thoughts from the literature. *University Chemistry Education, 5*, 42-51.

Justi, R. S., & Gilbert, J. K. (2002). Models and modelling in chemistry education. In: J. K. Gilbert, O. De Jong, R. Justi, D. F. Treagust, & J. H. Van Driel (Eds.), *Chemical education: Towards research-based practice* (pp. 47-68). Dordrecht: Kluwer.

Kalkanis, G., Hadzidaki, P., & Stavrou, D. (2003). An instructional model for a radical conceptual change towards quantum mechanics concepts. *Science Education, 87*, 257-280.

Kant, I. (1787). *Kritik der reinen Vernunft.* Riga: Alfred Kröner.

Kipins, M., & Hofstein, A. (2007). The inquiry laboratory as a source for development of metacognitive skills. *International Journal of Science and Mathematics Education, 6*, 601-627.

Korpan, C., Bisanz, G., Bisanz, J., & Henderson, J. (1997). Assessing literacy in science: Evaluation of scientific news briefs. *Science Education, 81*, 515-532.

Lederman, N. G. (1992). Students` and teachers` conceptions of the nature of science: A review of the research. *Journal of Research in Science Teaching, 29*, 331-359.

Lederman, N. G. (1999). Teachers' understanding of the nature of science and classroom practice: factors that facilitate or impede the relationship. *Journal of Research in Science Teaching, 36*, 916-929.

Lederman, N. G. (2007). Nature of science: Past, present and future. In: N. G. Lederman & S. K. Abell (Eds.), *Handbook of research on science education* (pp. 831-879). Mahwah: Lawrence Erlbaum.

Lederman, N. G., & Druger, M. (1985). Classroom factors related to changes in students` conceptions of the nature of science. *Journal of Research in Science Teaching, 22*, 649-662.

Lederman, N. G., & Zeidler, D. L (1987). Science teachers` conceptions of the nature of science: Do they really influence teaching behavior?. *Science Education, 71*, 721-734.

Lederman, N. G., Wade, P., & Bell, R. L. (1998). Assessing understanding of the nature of science: A historical perspective. In: W. F. McComas (Ed.), *The nature of science in science education: Rationales and strategies* (pp. 331-350). Dordrecht: Kluwer.

Lederman, N. G., Abd-El-Khalick, F., Bell, R. L., & Schwartz, R. (2002). Views of nature of science questionnaire: Toward valid and meaningful assessment of learner's conceptions of nature of science. *Journal of Research in Science Teaching, 39*, 497-521.

Lehn, J.-M. (2007). From supramolecular chemistry towards constitutional dynamic chemistry and adaptive chemistry. *Chemical Society Reviews, 36*, 151-160.

McComas, W. F. (1998). *The nature of science in science education: Rationales and strategies.* Dordrecht: Kluwer.

Meijer, M., Bulte, A. M. W., & Pilot, A. (2009). Structure–property relations between macro and micro representations: Relevant meso-levels in authentic tasks. In: J. K. Gilbert & D. F. Treagust (Eds.), *Multile respresentations in chemical education* (pp. 195-213). Dordrecht: Springer.

Müller, A., Dress, A., & Vögtle, F, (1995). *From simplicity to complexity.* Berlin: Springer.

Murcia, K., & Schibeci, R. (1999). Primary student teachers` conceptions of the nature of science. *International Journal of Science Education, 21*, 1123-1140.

Nott, M., & Wellington, J. (1996). When the black box springs open: Practical work in schools and the nature of science. *International Journal of Science Education, 18*, 807-818.

Palmquist, B. C., & Finley, F. N. (1997). Preservice teachers` views of the nature of science during a postbaccalaureate science teaching program. *Journal of Research in Science Teaching, 34*, 595-615.

Pajares, M. F. (1992). Teachers` beliefs and educational research: Cleaning up a messy construct. *Reviews in Educational Research, 62*, 307-332.

Pomeroy, D. (1993). Implication of teachers` beliefs about the nature of science: Comparison of the beliefs of scientists, secondary science teachers, and elementary teachers. *Science Education, 77*, 261-278.

Popper, K. C. (1959). *The logic of sientific discovery*. London: Hutchinson.

Price, W. S., & Hill, J. O. (2004). Raising the status of chemistry education. *University Chemistry Education, 8*, 13-20.

Reiners, C. S. (1996). Von der Stoffsystematik zu systemischen Aspekten der Naturwissenschaft Chemie. *Zeitschrift für Didaktik der Naturwissenschaften, 2*, 11-20.

Reiners, C. S. (1998). Amphoterie – ein Schlüsselbegriff für die Chemiedidaktik. In: A. Kometz (Ed.), *Chemieunterricht im Spannungsfeld Gesellschaft – Chemie – Umwelt* (pp. 160-170). Berlin: Cornelsen.

Rowell, J. A. (1982). Images of Science: An empirical study. *European Journal of Science Education, 4*, 79-94.

Rubba, P. A., & Harkness, W. L. (1993). Examination of preservice and in-service secondary science teachers` beliefs about science-technology-society interaction. *Science Education, 77*, 407-431.

Saborowski, J. (2000). *Computervisualisierung und Modelldenken*. Cologne: Dissertation.

Schmidt, W. H., & Kennedy. M. M. (1990). *Teachers´ and teacher candidates´ beliefs about subject and about teaching responsibilities*. East Lansing: Michigan State University (ERIC Document Reproduction Service No. ED 320 902).

Schwartz, R. S., Lederman, N. G., & Crawford, B. A. (2004). Developing views of nature of science in an authentic context: An explicit approach to bridging the gap between nature of science and scientific inquiry. *Science Education, 88*, 610-645.

Stefani, C., & Tsaparlis, G. (2009). Students' levels of explanations, models, and misconceptions in basic quantum chemistry: A phenomenographic study. *Journal of Research in Science Teaching, 46*, 520-536.

Taber, K., (2008). Towards a curricular model of the nature of science. *Science & Education, 17*, 179-218.

Taber, K., & Coll, R. K. (2002). Bonding. In: J. K. Gilbert, O. De Jong, R. Justi, D. F. Treagust, & J. H. Van Driel (Eds.), *Chemical education:Towards research-based practice* (pp. 213-234). Dordrecht: Kluwer.

Tasker, R., & Dalton, R. (2006). Research into practice: Visualisation of the molecular world using animations. *Chemistry Education Research and Practice, 7*, 141-159.

Tobin. K. (1990). Research on science laboratory activities: In pursuit of better questions and answers to improve learning. *School, Science and Mathematics, 90*, 403-418.

Tsaparlis, G. (1997). Atomic orbitals, molecular orbitals and related concepts: Conceptual difficulties among chemistry students. *Research in Science Education, 27*, 271-287.

Tsaparlis, G. (2007). Teaching and learning physical chemistry – review of educational research. In: M. D. Ellison & T. A. Schoolcraft (Eds.), *Advances in teaching physical chemistry* (pp. 75-112). Washington: Oxford University Press.

Van Driel, J. H., & Verloop, N. (1999). Teachers' knowledge of models and modelling in science. *International Journal of Science Education, 21*, 1141-1153.

Van Hoeve-Brouwer, G., & De Vos, W. (1994). Chemical Bonding or chemical structure?. In: H.-J. Schmidt (Ed.), *Problem solving and misconceptions in chemistry and physics* (pp. 238-245). Hong Kong: ICASE.

Warren, D. (2001). *The Nature of science*. London: RSC.

Zeichner, K. M., & Hoeft, K. (1996). Teacher socialisation for cultural diversity. In: J. Sikula (Ed.), *Handbook of Research on Teacher Education* (pp. 527-547). New York: Macmillan.

Context- and Problem-based Learning in Higher Level Chemistry Education

TINA L. OVERTON
University of Hull, United Kingdom

BILL BYERS
University of Ulster, United Kingdom

MICHAEL K. SEERY
Dublin Institute of Technology, Ireland

Context and problem-based learning are approaches to teaching that have been found to engage and motivate students and to develop a range of intellectual and transferable skills. This chapter discusses the literature related to these approaches and describes strategies to implement them in the teaching of chemistry within higher education.

Introduction

Teaching of chemistry at higher level has traditionally given priority to facts and theories with emphasis being placed on the learning of concepts. Only after the basic concepts have been learned have students been encouraged to try to apply what they have learned in any real world contexts. Underlying this traditional approach to chemistry teaching is an inherent assumption that students will readily be able to transfer knowledge and understanding from the academic context where learning is occurring to real world problems when they are subsequently encountered. The evidence however suggests that such transfer does not readily occur (Johnstone, 1991; DeHaan, 2005). Therefore introducing real world examples only after all the relevant theory has been covered may often not be the best method to promote student learning.

It is generally accepted that chemistry is inherently a difficult subject to learn. A major problem arises because the basic concepts can be expressed at three distinct levels which can be represented as corners of a triangle

Chapter consultant: Stuart W. Bennett, The Open University, Milton Keynes, United Kingdom

I. Eilks and B. Byers (Eds.). Innovative Methods in Teaching and Learning Chemistry in Higher Education, pp. 43-60. © 2009 RSC Publishing.

(Figure 1; Johnstone, 1991), with each of these levels complementing the others. The levels are

- the *macro*: what can be seen, touched and smelt;
- the *sub-micro*: atoms, molecules, structures, forces, etc,
- the *representational*: symbols, formulas, equations, etc.

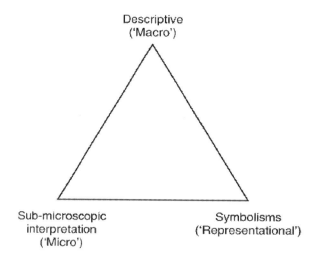

Figure 1. Three levels of science concept representation

Johnstone (1991) argued that it is only at the macro level that we encounter the real world and where students experience chemistry in the laboratory and indeed in real life. However, for chemistry to be more fully understood, it is usually necessary to move on to the sub-micro level where the behaviour of substances and physical phenomena can only be interpreted in terms of unseen conceptual models and recorded using some representational notation (see Floriano, Markic, Reiners, & Avitabile in this book). Chemistry, at university level, has traditionally been taught almost entirely at this level using a variety of representations. Real life, the macro level, is unfortunately often divorced from the rest of the subject or at best added on as an afterthought. All too often therefore, students fail to link chemistry at this sub-micro level with their everyday lives and thus fail to see the underlying relevance of much of the chemistry they are taught. However, where this approach has been reversed and real life contexts used to drive learning there is ample evidence to demonstrate that students engage much more enthusiastically with their learning (Reid, 2000; Belt, Evans, McCreedy, Overton, & Summerfield, 2002; Rayner, 2005). An interesting example of how the macro and sub-micro can be related to assist understanding of the limiting ingredient concept has been described by Hanson (2000).

Context and problem-based learning are approaches that are becoming increasingly popular in Higher Education as we try to address the difficulties of understanding and relevance outlined above. The aim of this chapter is to introduce these two approaches and provide some exemplars of their relevance to the teaching of chemistry in higher education.

What is context-based learning?

Foundations of context-based learning

Context-based learning (CBL) is possibly a misleading term as all learning surely occurs within some context (Hills, 2003). In its broadest sense CBL merely describes the cultural and social environment within which students, tutors and institutions operate. This context can of course be influenced by communications media to provide the academic community with a common culture. Hansman (2001) states that adult learning will only take place when this context and appropriate learning tools or methodologies come together to promote interaction between the learners.

A pragmatic approach to context-based learning simply involves the use of topical examples and applications to illustrate and illuminate the curriculum. For chemistry students this usually means providing them with opportunities to test theories with real world examples. Nonetheless the use of a meaningful and appropriate context has been shown to motivate and enthuse learners (Hennessy, 1993; Mandl, Gruber, & Renkl, 1993) and any effort to introduce topical issues into lectures is therefore to be strongly encouraged.

Using contexts as a scaffold for teaching chemical principles is justified in learning theory by the concept of situated cognition. According to this concept all our knowing and learning is bound into social, cultural and physical contexts (e.g. Greeno, 1998). This suggests that content learned through appropriate contexts will be better anchored in the memory and correspondingly more easily recalled and applied to real world problems associated with similar contexts that may be encountered in the future. This is unlikely to be the case for knowledge which is stored in our memory without connections to any real life contexts. The strategy of anchored instruction (Vanderbilt Group, 1990) makes use of these ideas by providing the learner with appropriate contexts as anchors for more effective learning.

Why use context?

The use of context is supported by both pedagogic and affective arguments. Referring back to the information processing model of learning as described in Byers and Eilks (in this book) and the theory of situated cognition and anchored instruction described above, we see that meaningful learning occurs when incoming information can be linked to and interpreted by what the learner already knows, or by what has meaning for him or her. Where no links can be made little significant learning will take place. All too often when chemistry is being taught at the sub-micro or particulate level, students fail to see its relevance to the real (macro) world. On the other hand the use of contexts that are familiar to the learner is likely to facilitate effective linking and therefore to catalyze learning. One way to show the relevance of the chemistry we teach is to put real life, relevant context into our teaching. By starting with a context that interests students, not only will they be much more likely to see the relevance and make the links, but they will also be more likely to be motivated to learn. An extensive review of 66 studies on interventions with 11-16 year old pupils found that the use of context motivates and fosters positive attitudes to science without compromising the learner's understanding of scientific ideas (Bennett, Hogarth, & Lubben, 2005).

Barbara Sitzman, 2001 American Chemical Society Conant Award Winner (JCE Editorial Staff, 2001), has suggested that the characteristics of great teachers are that they not only know their subject well but are also able to demonstrate how it relates to other disciplines. Fortunately Chemistry is ubiquitous and there is an almost infinite variety of contexts and issues that can be used and there is no reason why this should result in any loss of scientific rigour. For example, Holman and Pilling (2004) have described teaching the daunting topic of thermodynamics in context. The relationship between fine art and chemistry is particularly strong, with colour being a dominant feature of both (Orna, 2001). Chemistry is fundamental not only to the manufacture and characterisation of pigments but also to the authentication, conservation and restoration of works of art. The question, "Why are rubies red yet sapphires are blue?" provides an interesting context with which to introduce Crystal Field Theory (Byers, 2002).

Two further examples follow. The relationship between the molecular world and the macroscopic world is well illustrated by the work of Buckminster Fuller, the architect who designed the American pavilion for Expo 67 in Montreal while the characterisation and naming of C_{60} and other fullerenes only occurred some 20 years later (O'Driscoll, 1996). The C_{60} structure is familiar at the macro level being widely used for example for the manufacture of footballs. Chemists may have learnt from an architect but it seems likely that architecture and art in general can in turn learn much from molecular structures (Ball, 2008). Recently O'Connor and Hayden have discussed the advantages of contextualising the teaching of nanotechnology (O'Connor & Hayden, 2008).

Solubility is an example of how contexts can support teaching. Solubility is discussed in a rigid theoretical way in many chemistry programmes and therefore can appear dry and uninteresting. However it is a fundamental process with far reaching implications in our daily lives making it extremely easy to relate to a wide range of real world issues, such as environmental problems, living systems, nutrition and alcohol intoxication. Some contexts for the teaching of solubility are described below. Only about a third of the naturally occurring elements appear to be essential to life. It is now widely believed that life originated in the ancient oceans and utilised only elements that were both available and particularly suited to their intended role (Ochiai, 1978). Thus the widespread use of calcium in teeth, bones and shells becomes clearly understandable in terms of the ready availability of calcium and the low solubility of calcium salts of the predominant naturally occurring anions, hydrogen phosphate and carbonate (Ochiai, 1991).

The protein haemoglobin is a chemistry treasure chest (Childs, 2001). Unfortunately the fundamental reason that we need haemoglobin, or something like it, because the low solubility of O_2 in pure water is insufficient to satisfy our needs for aerobic respiration, is often lost in a background of sophisticated discussion of topics like cooperativity and high-spin/low-spin transitions. The fact remains that it is largely due to haemoglobin that the dissolved oxygen levels in mammalian blood are some 30 times greater than in distilled water thus enabling the existence of higher forms of life.

The effects of pressure on gas solubility can be seen all around us from the effervescence that accompanies the opening of a can of coca-cola to the agony of 'the bends' suffered by the unwary diver. Possibly the most dramatic illustration however, was provided by Lake Nyos in Western Cameroon where on an evening in August 1986 every living creature within a few kilometres of the lake died from asphyxiation (DeLorenzo, 2001). Lake Nyos in fact, lies in a volcanic crater and cracks in the crater floor allow the release of some five million cubic metres of carbon dioxide into the lake each year. The water in the lake is stratified and although natural mixing does allow enough CO_2 to escape to maintain constant levels, very high levels of CO_2 prevail in the high pressure region of the lower waters. On the evening in question it appears that some disturbance allowed the upper water to sink and the lower levels to rise. Gas solubility decreased with the decreasing pressure and the released CO_2 flooded over the crater's edge into the surrounding countryside, asphyxiating most life forms in the area. The recent suggestion that we might think about trying to control global warming by pumping CO_2 directly into the deep oceans will certainly need to consider such possibilities.

Spinach is undoubtedly a vegetable rich in the trace nutrients iron and calcium, and at first sight, Popeye's belief, that spinach is particularly good for you, might appear to be correct. However, on closer investigation we find that spinach is even richer in oxalate, which effectively blocks absorption of iron and calcium by forming insoluble salts (Walker, 1988). Thus contrary to popular belief eating spinach is unlikely to enhance intake of either metal and Popeye might just as well have stuck to eating peas.

A more sophisticated topic is the consideration of how alcohol levels in exhaled breath can be related to the level of alcohol in the blood. Discussion of the breathalyzer readily leads on to consideration of topics such as partition ratios and Henry's law (Thompson, 1997).

Context-based teaching

While there is much to be gained by supporting the established curriculum with topical issues and contexts we would suggest however, that true context-based teaching involves introducing relevant theory on a strictly need to know basis, by allowing principles to emerge directly from study of the context.

The use of true context-based teaching is currently increasing in pre-19 education. In the United Kingdom introduction of the *Salters* Chemistry scheme has proved both successful and motivating (Pilling, Holman, & Waddington, 2001; Holman & Pilling, 2001). The Salters A level course aims to 'emphasize the ways in which chemistry is applied and the work that chemists do' and includes modules on topics such as 'The Oceans' to teach enthalpy, entropy and solubility and a module called 'The Steel Story' to teach redox, electrochemistry and d-block chemistry. Similarly the *Salters Horners* A level physics course uses modules such as 'Transport on Track' to teach force, momentum, electromagnetic forces and 'Build or Bust' to teach simple harmonic motion, forces, vibrations, resonance and damping. Similar approaches are now implemented in different countries, e.g. *ChemConnections* in the United States (chemistry.beloit.edu). The Higher Education sector is now also seeing a growth in provision that presents science in real-world contexts, such as forensic science, sports science and astronomy (Belt & Overton, 2007; Potter & Overton, 2006).

A number of textbooks are now available to support context-based courses in the chemical sciences, starting with Ben Selinger's now classic text, 'Chemistry in the Marketplace' which contains chapters on such topics as 'Chemistry in the boudoir', 'Chemistry in the kitchen' and 'Chemistry in the medicine cabinet' (Selinger, 1989). More recent offerings include "'The Extraordinary Chemistry of Ordinary Things' (Snyder, 1997) and 'Chemistry in Context. Applying Chemistry to Society' (Stanitski, Eubanks, Middlecamp, & Pienta 2003).

When using context-based teaching it is important to ensure that assessment is also rich in context. The use of scenarios based on real world situations to present coursework or examination questions further establishes the relevance of the learning and is likely to promote the transfer of knowledge from one context to another.

What is problem-based learning?

Foundations of problem-based learning

Problem-based learning (PBL) can be considered to be a sub-category of context-based learning where the problem itself provides the context. The curriculum is carefully organised so that it is in effect driven by the real life contexts and PBL always involves working in small groups (see Eilks, Markic, Bäumer, & Schanze in this book). In PBL contexts are presented in the form of problem scenarios, an important feature being that the problems or scenarios are encountered before all the relevant learning has taken place and act as the driver for new learning. Thus PBL should be distinguished from problem solving where problems are generally encountered only after learning has taken place and is therefore concerned primarily with the application of knowledge rather than the learning itself. A course that is delivered entirely by PBL needs have no lectures and students work in small groups throughout the process, with tutors acting essentially as facilitators rather than teachers. A good introduction to PBL has been provided in a book by Boud and Feletti (1998) with short chapters grouped into themes, including getting started, design and implementation, and assessment and evaluation.

PBL first appeared in 1969 as a new approach to medical education at McMaster University, Canada. It was devloped as an educational approach drawing on philosophy, psychology, and educational research. According to Barrows and Tamblyn (1980), PBL can be explained as *"the learning that results from the process of working toward the understanding or resolution of a problem*". Savery and Duffy (1995) have used Barrow's model to demonstrate that PBL fits easily within the framework for effective learning described by the constructivist learning theory. Constructivism is a philosophy of learning founded on the premise that, by reflecting on our experiences, we construct our own understanding of the world we live in (see Byers & Eilks in this book). PBL learning is a process of building on prior knowledge, problem solving, using critical thinking approaches and reflecting (Maudsley, 2000).

According to Barrows (Barrows, 1996) PBL refers to learning which is facilitated by six core features:

1. Learning is student-centred;
2. Learning occurs in small peer-groups;
3. Teachers act as facilitators;
4. Problems provide the organizing focus and stimulus for learning;
5. Problems are the vehicle for the development of problem-solving skills;
6. New information is acquired through self-directed learning.

In this way, PBL aims to facilitate students' self-learning (Johnstone & Otis, 2006). As a result of the problem solving process, the outcomes for students who learn through the PBL method are that they are able to think critically and able to recognize and solve complex, real-world problems by finding and evaluating real-world resources; that they can work effectively in small groups; that they can demonstrate versatile communication skills and that they can use content knowledge and intellectual skills acquired at university to become lifelong learners (Duch, Groh, & Allen, 2001a).

There has been considerable research carried out that compares PBL trained medical students with traditional medical students. Many of these findings may be generalizable to the application of PBL in other disciplines. For example, research into reasoning skills found that PBL students tended to reason backwards from clinical information to theory whereas traditional students tended to reason forward from theory and stayed closer to clinical facts (Patel, Groen, & Norman, 1991). There is evidence that PBL students perform less well on written examinations testing knowledge (Mennin, Friedman, Skipper, Kalishman, & Snyder, 1993) but perform better on skills based assessments (Polglase, Parish, Buckley, Smith, & Joiner, 1989). Some studies have shown that PBL students use different study skills to those employed by conventional students. PBL students have been found to use a wider range of information sources and feel more confident in using information (Vernon & Blake, 1993). It has been suggested that problem-based curricula can lead to increased retention of knowledge, enhanced integration of basic scientific concepts into clinical thinking, development of self-directed learning skills and increasing intrinsic interest in the subject matter being learned (Dolmans & Schmidt, 1996). An interesting study found that graduates from a problem-based medical school considered that they had been better prepared for medical practice in a number of key areas than did graduates from a traditional medical school (Hill, Rolfe, Pearson, &

Heathcote, 1998). PBL students have been found to be more likely to study for meaning than conventional students (Newble & Clarke, 1986) though Groves (2005) suggests that this is unlikely to occur where the assessment is not supportive or the workload excessive.

How does problem-based learning work?

PBL is different from other forms of learning in that the students work in teams throughout and move towards a solution to the problem together by gathering and sharing information and ideas. There are several formal models of PBL and these are strictly adhered to in some disciplines, particularly medicine and associated professional disciplines, such as nursing. As PBL is relatively new in the sciences, practitioners are developing flexible models and implementing them in ways that suit their own particular context. Some examples are discussed later. However, the main features of PBL are real world context, group work, problem solving, acquisition of new knowledge, and presentation of outcomes or product.

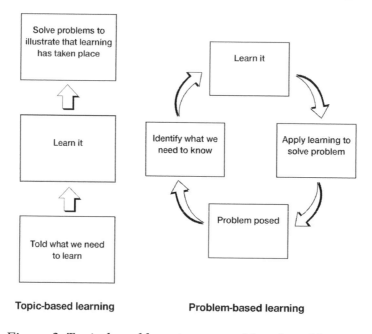

Figure 2. Topic-based learning vs. problem-based learning

Generally, during the first classroom session the students are divided into groups and presented with the problem. They may brainstorm in order to clarify the nature of the problem and identify their learning needs. They may delegate roles within the groups and share existing knowledge. The tutor's role is one of observation, guidance and support. Outside the classroom session, the students engage in independent study in order to fill any gaps in their subject knowledge. They come together again in a group or classroom session to share and critically evaluate any resources and information they have been able to gather. Using the newly acquired information they work towards a solution to the problem. Again, the tutor's role is one of guidance and support. This cycle of independent study, group interaction and critical analysis may be repeated as many times as dictated by the problem. Eventually the students present their solution and reflect on the process and solution. The cyclic nature of the process and the difference between a problem based approach and the more traditional topic based approach to learning is illustrated in Figure 2.

What about assessment?

As PBL is a very different type of learning activity it may not be appropriate to assess students in a traditional way. The assessment should be matched to the desired learning outcomes. Assessment may focus on the solution to the problem, or the problem solving process or the skills development aspect. Tutors must decide whether they wish to give each member of a group the same mark or whether they wish to build an individual element into the assessment. Students may be involved in assessing each other's contribution to the activity or may even be required to carry out self-assessment and reflection. Useful assessment tools include: reflective logs and diaries, written reports, oral presentations, posters or the product from practical activity (Chin & Overton, 2005). A good discussion on the assessment of a problem based laboratory module has recently been published by McDonnell, O'Connor, and Seery (2007).

Examples and implementation

Examples from Chemistry

Context and problem-based learning in Chemistry has grown in popularity over the past five years and new and innovative examples are continuing to appear. Belt et al. (2002) have produced a suite of C/PBL resources for analytical chemistry drawing on contexts in industrial, pharmaceutical, environmental and forensic chemistry (also Summerfield, Overton, & Belt, 2003). These resources deliver learning outcomes in analytical chemistry as well as a range of transferable skills. Green chemistry has also been used as a context for chemistry teaching (Grant et al., 2004; Heaton, Hodgson, Overton, & Powell, 2006) where the aim has been to raise the issue of green chemistry as it relates to the chemical industry. In another example, sport was used as the context to meet learning outcomes in biochemistry, simple thermodynamics and materials chemistry (Potter & Overton, 2006). Environmental chemistry is another context that lends itself to delivery of the chemistry curriculum (Kegley, Stacy, & Carroll, 1996). It might be expected that the traditional branches of Chemistry; inorganic, organic and physical, would be more difficult to deliver via context or problem-based learning as the applications and real life contexts are less obvious. Some success has been achieved however and a collection of resources in these branches has been published by the Royal Society of Chemistry (Belt & Overton, 2005). PBL is used in University of Delaware, United States, chemistry teaching programme for first year undergraduate honours chemistry (Groh, 2001; Groh, 2004). Students are given three problems, and assigned to groups of about four, with specific group roles such as leader, recorder, advocate taken by students in rotation. Marks are awarded for attendance and participation at the group sessions (5%). There is no parallel lecture course; students are assigned independent study topics to review and revise, and there are three one hour tests to check students' knowledge and understanding during the module (45%). There is a concurrent laboratory programme (20%), which aims to complement and expand on the theoretical programme. Students' work on the problem is assessed by group or individual reports and reflective statements (15%). A final exam is also given (15%). Some example problems, covering the areas of physical properties of materials (specific heat, heat of fusion) and acids/bases/pH are available on the University of Delaware website (see resources at the end of this chapter).

Another study using PBL described its implementation into a module on Instrumental Analysis (Zhang, 2002). In this case, students are given a few lectures to provide some information or ideas relevant to their problems, which consist of a number of short problems and one semester-long problem. Students are divided into groups of four and work on their problems in and out of class time. The tutor acts as a "wandering tutor", going from group to group and temporarily becoming part of each group to facilitate the process. Zhang describes in detail in his work the format of the small group projects and the main project, including group requirements and assessment strategies. Additionally, he describes some problems that he has encountered as a tutor.

The University of Southern California, United States, uses PBL and CBL to teach Pharmaceutical Chemistry (Romero, Eriksen, & Haworth, 2004). The authors describe their implementation and experiences of PBL over a decade. The structure of the course is built on case-studies based on pharmaceutical formulation problems, and the instructors use group-based work and instructor-led discussion sessions. Assessment includes oral assessment and essay-based problem-solving examinations. The authors provide an example of a case-study problem. A detailed analysis of the course in terms of assessment effectiveness, how course grading has changed and the effectiveness of the case-study is also provided.

The PBL approach has also be applied successfully to the undergraduate chemistry laboratory. McGarvey (2004) has collaborated with industry to produce a suite of physical chemistry experiments and McDonnell et al. (2007) have produced PBL mini-projects which utilise contexts such as cosmetics, food and forensic science. A recent study by Domin (2007) suggests that while learning associated with traditional expository experiments tends to occur mainly after the experiment has been completed, learning tends to be maximized while the activity is being carried out in problem-based laboratories.

Examples from Physics

Problem-based learning in physics has emerged in the United Kingdom and Ireland over the last 5 years, largely stimulated by the efforts of groups at the University of Leicester and Dublin Institute of Technology. A comprehensive guide to PBL in physics which contains a large number of examples, including the work of these two groups, has been published by the Higher Education Academy Physical Sciences Centre (Raine & Symons,

2005). For example PBL has been used in the undergraduate physics laboratory (Howard, 2004) and in small group projects (Mowbray, 2005). One interesting application of PBL has involved the use of images, rather than textual questions, equations and formulas (Collett, 2004). An extensive post-16 curriculum uses contexts in sport, food, and the environment to teach basic physics concepts (Whitelegg & Parry, 1999). The authors of this curriculum warn against using contexts which potentially alienate sections of the student population and to take care to consider gender and cultural issues

Implementation strategies and consequent issues

Several educators cited here have described the process of change on going from traditional to PBL paradigms, and several useful lessons can be derived from their experiences. A suggested implementation strategy is outlined below:

1. Determine the learning outcomes of the course/module: what are the goals of your module (based on the goals of the programme) and do these goals suit the PBL paradigm?
2. What resources do you have available to you – what are the number of students, the number of tutors, how many contact hours, what is the physical environment (e.g. fixed/movable chairs), what are the timetable restrictions?
3. Based on the resources and learning outcomes, consider how you wish to assess the module.
4. Develop a learning matrix, listing the learning outcomes. For each problem you devise, ensure that some of the learning outcomes you list are addressed. Ensure all learning outcomes are covered by at least one of the problems set. An example of a learning matrix can be found in an article by Ram (1999).
5. In writing problems, provide students with a clear role. This gives them ownership and responsibility for the work, and for the outcomes– *i.e.* they are accountable, which has inherent motivational aspects. It is also likely to be motivating as it is more enjoyable for the students. Ensure the problems are challenging enough so that they require team work but not so challenging that the students will be put off by their level of difficulty.

The PBL process requires the role of the instructor to change from that of educator to that of facilitator. The process involved in tutoring is as follows (Bowe, 2005):

1. Delegate roles – who is the chair, who will record, and decide whether these roles will rotate, and how often; note that you may need different assessment criteria for each role.
2. Allow the students to brainstorm, develop a hypothesis and gauge their current knowledge and understanding.
3. Identify students learning issues – what is needed to solve the problem, and how will this be done. The role of the tutor here is to check the process. The students can list their ideas, what facts they know, what

they need to find out and who is responsible for this as a record of the session.

4. Each group member then completes their assigned tasks independently.
5. At the next session, the group reviews, and repeats the process until the problem is solved. The tutor can check for understanding by asking questions while group members are giving their feedback. Peer tutoring can be facilitated by allowing students to question each other.

Within the PBL process, there are several issues that arise. These can be divided into three categories: (i) resource and administrative issues, (ii) instructor issues and (iii) student issues. Again, several of the case studies described herein outline approaches to resolving these issues, and an excellent book devoted to the topic covers some useful points from all three perspectives (Schwartz, Mennin, & Webb, 2001). Some useful issues from the point of view of the instructor include the following:

1. The need to give timely, regular feedback;
2. Encouraging 'self-directed learning';
3. Dealing with group issues such as 'mature' students who control the process or with students who don't wish to be involved in a group process; individual accountability;
4. Considering appropriate assessment (probably the single most important aspect when introducing PBL).

Resources

A search under 'problem based learning' using *Google* finds eight million hits with no trouble at all. Most PBL websites give a definition of the key characteristics and extol the virtues of the approach. Most give extensive link-lists and, consequently, almost any PBL website is a reasonable starting point. Few attempt to give any sort of realistic advice on implementation, overcoming difficulties, preparing staff and students or writing problems. Even fewer sites give examples of problems and many that do give materials which are, to say the least, disappointing. Much of what is presented is really no more than reasonably creative problem solving.

Most quality PBL sites originate in the USA, Canada and Australia. Much of what is available is in medical education but is often still applicable to other disciplines. Many of the sites are interdisciplinary and provide resources and ideas which many practitioners may find useful. What follows here are brief summaries of some of the more interesting and useful aspects of several sites on PBL.

LeAP (Problem-based Learning in Astronomy and Physics, www.le.ac.uk/leap) was a three-year fund for the development of teaching and learning project. The project aimed to increase the profile of problem-based learning in university Physics and Astronomy courses. The University of Leicester, United Kingdom, led the project consortium, with the Universities of Hertfordshire, Reading, and Sheffield as partners. The site includes a comparative analysis of PBL within physics, case studies, exemplar support materials for students and tutors, and original PBL problems. Although the project is now completed the webpage remains updated and the PBL work is now sustained under the activities of the Centre for Excellence in Teaching and Learning (π-CETL; www.open. ac.uk/picetl/). An annual PBL summer school is organised each July.

The University of Adelaide's Advisory Centre for University Education is home to the 'Leap into PBL'. This site is aimed primarily at the university teacher who wishes to explore this approach for the first time, but may also be useful to the teacher who has dabbled with PBL. The site aims to provide a structure around which practitioners can build their own course. It includes a step by step induction to PBL and covers a wide range of issues such as staff training, preparing students, assessment, evaluation, dealing with non-participation, keeping the groups going, timetabling sessions, etc. It also provides guidance on writing problems that does not gloss over the effort and time involved. This s a very useful and practical site and is a good starting point, especially for the lecturer new to PBL (www.adelaide.edu. au/clpd/materia/leap/leapinto/ProblemBasedLearning.pdf).

The National Center for Case Study Teaching in Science, United States, (ublib.buffalo.edu/libraries/projects/cases/ubcase.htm) is a real treasure trove of context-based case studies. There are many examples of cases covering many areas of science and links to a large number of sites which could provide ideas for new cases.

The Problem-based Learning Initiative at Southern Illinois University, United States, (www.pbli.org/core.htm) concentrates mainly on medical education but is very useful for the basics such as the essential requirements for PBL. If you are interested in medical education then they have a range of books, videos, PBL modules and patient simulations to buy. The bibliography is very comprehensive.

The San Diego State University, United States, Distributed Course Delivery for PBL site (edweb.sdsu.edu/clrit/home.html) provides an on-line workshop in PBL which could form the basis of do-it-yourself staff development. This could be another good starting point for academics new to PBL. The 'Learning Tree' section provides comprehensive coverage of the subject and is particularly strong on assessment, implementation and overcoming barriers and obstacles. The site also includes an extensive bibliography.

The University of Delaware, United States, site (www.udel.edu/pbl/courses. html) hosts a number of sample problems taken mainly from the sciences. By far the most useful feature of this site is the PBL Clearinghouse which is a searchable collection of many peer reviewed problems. The Clearinghouse is accessed via an email user name and password but these are available easily and you can be signed up within minutes. Once into the Clearinghouse users can search by keyword, author or discipline. There is also an invitation to become an author or reviewer.

McMaster University, Canada, (www.fhs.mcmaster.ca/pbls) has a long tradition in PBL. One staff member, P. K. Rangachari, has some very useful advice related to writing problems in his 'Writing Problems: A Personal

Casebook'. This casebook discusses the many aspects of writing good quality problems and includes many examples drawn mainly from the biomedical and biological sciences.

The Maricopa Center for Learning and Instruction, United States, hosts a searchable database of links (www.mcli.dist.maricopa.edu/pbl/problem. html) which is more useful than most as the search can be refined so producing a sensible number of more relevant links.

Other useful printed information can be found in Raine and Symons (2005), Duch, Groh, and Allen (2001b), Savin-Baden and Major (2004), or Savin-Baden, and Wilkie (2004).

References

Ball, P. (2008). The Crucible. *Chemistry World*, March, 42-43.

Barrows, H., & Tamblyn, R. (1980). *Problem-based learning: An approach to medical education*. New York: Springer.

Barrows, H. S. (1996). Problem-based learning in medicine and beyond: A brief overview. In: L. Wilkerson & W. H. Gijselaers (Eds.), *New directions for teaching and learning* (Vol. 68, pp. 3-11). San Francisco: Jossey-Bass.

Belt, S., Evans, E. H., McCreedy, T., Overton, T. L., & Summerfield, S. (2002). A problem based learning approach to analytical and applied chemistry. *University Chemistry Education, 6*(2), 65-72.

Belt, S., & Overton, T. L. (2005). *Case studies for undergraduate chemistry courses*. Cambridge: RSC.

Belt, S., & Overton, T. L. (2007). Context-based case studies in analytical chemistry. In: P. A. Mabrouk (Ed.), *Active learning: Models from the analytical sciences* (pp. 87-99). Washington: ACS.

Bennett, J., Hogarth, S., & Lubben, F. (2005). *A systematic review of the effects of context-based and Science-Technology-Society (STS) approaches in the teaching of secondary science*. York: University of York.

Boud, D., & Feletti, G. (1998). *The challenge of problem-based learning*. London: Kogan Page.

Bowe, B. (2005). Assessing problem-based learning: A case study of a physics problem-based learning course. In: T. Barrett & I. MacLabhrainn (Eds.), *A handbook of enquiry and problem-based learning in higher education: Irish case studies and international perspectives* (pp. 103-111). Galway: National University of Ireland.

Byers, W. (2002). Cultured pearls or tasty truffles: Teaching chemistry for the 21st century. *Chemistry in Action*, 66, 20-24.

Childs, P. E. (2001). Haemoglobin - A molecular lung. *Chemistry in Action*, 64, 36-38.

Chin, P., & Overton, T. (2005). *Assessing group work*. Retrieved April 21, 2009, from www.heacademy.ac.uk/assets/ps/documents/primers/primers/ps0083_assessing_group_work_mar_2005_1.pdf.

Collett, J. (2004). *Image-based PBL. PosiBiLities: PBL in Physics and Astronomy*. Hull: Higher Education Academy Physical Sciences Centre.

DeHaan, R. L. (2005). The impending revolution in undergraduate science education. *Journal of Science Education and Technology, 14*, 253-269.

DeLorenzo, R. (2001). From chicken breath to the killer lakes of Cameroon: Uniting seven interesting phenomena with a single chemical underpinning. *Journal of Chemical Education, 72*, 191-194.

Dolmans, D., & Schmidt, H. (1996). The advantages of problem-based curricula. *Postgraduate Medical Journal, 72*, 535-538.

Domin, D. S. (2007). Students' perceptions of when conceptual development occurs during laboratory instruction. *Chemistry Education Research and Practice, 8*, 140-152.

Duch, B. J., Groh, S. E., & Allen, D. E. (2001a). Why problem-based learning?. In: B. J. Duch, S. E. Groh & D. E. Allen (Eds.), *The power of problem-based learning: A practical "how to" guide for teaching undergraduate courses in any discipline* (pp. 3-

12). Virginia: Stylus.

Duch, B. J., Groh, S. E., & Allen, D. E. (Eds.) (2001b). *The power of problem-based learning: A practical "how to" guide for teaching undergraduate courses in any discipline*. Virginia: Stylus.

Grant, S., Freer, A. A., Winfield, J. M., Gray, C., Overton, T. L., & Lennon, D. (2004). An undergraduate teaching exercise that explores contemporary issues in the manufacture of titanium dioxide on the industrial scale. *Green Chemistry, 6*, 25-32.

Greeno, J. G., & Middle School Mathematics Through Applications Projects Group. (1998). The situativity of knowing, learning, and research. *American Psychologist, 53*, 5-26.

Groh, S. E. (2001). Writing problems for deeper understanding. In: B. J. Duch, S. E. Groh & D. E. Allen (Eds.), *The power of problem-based learning: A practical "how to" guide for teaching undergraduate courses in any discipline* (pp. 207-222). Virginia: Stylus.

Groh, S. E. (2004). *Problem-based learning at the University of Delaware: Sample syllabi and problems*. Retrieved December 1, 2007, from udel.edu/~sgroh/chem104syll.html.

Groves, M. (2005). Problem-based learning and learning approach: Is there a relationship?. *Advances in Health Science Eduction, 10*, 315-326.

Hansmann, C. (2001). Context-based adult learning. *New Directions for Adult and Continuing Education, 89*, 43-51.

Hanson, D., & Wolfskill, T. (2000). Process workshops - A new model for instruction. *Journal of Chemical Education, 77*, 120-130.

Heaton, A., Hodgson, S., Overton, T., & Powell, R. (2006). The challenge to develop CFC (chlorofluorocarbon) replacements: A problem-based learning case study in green chemistry. *Chemistry Education Research and Practice, 7*, 280-287.

Hennessy, S. (1993). Situated cognition and cognitive apprenticeship: Implications for classroom learning. *Studies in Science Education, 22*, 1-41.

Hill, J., Rolfe, E. I., Pearson, S., & Heathcote, A. (1998). Do junior doctors feel that they are prepared for hospital practice? A study of graduates from traditional and non-traditional medical schools. *Medical Education, 32*, 19-24.

Hills, G. (2003). Warning: Keep chemistry in context. *Education in Chemistry, 40*(3), 84.

Holman, J., & Pilling, G. (2001). All you need to know about chemistry. *Education in Chemistry, 38*(1), 11.

Holman, J., & Pilling, G. (2004). Thermodynamics in context. A case study of contextualised teaching for undergraduates. *Journal of Chemical Education, 81*, 373-375.

Howard, R. G., & Bowe, B. (2004). Problem-based learning in the first year physics laboratory. Paper presented at the PBL conference, Cancun, Mexico.

JCE Editorial Staff (2001). An Interview with Barbara Sitzman 2001 Award Winner. *Journal of Chemical Education, 78*, 1151-1157.

Johnstone, A. H. (1991). Why is science difficult to learn? Things are seldom what they seem. *Journal of Computer Assisted Learning, 7*(7), 75-83.

Johnstone, A. H., & Otis, K. H. (2006). Concept mapping in problem-based earning: A cautionary tale. *Chemistry Education Research and Practice, 7*, 84-95.

Kegley, S., Stacy, A. M., & Carroll, M. K. (1996). Environmental chemistry in the general chemistry laboratory, Part I: A context-based approach to teaching chemistry. *The Chemical Educator, 1*(4), 1-14.

Mandl, H., Gruber, H., & Renkl, A. (1993). Misconceptions and knowledge compartmentalisation. In: G. Strube & K. F. Wender (Eds.), *The cognitive psychology of knowledge* (pp. 161-176). Amsterdam: North-Holland.

Maudsley, G. (2000). Promoting professional knowledge, experiential learning and critical thinking for medical students. *Medical Education, 34*, 34.

McDonnell, C., O'Connor, C., & Seery, M. K. (2007). Developing practical chemistry skills by means of student-driven problem-based learning mini-projects. *Chemistry Education Research and Practice, 8*, 130-139.

McGarvey, D. J. (2004). Experimenting with undergraduate practicals. *Chemistry Education Research and Practice, 8*, 54-65.

Mennin, S. P., Friedman, M., Skipper, B., Kalishman, S., & Snyder, J. (1993). Performances by medical students in the problem-based and conventional tracks at the University of New Mexico. *Academic Medicine, 68*, 616-625.

Mowbray, D. J., Booth, C. N., & Buttar, C. M. (2005). Laboratory PBL at the University of Sheffield. In: D. Raine & S. Symons (Eds.), *PossiBiLities: PBL in Physics and Astronomy* (pp. 34-35). Hull: Higher Education Academy Physical Sciences Centre.

Newble, D. I., & Clarke, R. M. (1986). The approaches to learning of students in a traditional and in an innovative problem-based medical school. *Medical Education, 20*, 267-273.

O'Connor, C., & Hayden, H. (2008). Contextualising nanotechnology in chemical education. *Chemistry Education Research and Practice, 9*, 35-42.

O'Driscoll, C. (1996). Designs on C_{60}. *Chemistry in Britain*, 32(9), 32-36.

Ochiai, E.-I. (1978). Principles in bioinorganic chemistry. *Journal of Chemical Education, 55*, 631-633.

Ochiai, E.-I. (1991). Why Calcium?. *Journal of Chemical Education, 68*, 10-12.

Orna, M. V. (2001). Chemistry, color and art. *Journal of Chemical Education, 78*, 1305-1311.

Patel, V. L., Groen, G. J., & Norman, G. R. (1991). Effects of conventional and problem-based medical curricula on problem solving. *Academic Medicine, 66*, 380-389.

Pilling, G., Holman, J., & Waddington, D. (2001). The Salters experience. *Education in Chemistry, 38*, 131-133.

Polglase, R. F., Parish, D. C., Buckley, R. L., Smith, R. W., & Joiner, T. A. (1989). Problem-based ACLS instruction: A model approach for undergraduate emergency medical education. *Annals of Emergency Medicine, 18*, 997-1000.

Potter, N., & Overton, T. L. (2006). Chemistry in sport - Context-based e-learning in chemistry. *Chemistry Education Research and Practice, 7*, 195-202.

Raine, D., & Symons, S. (2005). *PossiBiLities - Problem-based learning in Physics and Astronomy*. Hull: Higher Education Academy Physical Sciences Centre.

Ram, P. (1999). Problem-based learning in undergraduate education: A sophomore chemistry laboratory. *Journal of Chemical Education, 76*, 1122-1126.

Rayner, A. (2005). Reflections on context-based science teaching: A case study of physics for students of physiotherapy. Paper presented at the Uniserve Science Blended Learning Symposium, University of Sydney, Australia.

Reid, N. (2000). The presentation of chemistry: Logically driven or applications led?. *Chemistry Education Research and Practice, 1*, 38-39.

Romero, R. M., Eriksen, S. P., & Haworth, I. S. (2004). A decade of teaching pharmaceutics using case studies and problem-based learning. *American Journal of Pharmaceutical Education, 68*(2), Article 31. See also: Haworth, I. S., Eriksen, S. P., & Chmait, S. H. (1998). A problem-based learning, case study approach to pharmaceutics: Faculty and student perspectives. *American Journal of Pharmaceutical Education, 62*, 398-405.

Savery, J. R., & Duffy, T. M. (1995). Problem-based learning: An instructional model and its constructivist framework. *Educational Technology, 35*(5), 31-37.

Savin-Baden, M., & Major, C. H. (2004). *Foundations of problem-based learning*. Milton Keynes: Open University Press.

Savin-Baden, M., & Wilkie, K. (2006). *Problem-based learning online*. Milton Keynes: Open University Press.

Schwartz, P., Mennin, S. P., & Webb, G. (2001). *Problem-based learning: Case studies, experience and practice*. London: Kogan Page.

Selinger, B. (1989). *Chemistry in the market place*. Sydney: Harcourt Brace Jovanovich.

Snyder, C. H. (1997). *The extraordinary chemistry of ordinary things*. New York: Wiley.

Stanitski, C. L., Eubanks, L. P., Middlecamp, C. H., & Pienta, N. J. (2003). *Chemistry in context: Applying chemistry to society*. New York: McGraw Hill.

Summerfield, S., Overton, T., & Belt, S. (2003). Problem-solving case studies. *Analytical Chemistry, 75*(7), 181-182.

Thompson, R. Q. (1997). The thermodynamics of drunk driving. *Journal of Chemical Education, 74*, 532-536.

Vanderbilt Group: Cognition and Technology Group at Vanderbilt (1990). Anchored instructions and its relationship to situated cognition. *Educational Researcher, 19,* 2-10.

Vernon, D. T. A., & Blake, R. L. (1993). Does problem-based learning work: A meta-analysis of evaluative research. *Academic Medicine, 68,* 550-563.

Walker, N. (1988). Oxalate blockage of calcium and iron. *Journal of Chemical Education, 65,* 533.

Whitelegg, E., & Parry, M. (1999). Real-life contexts for learning physics: Meanings, issues and practice. *Physics Education, 34*(2), 68-72.

Zhang, G. (2002). Using problem-based learning and cooperative group learning in teaching instrumental analysis. *China Papers*, October, 4-8. Retrieved May 1, 2009, from science.uniserve.edu.au/pubs/china/vol1/guiling.pdf.

62

.

Research-based Teaching in Higher Level Chemistry Education

MARTIN J. GOEDHART
University of Groningen, The Netherlands

ODILLA E. FINLAYSON
Dublin City University, Ireland

SARI LINDBLOM-YLÄNNE
University of Helsinki, Finland

Many graduates from science programmes move on to higher research degrees (M.Sc., Ph.D) or pursue research careers in industry or research centres. This chapter addresses whether undergraduate programmes in chemistry adequately prepare graduates for such research and examines the relationship between teaching and research. Finally specific examples are given which show how undergraduate students can become engaged in research and research-like activities.

Introduction

Preparation for a career in research has always been seen as a key objective of chemistry programmes at research universities. However, critical analyses of courses and curricula in chemistry have raised doubts about the effectiveness of the traditional curriculum to attain this goal (Laws, 1996; Sunal, Wright, & Bland Day, 2004).

Many lecture courses at universities aim at transmitting knowledge from lecturers to students (see Byers & Eilks in this book) and laboratory courses consist in many cases of standardized experiments, in which the conclusions can hardly be a surprise to the students (see Bennett, Seery, & Sövegjarto-Wigbers in this book). These traditional teaching approaches have their merits - for example traditional lectures may be more cost effective for knowledge transmission to large numbers of students and traditional laboratories may be used to promote the development of manipulative skills. However, these approaches are quite limited in contributing to students'

Chapter consultant: Maria Limniou, University of Manchester, United Kingdom

I. Eilks and B. Byers (Eds.). Innovative Methods of Teaching and Learning Chemistry in Higher Education, pp. 61-84. © 2009 *RSC Publishing.*

insights into the process of chemical research and in developing academic attitudes. The question is raised as to whether such traditional teaching approaches can in fact adequately prepare students for a research career. We fear that students tend to be very dependent when they first undertake research, for example when they enter graduate school. This suggests that many key skills still remain to be learned within the graduate phase, thus making the early period of research relatively unproductive.

There has been a continuing intense debate among chemistry educators on more effective ways to prepare students to conduct research since the 1980s, and several pilot studies have been undertaken to try to teach research skills more explicitly, for example by the introduction of more open-ended or so-called inquiry-based practical work (see Bennett, Seery, & Sövegjarto-Wigbers in this book). Interestingly, such approaches had been used earlier, but in secondary schools rather than in higher education. Other methods, such as project work or problem-based teaching, have now become the basis of curricula at some universities and penetrated the curricula of others by being incorporated within particular courses (see Overton, Byers, & Seery in this book). Changes have also been introduced due to calls by employers for graduates with particular skill sets; e.g. Duckett, Garratt, and Lowe (1999) matched responses from graduates and industrial employers to identify the range of skills required and they concluded that emphasis in teaching should be placed on creating more opportunities for the development of specific skills.

Research skills may be considered, at least in part, as generic skills. The importance of teaching generic skills has been recognized for some time, mainly as a result of the emphasis employers now place on the relevance of such skills to professional practice, and has been further stimulated by the harmonization of higher education at bachelor and master levels throughout the European Union following the Bologna Declaration in 2000. Building upon the Bologna Declaration, the Dublin descriptors are used as a framework for standards for European higher education and these emphasize the learning of generic skills. Although research skills have a generic character, it must be emphasized that research skills tend to be strongly embedded in specific domains. For example, research in biochemistry is likely to be entirely different from research in organic chemistry. For this reason, it is widely accepted that research skills should not be taught in separate courses within the university programme, but should preferably be integrated within domain-specific courses (Clanchy & Ballard, 1995).

Research skills cover a wide area involving knowledge, skills and attitudes. It is not always easy to distinguish between these categories and for this reason, the term *competencies* is often used to emphasize the interrelatedness of knowledge, abilities and attitudes. Based on the many different listings of research skills that have been published in the literature, we suggest the following compilation:

1. Information skills (to find and analyse information):
2. Collaboration skills (to work in a team and in a community of researchers);
3. Inquiry skills (to apply methods of inquiry, including planning, data collection and data analysis);
4. Communication skills (to present research findings orally and in written format);
5. Reflective skills (to evaluate the research process).

In a number of publications other skills relevant for carrying-out research are mentioned, including critical thinking, computer literacy skills, skills in using scientific software, and organizational skills (e.g. Milne, 2000).

In this chapter we will describe some examples of teaching research skills. We have used the term *research-based teaching* to characterize teaching methods that try to bridge the gap between teaching and research by engaging students in research and research-like activities. The term research-based teaching originates from analyses of the relation between teaching and research in university curricula. Furthermore, we try to answer the question of what characterizes chemical research and the consequences that this has for the curriculum in higher level chemistry education. The last part of this chapter describes actual examples of how students can be engaged in research and research-like activities as part of their undergraduate programmes.

The relation between teaching and research

In our analysis of the relationship between teaching and research we follow the typology used by Healey (2005) and others. In their analysis of the relation between teaching and research in universities they distinguish between *research-led, research-oriented* and *research-based* curricula.

The main teaching approach in a *research-led curriculum* is the transmission of information (research findings) and skills (research methods). Following the description above, it may be inferred that the traditional chemistry curriculum is best characterized by this term. The basic idea is that knowledge and skills are taught first – mainly in the undergraduate programme – and that these are subsequently applied in research – that is, mainly in the graduate phase. This means that students learn research findings as facts from lectures and textbooks, and learn research methods by following cookbook-like manuals in laboratory courses. As a consequence of this teaching philosophy a separation between lecture courses, where knowledge is taught, and laboratory courses, where experimental procedures are taught, occurs. Teacher-centred approaches tend to be dominant for research-led curricula (Prosser & Trigwell, 1999; Kember, 1997).

As stated in the introduction, since the 1980s educators and academic staff members have questioned the adequacy of this approach, and put forward several objections to the research-led curriculum. Firstly, as the emphasis is on *research products* and not on the *research process,* it may be questioned whether students get an adequate preparation for research or even if they know what research entails. Secondly, students are not stimulated to develop an academic attitude (i.e. to become creative, spirited, curious, flexible, ambitious, critical, engaged, etc.). Most researchers will quickly admit that these attitudes are necessary to become a good researcher, but these capabilities are hardly developed in a research-led curriculum. Thirdly, students may be bored by the cut-and-dried extent of factual knowledge they learn instead of being engaged in more exciting and challenging research activities. Every researcher remembers being involved in real research for the first time and experiencing a stimulating influence from it. Fourthly, in the research-led curriculum, students often consider scientific knowledge as true, factual, non-problematic and not as the endpoint of a, sometimes long, evolutionary process (Ryder, Leach, & Driver, 1999). This conception is undoubtedly reinforced by the nature of textbooks, which present scientific knowledge as a 'rhetoric of conclusions' (Schwab, 1966). Fifthly, development of research skills requires time, and for this reason, short research projects carried out in the final year of a degree course can only serve as a brief introduction to research, and are certainly inadequate to build up desired research competencies. The fact that this *research-led* approach has survived over time, despite reforms at universities and in university curricula, implies that this approach has its merits and won't easily be put aside. However, it is evident that such an approach is not tailored to developing students' research skills.

In the *research-oriented curriculum* the development of research skills is more explicitly visible in the curriculum. In the research-oriented curriculum students are involved in processes of knowledge creation by engaging in research (-like) activities. These activities include literature search and review, inquiry-based laboratory work, mini-research projects, etc. The laboratory is a key place to learn chemical research and this means that laboratory courses are mostly used for teaching research skills. The teaching of research skills in inquiry-based laboratory work has been discussed by many authors (e.g. Hegarty-Hazel, 1990; Gott & Duggan, 1995; Reid & Shah, 2007). The research literature on the development of research skills (most of it in secondary schools) shows three main approaches. The first approach is the teaching and learning of individual separate skills necessary to do research (like formulating a research question, making a research plan etc.). The second approach is that research is considered as a form of problem solving (with the heuristic used in the teaching of problem-solving: problem analysis and definition, development of solution strategies, and evaluation). The third approach considers research as a holistic activity in that research is considered as a process, strongly connected to a specific domain (Wellington, 1989). This holistic approach means that students perform entire research tasks, instead of training specific elements. To cite Derek Hodson (1993): *"... science is a holistic and fluid activity, not a matter of following a set of rules that requires particular behaviour at particular stages. It is an organic, dynamic, interactive activity, a constant interplay of thought and action."* One example of the holistic approach is the PACKS model (procedural and conceptual knowledge in science) described by Millar, Gott, Lubben, and Duggan (1994). In this approach research skills are integrated with the development of domain knowledge.

In the development of students' research abilities, Gott & Duggan (1995) emphasize the role of *concepts of evidence*. These are particularly relevant in measurement and include concepts like accuracy, reliability and validity, which deal with the quality of the result of a measurement. Research has provided evidence that students tend to find difficulty in understanding these concepts, which have a central role in measurement (Goedhart & Verdonk, 1991; Séré, 1993; Allie, Buffler, Kaunda, Campbell, & Lubben, 1998; Lubben, Buffler, Allie, & Campbell, 2001). Goedhart and Verdonk (1991) have advocated that development of these concepts and the design of measurement procedures by students should go together.

In a *research-based curriculum,* students learn as researchers through engagement in authentic research. In fact, graduate and post-graduate programmes frequently use this model. Students are considered as apprentice researchers. The theoretical basis which best fits with this model is cognitive apprenticeship (Brown, Collins, & Duguid, 1989). Research-based undergraduate curricula are rare. One example is the Aalborg model in engineering studies at Aalborg University, Denmark (Kjersdam & Enemark, 1994). The Aalborg model is based on problem-based learning (PBL) in which problem situations from authentic practices are used to teach students professional competencies. PBL approaches are tailored for more practically oriented programmes with a clear focus on a professional practice, like engineering and medicine (for more information on PBL see Overton, Byers & Seery in this book or the special issue of the *International Journal of Engineering Education* (2003) vol. 19, no. 5).

Although the three terms above *(research-led, research-oriented,* and *research-based)* were originally used to categorize curricula, it might be more appropriate in this chapter to use this categorization for courses, or even parts of courses. The reason for this is that *research-oriented* and *research-based* curricula are rare, especially when we focus on chemistry programmes.

The nature of chemical research

What are the characteristics of chemical research? A problem in defining chemical research is that the field is very varied and heterogeneous and it is almost impossible to find a common denominator for the methods applied in chemical research. An answer cannot simply be found by examining the current research that is carried out in chemistry departments, because each research group has its own historic roots and this means that research in, for instance, organic chemistry might be very different in different research institutions. Furthermore, chemical research has now frequently become a part of interdisciplinary fields such as environmental research or materials science.

The classical division of chemistry into the disciplines of physical, analytical, organic, inorganic and biochemistry is well known. However, because of the evolvement of interdisciplinary fields this distinction is now considered out-dated (Hammond & Nyholm 1971, Hoffmann 1995), although it is still used as the organizing principle in many university curricula and many introductory textbooks classify themselves as physical, organic, biochemical, etc.

Goedhart (2007) proposed a new division of chemistry from the viewpoint of teaching research abilities to students at the undergraduate level. He distinguishes between three context areas in chemistry: *synthesis, analysis* and *theory development.* These three different areas use different frameworks and apply different research approaches and different research methods. Goedhart gives examples of how students' learning problems can be caused by not making the differences between these research approaches explicit.

Analysis and synthesis are familiar terms to chemists, although Goedhart gives these concepts a somewhat different meaning. Analysis is the acquisition of knowledge of the chemical composition of substances (in elements) and mixtures (in substances), both qualitative and quantitative, and the structure of substances and mixtures at the molecular and atomic levels (see Table 1). This differs from familiar definitions of analysis in that it also includes structural analysis. The justification for this is that from a competencies perspective, both areas are similar with respect to the methods used. Synthesis is defined as the making of substances and mixtures with specific properties (see Table 2). This encompasses not only traditional organic and inorganic syntheses but also the preparation of mixtures and the isolation of substances from mixtures, aimed at isolating purified substances not at investigating their composition.

For most chemists, theory development would not normally be considered as an area of chemical research. This area is defined as 'development and validation of scientific explanations of the properties of substances and reactions' (Table 3). As well as containin physical chemistry and biochemistry, theories on analysis and synthesis are also included. This area is about developing theories, models and new concepts. The so-called scientific method, which works with the testing of hypotheses, is applicable in this area.

The importance of this distinction into three areas is that, when we consider the structure of the chemistry curriculum in higher education, it offers three clear curriculum lines. It might also give a focus for courses in chemistry. In Tables 1-3, concepts and competencies are given which are relevant in each of these three areas of chemical research.

From the perspective of this chapter, this means that if we want students to be introduced to research, we have to identify which kind of research we aim at. More than likely it will be to all three, but in teaching to chemistry undergraduates, we have to make explicit the differences between these three areas.

Table 1: Key competencies and knowledge areas in the context area analysis (adapted from Goedhart, 2007)

Context area *Analysis*

Aim	Acquiring information about composition and structure of substances and mixtures
Key competencies	Sampling Using instruments adequately (sensitivity, detection limit, calibration, instrument errors) Knowing physical measurement principles (signal transformation etc.) Judging quality of the information (accuracy, precision, reliability, validity etc.)
Knowledge areas	Sampling and sample preparation procedures Instruments, methods, techniques (i.e. chemical methods, spectrometric methods, surface analysis methods) (analytical chemistry, structure analysis) Methods of data analysis

Table 2: Key competencies and knowledge areas in the context area synthesis (adapted from Goedhart, 2007)

Context area *Synthesis*

Aim	Making products with specified properties
Key competencies	Using design principles (retrosynthesis) Using synthetic methods, incl. separation and isolation (group protection, multistep synthesis, combinatorial chemistry) Controlling reaction processes (temperature, pressure, solvent, catalysts) Judging quality of process (purity, yield) Judging quality of product (characterization, identification)
Knowledge areas	Design principles (retrosynthesis) Substance properties and reactions (descriptive organic and inorganic chemistry) Processes and influence of variables on chemical processes (thermodynamics, kinetics) Synthetic methods (group protection, multistep synthesis, combinatorial chemistry) and procedures (incl. separation and isolation) Characterization and identification methods

Table 3:   Key competencies and knowledge areas in the context area theory development (adapted from Goedhart, 2007)

Context area *Theory development*

Aim	Development and validation of scientific explanations of properties of substances and reactions
Key competencies	Using experimental method in testing scientific explanations
	Understanding the nature and structure of scientific explanations
	Using instruments to measure physical quantities
	Using methods of data analysis
Knowledge areas	Models and theories at the microscopic and macroscopic level (i.e. bonding theory, thermodynamics)
	Instruments, methods and techniques
	Methods of data analysis

Examples of case studies

There are many good examples of research-based chemistry teaching in the educational literature. These are designated by different terms like student (research) projects, inquiry-based (oriented) teaching (laboratory work), undergraduate research, problem-based learning etc.

In Table 4 some examples of published research-based practices are listed. This table is not intended to provide a comprehensive overview but to provide interested readers with typical examples. Table 4 is divided into three sections, namely undergraduate research, inquiry-based approaches (including guided inquiry) and research-based approaches. The terminology used by the authors of the papers was used to classify them; however, we realize that distinct borders between the three categories are not always clear. In the US there is a long tradition of involving undergraduates in research projects (see e.g. Doyle (2000), and a special issue of the *Journal of Chemical Education* (1984) 61 (6)).

In the text below we present some more extended descriptions of research-based chemistry teaching showing the opportunities for this approach. In our examples we have attempted to present different approaches showing the variety in this area. More information on these examples can be found through websites, publications in journals or through the staff members involved. Our selection has been based on highlighting a variety of approaches where their effectiveness has been at least partially evaluated.

Table 4: Literature examples of research based teaching practices

Undergraduate research:

Bunnett (1984), Pladziewicz (1984), Krantz (1981), Goodwin (1984), Hansch & Smith (1984), Karukstis & Wenzel (2004), Council on Undergraduate Research (www.cur.org)

Guided-inquiry/ inquiry-based:

General Chemistry: Pavelich & Abraham (1977), Pavelich & Abraham (1979), Farrell et al. (1999), Wenzel (2001), Green et al. (2004)
Biochemistry: Hutchinson et al. (2005)
Environmental chemistry/organic chemistry: Clarke et al. (2006)
Physical chemistry: Deckert et al. (1998)
Organic chemistry: Gaddis & Schoffstall (2007), Mohrig et al. (2007), Gilbert et al. (2001)
Inorganic chemistry: Widstrand et al. (2001)

Research-based/simulations of research/research projects:

General chemistry: Holme (1994), Kelly & Finlayson (2007)
Environmental chemistry: Thorne & Matheson (1977), Baum et al. (2005)
Organic chemistry/analytical chemistry: Bobbitt & Huang (1974), Kroll (1985), Dunn & Phillips (1998), Dunn et al. (1997), Newton et al. (2006)
Analytical chemistry: Toh (2007)
Miscellaneous: Gron et al (2007), Hanks & Wright (2002), Schmidt (1997)
ACELL (Advancing Chemistry by Enhancing Learning in the Laboratory) and APCELL (Australian Physical Chemistry Enhanced Laboratory Learning, acell.chem.usyd.edu.au), see also Barrie (2001a, 2001b), Buntine et al. (2007), Read & Kable (2007).

Example 1: Chemistry research projects (University of Amsterdam, The Netherlands)

In the bachelor programme for chemistry majors at the University of Amsterdam, The Netherlands, the development of generic and subject-specific skills is integrated with the learning of chemistry subject knowledge. During the laboratory courses in the first year students learn basic laboratory skills, but during the second and third years, students develop their research skills in the authentic environment of research groups. During two periods in the second year students join two different research groups for a research project, and in the third year they work individually in a research group on their bachelor research project. The second year projects take four weeks in January and four weeks in June.

All research groups in the chemistry department offer research projects to students (see Figure 1). A pair of students may apply for one of the projects.

71

During the first week of the project, students spend their time on a literature study. Further, they get acquainted with their research group and with the specific experimental procedures to be used. Some research groups require students to prove their knowledge by passing a test before starting a project.

Students develop their research plans during the first week of the project. In weeks two and three they spend most of the time in the laboratory carrying out experiments. Although each of the pair of students works independently on their research project, they are supervised by a PhD student and a staff member.

During the final week, pairs of students write a report and prepare a presentation. Students present their results at a 'project conference' where students chair the sessions and lead the discussions which follow each presentation. The students give and receive peer-feedback on the first draft of their project report and detailed feedback is given by the supervisor on their final report. The assessment includes the research plan, experimental results, report and presentation. The presentations given at the conference are evaluated by a panel consisting of several lecturers.

- Comparison of the physiology of two lactic acid bacteria *Lactococcus lactis* and *Enterococcus faecalis*
- Capillary isoelectric focusing of proteins
- On the reduction state of the quinone-pool: Effect of different cytochromes on % UQ8-H2
- Gradient LC for the separation and characterization of lignosulfonates
- Novel triazole-based multichromophores: synthesis, characterisation and advanced spectroscopy
- Ultrafast dynamics of bifunctional nanocrystals
- Colourful chemistry of rhenium carbonyl ortho-quinone complexes
- Stereoselective organocatalytic synthesis of 5-(indole-3-yl)-proline
- The synthesis of fluoro containing allenes and their applications
- Supramolecular bidentate ligands: Synthesis of novel building blocks and their application in catalysis
- High-resolution spectroscopy on the chromophore of the Green Fluorescent Protein

---

Figure 1. Examples of student research projects (University of Amsterdam)

During the two chemistry research projects students acquire not only research skills and other generic skills, such as communication and literature searching skills, but they also get acquainted with chemistry knowledge and skills within a specific modern research area. In our opinion, this cannot be achieved in a traditional course setting. For the students these projects also fulfil an orientation function. Many students choose the discipline of one of their chemistry research projects when they proceed on to a master's programme.

Since the start of these courses in 2004, the student evaluations have always been very positive. Students stated that they liked working independently, and they thought that it was a useful experience for them to meet technical and/or scientific problems which are usually unavailable to them in traditional laboratory courses.

Example 2: Teaching synthetic design (Utrecht University, The Netherlands)

Innovative laboratory courses in synthetic design, for first and third year undergraduates, have been in use at Utrecht University, The Netherlands, since the 1980s. An important feature of this innovative laboratory course is that it was informed by pedagogical research. The method used was that of research design (Van den Akker, Gravemeijer, McKenney, & Nieveen, 2006). The project started with a critical evaluation of the traditional laboratory courses in use at the university. This led to a revision of the objectives of these courses and to the subsequent design, implementation and evaluation of a new approach. Application of the methods of research design and the evaluation of teaching materials led to the production of the new course.

De Jager (1985) developed and evaluated student projects for a third year undergraduate course, in which students were required to select synthesis conditions (reaction temperature, solvent, proportions of reagents, etc.) and separation and purification methods (distillation, extraction, crystallization, etc.). The course replaced earlier laboratory courses in organic and inorganic chemistry.

During the course students were assigned different tasks, such as to design efficient separation and purification procedures. Towards the end of the course full synthetic design tasks were given to the students. These syntheses were selected to illustrate and develop key concepts in chemical synthesis, such as the role of reaction temperature or solvent on product formation. In the synthetic design tasks, students were provided with a synthetic route but were required to select the conditions to achieve maximum yield and/or purity. The underlying idea was to stimulate students to use knowledge from previous lecture courses in organic, inorganic, physical (kinetics, thermodynamics) and analytical chemistry (separation and purification procedures, analysis methods).

Students worked in pairs on so-called twin experiments. These were pairs of similar syntheses. Two types were used: convergent twin experiments, with different substances leading to the same product, or divergent twin experiments, with the same substances leading to different products, depending on the reaction conditions (see Figure 2 for examples).

During the planning phase, in which students searched the literature to identify a suitable method for their synthesis, they worked in pairs. However once in the laboratory students worked individually. Students were required to design different stages of the synthesis.

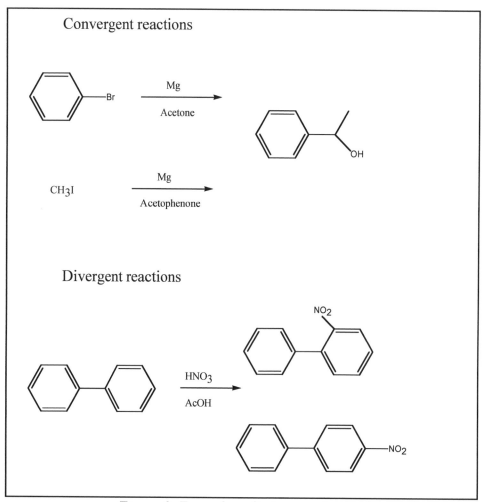

Figure 2. Examples of twin experiments

Although student evaluations were generally positive, it appeared that the approach was not entirely successful. It is therefore useful to mention the problems identified by the researchers, because these provide insight into the obstacles students and instructors meet when working with this kind of assignment. Firstly, problems arose because the teaching assistants (mainly graduate and PhD students) were not always capable of guiding the students properly. Students should be provided with hints and encouragement to 'scaffold' them as they develop their chosen design. In many cases however, the assistants, who often had only limited teaching experience, did not give adequate support and either told the students the solution to the problems immediately or remained silent, believing that the students must find the solutions for themselves. Secondly, students' knowledge was often not sufficiently advanced to enable informed decisions on reaction conditions to be made. This can be thought of as an example of a fundamental learning problem, known as the transfer problem. This means that knowledge acquired in one context (in this case from textbooks and lectures) cannot be easily applied in another context (in this case the laboratory).

However, the strategy used in this course was certainly challenging to both students and teachers, and explored new approaches to the teaching of synthesis, while trying to overcome the shortcomings associated with a traditional synthesis laboratory.

Example 3: PBL mini-projects (Dublin Institute of Technology, Ireland)

McDonnell, O'Connor, and Seery (2007) described problem based learning mini projects which occupied five 3-hour laboratory sessions in a second year degree course in the Dublin Institute of Technology (DIT), Ireland. The mini-projects ran concurrently with 'traditional' laboratory sessions. Groups of 3-4 students were assigned contextualized problems dealing with e.g. fluorescence, cosmetics, sunglasses, calorific value of crisps, and forensic chemistry (see for more extensive list: McDonnell et al., 2007). Supervisors are encouraged to propose their own projects.

An overview of the process is presented in Figure 3. The process started with a pre-project talk by the supervisor in which the intended learning outcomes and project planning were explained. Students searched libraries and the internet for information about the research theme, especially on experimental procedures and risk assessment. Students were required to keep a diary throughout the project and this was graded by the supervisor. As in real research some students had frustrating experiences because of the lack of immediate success with their projects. From evaluations it appeared that students appreciated the projects very much. Compared with the traditional laboratory, students ranked the mini-projects as fun and interesting, and said that they felt confident in the laboratory and in the use of new instruments. A major criticism however was 'team incompatibility', caused by students' lack of experience in working in groups.

Staff members were positive and found that students became more enthusiastic, even during lectures. Class attendance, which usually declined as the academic year progressed, was found to increase after initiation of the projects. Staff also noticed that students were better prepared for projects in their third year.

The authors of the article conclude that the mini-projects were more time-consuming than the traditional approach, but evaluate the project as positive because they believe that students gained a much greater understanding of principles and procedures, that experiments proved more interesting to students and that the projects better reflect real-life problem solving.

This means that it is not only possible to change a course from a traditional approach to a research-based approach, but that its effects can influence students' learning in a positive way in other courses in the programme.

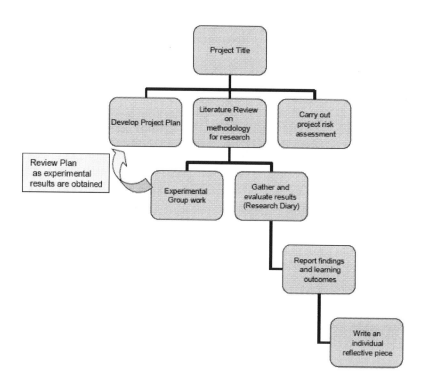

*Figure 3. Flowchart showing requirements from students at each stage
(from McDonnell et al., 2007)*

Example 4:   Multidisciplinary problems (Dublin City University, Ireland)

As noted earlier, research skills take time to develop and therefore the authors of this project felt that students should be given the opportunity to start developing research skills in their first year of university study particularly in communication, problem solving and group working / team working skills (McLoughlin & Finlayson, 2008). To this end, a module for first year students (class size of approximately 180) based on small group work (4-5 students per group) where each group must tackle a number of problems has been running since 2007 in Dublin City University, Ireland. This module is based on paper exercises and is research-oriented in terms of the distinctions made earlier. It therefore allows first year students to become familiar with skills such as finding information, assessing suitable information, generating conclusions, working within a team, etc. without the added difficulty of mastering laboratory skills.

The module consists of a range of problems, multidisciplinary in nature, that students tackle in a group work setting. Characteristics of the problems were that they:

· Were based on the first year science modules, i.e. students should have met the underlying science in their course work. The aim was not to teach new material through the problems but to reinforce students' own knowledge and skills.

· Included an element of each of the disciplines physics, chemistry and biology in each or at least most of the problems.

- Were mixtures of open and closed problems where the output ranged from either one coherent answer to where the output was a debate based on the facts given to the groups.
- Were relevant and interesting to the group of students – this was not always easy to implement as the range of interests within the student body varied widely.

The module had a broad range of assessments – from poster presentations, scientific evaluation reports to debates. Additionally, some problems introduced other topics where students challenged their own views on scientific issues, including ethics. Table 4 lists some of the problem scenarios, outlines the scope of each problem, the content and the output required.

Table 4:   Problem scenarios showing range of scope, content and output

Problem Title	Scope	Content	Output
Morning in the life	Explanation of everyday applications of chemistry, physics, and biology.	Open	Poster/ Critique
Nuclear Energy	Process; reading of scientific articles; extracting arguments.	Given number of reference papers	Letter to Minister
Shrinking Man	Cell structure and function, Immune response system, DNA, Electronic configuration, Reduction /enlargement.	Series of questions to solve	Scientific report
Genetic Screening	Genetic screening. Ethics arguments.	Representative of particular lobby group	Debate
Home Brewing	Thermodynamics, Energy calculations, Organic synthesis of ethanol. Sterilization techniques.	Process and data re-scale	Report - profit

Taking as an example the Home Brewing problem, students had to research the fermentation process, determine the likely impurities and suggest ways of both monitoring and minimising them, examine the energy changes involved and finally, to plan a small production process with appropriate costings to show a profit. Within each session, the lecturer and postgraduate tutors moved round the student groups and offered any necessary support and guidance.

Throughout the module, students are introduced to a range of problems that require different skills. In all cases, the group must manage the problem, dividing up the tasks, finding information and bringing it back to the group who then are responsible for composing a group answer. Therefore team working and literature searching skills are being developed.

Communication skills in terms of oral presentation, poster presentation and defence of one's opinions as well as scientific debate are all assessed within the module. Students are also communicating within the groups. Development of scientific arguments and production of facts to support their arguments is also supported within the module. In addition, students start to realize that to solve 'real' problems generally requires some understanding of all three science disciplines.

Following detailed student evaluation and focus group discussions over two years of implementation, the following conclusions were drawn. The problems were challenging but solvable by the students who generally both liked and learned from each problem, though the extent of the learning varied from problem to problem. The problems were used to allow the students a chance to develop a range of additional skills that would not normally be introduced during the first year such as developing arguments, finding scientific data and evidence (literature search and synthesis of the literature data), presentation skills, poster presentation, scientific writing, concise arguments and responding to the lack of a 'right' answer. These skills are essential for the development of successful scientists and potential researchers. In focus group discussions, one group indicated that they felt better prepared to implement these skills in later years of their study as a result of this first year experience. In contrast, the other focus group (consisting mainly of girls) was more negative about this skill development module and wanted just to be given the information and left to develop these skills later when they were required.

In terms of the group work, students liked working in groups and preferred to tackle these problems as part of a group rather than as individuals and stated that they felt that they had contributed well to the working of their group. In terms of assessment, students generally achieved higher marks in this module than in the other scientific modules. We did not expect to see a correlation in marks as in this module, other skills were being assessed and also it was a group assessment. Additionally, we did not determine the extend of scientific knowledge that had been acquired by individual students at the end of the module so we cannot really determine if their scientific knowledge had increased. However, they were certainly exposed to more independent and cooperative learning opportunities than in lecture modules and were also given the chance to develop alternative skills such as finding information, generating arguments, etc. The social dynamics within the groups should not be overlooked. Here were groups of first year students actually discussing science.

78

Example 5:   NetLab - Portal for students to work as researchers within a laboratory course (University of Helsinki, Finland)

Laboratory courses at the University of Helsinki, Finland, are arranged throughout the year and about 40 students take each course. Due to the large number of student groups in a single laboratory course the teachers have little time for individual supervision. Students generally experience problems while studying chemistry related to learning the language of chemistry and to understanding the invisible world of chemistry. In particular, students often have difficulty in understanding reaction mechanisms and in visualizing the 3D-structures of molecules. Students find laboratory courses time consuming and many have difficulty in managing their time in relation to practical activities. This may result in prolonged periods of study and delayed graduation. Students also often feel that the curriculum is fragmented and fail to see the connection between the theory covered in lectures and their practical laboratory courses.

Therefore to enable better bridging between lectures, theory, and practical laboratory work and to encourage students to work more like a chemistry researcher, a new web-based NetLab-portal was developed. NetLab provided opportunities for:

- Active learning processes
- Increased motivation of students
- Visualization – the invisible into the visible
- Interaction between lectures and practical work – making productive participation in laboratory courses easier
- Illustration of laboratory procedures – safety and economy in the laboratory
- Planning of personal schedules and developing time management skills
- Skills for searching for chemical information – The Chemical Registry
- Electronic feedback
- Making organic chemistry more attractive

NetLab utilizes web-based learning as a support and as a connection point to practical work being carried out in the laboratory (see also Lagana et al. or Bennett, Seery, & Sövegjarto-Wigbers both in this book), the comprehension of 3D-structures and theoretical lectures. It provides a web-based interface where students can find, for example, instructions on how to perform syntheses, instructions for the analysis of products, details of equipment and material to be used, safety data sheets for the chemicals the will be using, and interactions and necessary forms for submitting reports (Figure 4).

The main purpose of NetLab is to guide the students towards learning to work and study independently in the laboratory. Web-based materials provide students with opportunities to learn independently and to access material regardless of time and place. NetLab can provide students with detailed laboratory methods and instructions for operating particular instruments (with pictures) or for carrying out particular procedures. For example, Figure 5 shows a screenshot of a page where a distillation method is introduced.

The reaction mechanism module on NetLab provides 3D-models of the synthesis products which can help students to discern spatial structures of molecules and reaction mechanisms at the atomic and electronic level. There are also animations with detailed explanations of the most common reaction mechanisms.

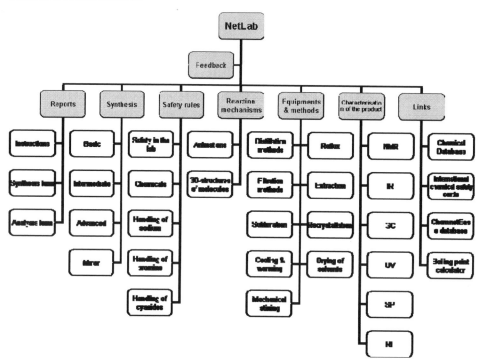

Figure 4. Schematic diagram of the NetLab

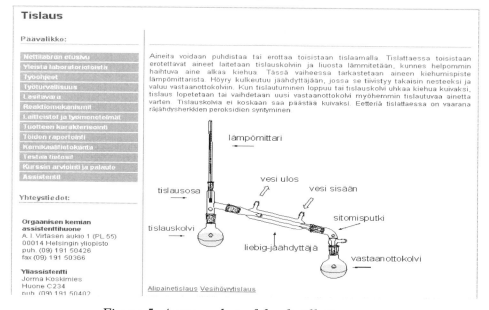

Figure 5. A screenshot of the distillation page.

NetLab provides a useful portal where students can find all information relevant to their practical activities and for linking these activities to their lecture programme. It provides a resource where relevant information may be easily found, thus encouraging greater student engagement.

Conclusions

In this chapter several examples of attempts to integrate teaching and research have been described. Each of the examples has its own features. In example 1 from the University of Amsterdam, The Netherlands, students are authentically engaged in research. This authenticity is achieved through students actually becoming part of a social community of researchers, and because students work on problems that are derived from the research work of the staff of the chemistry department. Example 2 (Utrecht University, The Netherlands) focuses on the design of laboratory procedures in synthetic chemistry. This has been designated as a simulation-of-research. Although this course does not include authentic research, the students are nonetheless trained in competencies that are necessary in research environments. The emphasis in this course is on applying theoretical knowledge to synthetic design. Example 3 (Dublin Institute of Technology, Ireland) describes mini-projects, in which students perform a small research project as part of their second year studies. Although this research is not completely authentic, students are nonetheless placed in the position of a researcher. Students follow their own plans and seek solutions to research questions where the answers are not already known by the students. Example 4 from Dublin City University, Ireland, shows that students can be introduced to research-like activities in terms of group work exercises involving multidisciplinary problems even with large classes. The example from Helsinki, Finland, describes a repository providing resources including manuals, data, and theoretical backgrounds to help students to plan synthesis experiments. These first year undergraduates are still inexperienced and it cannot be expected that they will be ready to solve real research problems. Following the definitions we gave at the beginning of this chapter, the first example is of a research-based course while the other four examples may be called research-oriented courses.

These examples and other examples from the literature can give us insights into the factors which lead to success with this approach to teaching.

- The first important factor is the open-endedness of the research problems. We recommend that students should be given freedom to make and follow their own decisions, and even that students should be encouraged to select their own projects. The openness is, of course, restricted by a student's pre-knowledge. If the gap between what a student knows, and the knowledge that will be required is too large, the student may well become frustrated and demotivated.
- It is important that students have ownership of the task. This can be facilitated by providing students with authentic problems that are close to real research. Ownership can be stimulated by involving students in all stages of the research, i.e. in the planning, performance and reporting of the project. Authenticity might also be improved by letting students write a report as a research paper (where students have done an excellent job it may even be possible to have this paper published in a journal), by using a peer review procedure on the reports and by letting students present their work at a student conference.

- Student research projects can only be successful if they are adequately guided by a supervisor. The supervisor's task is not easy. It is our experience that supervisors are not always patient and tend to show 'correct solutions' to students before they have had the opportunity to reflect on the problems for themselves.
- It is important to scaffold the learning process by dissecting the project into different stages: the research planning, the laboratory work and the report stages. It is important that strict deadlines are used and that every step is discussed by the student and the supervisor and that the supervisor gives permission to proceed to the next stage. It is recommended that students keep diaries of their work.
- Clear assessment criteria should be used and communicated to students. In research projects assessment should not only be based on the result of the work but also on the process. This might be new to some students and it is important to be as clear as possible about what is expected.
- Evaluation of the process and students' reflections on what they did and learned is essential. For many students a research project might seem to be a set of unrelated activities. It is therefore important to show students how the different stages interact.

Even when the success factors described above are present, learning outcomes for research-based teaching methods can still be disappointing to both teachers and students. Often, our expectations are too high. Research-based courses focus on the development of domain-specific and generic research skills and attitudes, which takes time. Knowledge acquisition is not the first objective in research-based activities. Moreover, we should not overestimate the outcomes of traditional courses. In traditional courses it seems that students acquire a lot of knowledge but it is by no means certain that this knowledge is sustainable or capable of being applied in new situations. There are numerous reports on the problems related to the application or transfer of knowledge which students are believed to have mastered in other courses, to new situations. In general, the transfer of knowledge to new situations is disappointing. Educational researchers have identified this transfer problem as one of the major fields of educational research and have tried to find conditions under which such transfer becomes easier (Bransford et al., 2000).

One of the threats to the incorporation of research projects into the chemistry curriculum is that implementation sometimes depends on one or a small group of staff members, so that these projects do not always survive curriculum changes. Research projects are not considered by everybody as valuable parts of the curriculum. However, we believe that research-based courses are increasingly being recognized as essential steps on the way to developing students as future researchers.

Acknowledgement

We thank Natasa Brouwer (University of Amsterdam), Nina Aremo and Kristiina Wähälä (University of Helsinki) for providing of heretofore unpublished work that we have used as examples in this chapter.

References

Allie, S., Buffler, A., Kaunda, L., Campbell, B., & Lubben, F. (1998). First year physics students' perceptions of the quality of experimental measurements. *International Journal of Science Education, 20*, 447-459.

Barrie, S. C., Buntine, M. A., Jamie, I. M., & Kable, S. H. (2001a). APCELL: The Australian physical chemistry enhanced laboratory learning project. *Australian Journal of Education in Chemistry, 57*, 6-12.

Barrie, S. C., Buntine, M. A., Jamie, I. M., & Kable, S. H. (2001b). Physical chemistry in the lab. *Chemistry in Australia, 2*, 58-62.

Baum, M. M., Krider, E. S., & Moss, J. A. (2006). Accessible research experiences: A new paradigm for in-lab chemical education. *Journal of Chemical Education, 83*, 1784-1787.

Bobbitt, J. M., & Huang, S. J. (1974). A simulated research project in synthetic organic chemistry: An undergraduate laboratory. *Journal of Chemical Education, 51*, 58-60.

Bransford, J. D., Brown, A. L., & Cocking, R. R. (Eds.) (2000). *How people learn. Brain, mind, experience, and school*. Washington: National Academy Press.

Brown, J. S., Collins, A., & Duguid, P. (1989). Situated cognition and the culture of learning. *Educational Researcher, 18*(1), 32-42.

Bunnett, J. F. (1984). Undergraduate research as chemical education - A symposium: The education of butchers and bakers and public policy makers. *Journal of Chemical Education, 61*, 509-510.

Buntine, M. A., Read, J. R., Barrie, S. C., Bucat, R. B., Crips, G. T., & George, A. V. (2007). Advancing chemistry by enhancing learning in the laboratory (ACELL): A model for providing professional and personal development and facilitating improved student laboratory learning outcomes. *Chemistry Education Research and Practice, 8*, 232-254.

Clanchy, J., & Ballard, B. (1995). Generic skills in the context of higher education. *Higher Education Research and Development, 14*, 155-166.

Clarke, N. R., Casey, J. P., Brown, E. D., Oneyma, E., & Donaghy, K. J. (2006). Preparation and viscosity of biodiesel from new and used vegetable oil: An inquiry-based environmental chemistry laboratory. *Journal of Chemical Education, 83*, 257-259.

De Jager, H. (1985). *Leren synthetiseren. Symbiose van ambacht en wetenschap* [Learning synthesis. Symbiosis of practice and science]. Utrecht University, Utrecht.

Deckert, A. A., Nestor, L. P., & DiLullo, D. (1998). An example of a guided-inquiry, collaborative physical chemistry laboratory course. *Journal of Chemical Education, 75*, 860-863.

Doyle, M. P. (Ed.) (2000). *Academic excellence: The sourcebook. A study on the role of of research in the physical sciences at undergraduate institutions*. Tucson: Research Corporation.

Duckett, S. B., Garratt, J., & Lowe, N. D. (1999). Key skills: What do chemistry graduates think?. *University Chemistry Education, 3*, 1-7.

Dunn, J. G., & Phillips, D. N. (1998). Introducing second-year chemistry students to research work through mini-projects. *Journal of Chemical Education, 75*, 866-869.

Dunn, J. G., Phillips, D. N., & Van Bronswijk, W. (1997). Introducing third-year chemistry students to the planning and design of an experimental program. *Journal of Chemical Education, 74*, 1186-1188.

Farrell, J. J., Moog, R. S., & Spencer, J. N. (1999). A guided inquiry general chemistry course. *Journal of Chemical Education, 76*, 570-574.

Gaddis, B. A., & Schoffstall, A. M. (2007). Incorporating guided-inquiry learning into the organic chemistry laboratory. *Journal of Chemical Education, 84*, 848-851.

Gilbert, R. G., Fellows, C. M., McDonald, J., & Prescott, S. W. (2001). An introduction to the scientific process: Preparation of poly(vinyl acetate) glue. *Journal of Chemical Education, 78*, 1370-1372.

Goedhart, M. J. (2007). A new perspective on the structure of chemistry as a basis for the undergraduate curriculum. *Journal of Chemical Education, 84*, 971-976.

Goedhart, M. J., & Verdonk, A. H. (1991). The development of statistical concepts in a design-oriented laboratory course in scientific measuring. *Journal of Chemical Education, 68*, 1005-1009.

Goodwin, T. E. (1984). Undergraduate research as chemical education-A symposium: An undergraduate laboratory experiment: The total synthesis of maytansine. *Journal of Chemical Education, 61*, 511-512.

Gott, R., & Duggan, S. (1995). *Investigative work in the science curriculum.* Buckingham: Open university press.

Green, W. J., Elliott, C., & Cummins, R. H. (2004). "Prompted" inquiry-based learning in the introductory chemistry laboratory. *Journal of Chemical Education, 81*, 239-241.

Gron, L. U., Hales, D. A., & Teague, M. W. (2007). Creating a research-rich chemistry curriculum with an integrated, upper-level-undergraduate laboratory program. *Journal of Chemical Education, 84*, 1343-1347.

Hammond, G., & Nyholm, R. (1971). The structure of chemistry. *Journal of Chemical Education, 48*, 6.

Hanks, T. W., & Wright, L. L. (2002). Techniques in chemistry: The centerpiece of a research-oriented curriculum. *Journal of Chemical Education, 79*, 1327-1330.

Hansch, C., & Smith, R. N. (1984). Undergraduate research as chemical education-A symposium: Research and its support in the undergraduate chemistry department. *Journal of Chemical Education, 61*, 517-519.

Healey, M. (2005). Linking research and teaching: Exploring discilinary spaces and the role of inquiry-based learning. In: R. Barnett (Ed.), *Reshaping the university: New relations between research, scholarship and teaching* (pp. 67-78). Poland: Society for Research into Higher Education and the Open University Press.

Hegarty-Hazel, E. (Ed.) (1990). *The student laboratory and the science curriculum.* New York: Routledge.

Hodson, D. (1993). Re-thinking the old ways: Towards a more critical approach to practical work in school science. *Studies in Science Education, 22*, 85-142.

Hoffmann, R. (1995). *The same and not the same.* New York: Columbia University Press.

Holme, T. A. (1994). Providing motivation for the general chemistry course through early introduction of current research topics. *Journal of Chemical Education, 71*, 919-921.

Hutchinson, K. M., Bretz, S. L., Mettee, H. D., & Smiley, J. A. (2005). A guided inquiry experiment for the measurement of activation energies in the biophysical chemistry laboratory: Decarboxylation of pyrrole-2-carboxylate. *Biochemistry and Molecular Biology Education, 33*, 123-127.

Karukstis, K. K., & Wenzel, T. J. (2004). Enhancing research in the chemical sciences at predominantly undergraduate institutions: Recommendations of a recent undergraduate research summit. *Journal of Chemical Education, 81*, 468-469.

Kelly, O. C., & Finlayson, O. E. (2007). Providing solutions through problem-based learning for the undergraduate 1st year chemistry laboratory. *Chemistry Education Research and Practice, 8*, 347-361.

Kember, D. (1997). A reconceptualisation of the research into university academics' conceptions of teaching. *Learning and Instruction, 7*, 255-275.

Kjersdam, F., & Enemark, S. (1994). *The Aalborg experiment - project innovation in university education.* Aalborg: Aalborg University Press.

Krantz, W. B. (1981). Undergraduate research in chemical engineering. *Chemical Engineering Education, 15*, 137-140.

Kroll, L. (1985). Teaching the research process via organic chemistry lab projects. *Journal of Chemical Education, 62*, 516-518.

Laws, P. M. (1996). Undergraduate science education: A review of research. *Studies in Science Education, 28*, 1-85.

Lubben, F., Buffler, A., Allie, S., & Campbell, B. (2001). Point and set reasoning in practical science measurement by entrant university freshmen. *Science Education, 85*, 311-327.

McDonnell, C., O'Connor, C., & Seery, M. K. (2007). Developing practical chemistry skills by means of student-driven problem based learning mini-projects. *Chemistry Education Research and Practice, 8*, 130-139.

McLoughlin, E., & Finlayson, O. E. (2008). A multidisciplinary Approach – does it encourage engagement with all the sciences. Presentation at SMEC Conference 2008. Retrieved May 1, 2009, from www.dcu.ie/smec/2008/pdf/B1_E_McLoughlin.pdf.

Meester, M. A. M., & Maskill, R. (1995). First-year chemistry practicals at universities at England and Wales: Aims and the scientific level of the experiments. *International Journal of Science Education, 17*, 575-588.

Millar, R., Gott, R., Lubben, F., & Duggan, S. (1994). Investigating in the school science laboratory: Conceptual and procedural knowledge and their influence on performance. *Reseach Papers in Education, 9*, 207-248.

Milne, C. (2000). Tertiary literacies: Integrating generic skills into the curriculum. In: S. Fallows & C. Steven (Eds.), *Integrating key skills in higher education. Employability, transferable skills and learning for life* (pp. 87-97). London: Kogan Page.

Mohrig, J. R., Hammond, C. N., & Colby, D. A. (2007). On the successful use of inquiry-driven experiments in the organic chemistry laboratory. *Journal of Chemical Education, 84*, 992-998.

Newton, T. A., Tracy, H. J., & Prudente, C. (2006). A research-based laboratory course in organic chemistry. *Journal of Chemical Education, 83*, 1844-1849.

Pavelich, M. J., & Abraham, M. R. (1977). Guided inquiry laboratories for general chemistry students. *Journal of College Science Teaching, 7*, 23-26.

Pavelich, M. J., & Abraham, M. R. (1979). An inquiry format laboratory program for general chemistry. *Journal of Chemical Education, 56*, 100-103.

Pladziewicz, J. R. (1984). Undergraduate research as chemical education-A symposium: Factors important to the maintenance of undergraduate research programs. *Journal of Chemical Education, 61*, 515-516.

Prosser, M., & Trigwell, K. (1999). *Understanding learning and teaching: The experience in Higher Education.* Philadelphia: Open University Press.

Read, J. R., & Kable, S. H. (2007). Educational analysis of the first year chemistry experiment 'thermodynamics think-in': An ACELL experiment. *Chemical Education Research and Practice, 8*, 255-273.

Reid, N., & Shah, I. (2007). The role of laboratory work in university chemistry. *Chemistry Education Research and Practice, 8*, 172-185.

Ryder, J., Leach, J., & Driver, R. (1999). Undergraduate science students' images of science. *Journal of Research in Science Teaching, 36*, 201-220.

Schmidt, M. H. (1997). Using "Household chemistry projects" to develop research skills and to teach scientific writing. *Journal of Chemical Education, 74*, 393-395.

Schwab, J. J. (1966). The teaching of science as scientific enquiry. In: J. J. Schwab & P. F. Brandwein (Eds.), *The teaching of science* (pp.1-103). Cambridge: Harvard University Press.

Séré, M.-G., Journeaux, R., & Larcher, C. (1993). Learning the statistical analysis of measurement errors. *International Journal of Science Education, 15*, 427-438.

Sunal, D. W., Wright, E. L., & Bland Day, J. (Eds.) (2004). *Reform in undergraduate science teaching for the 21st century.* Greenwich: Information Age publishing.

Thorne, J. M., & Matheson, K. L. (1977). A simulated research experience for chemists and non-chemists. *Journal of Chemical Education, 54*, 165-166.

Toh, C.-S. (2007). An experiential research-focused approach: Implementation in a nonlaboratory-based graduate-level analytical chemistry course. *Journal of Chemical Education, 84*, 639-642.

Van den Akker, J., Gravemeijer, K., McKenney, S., & Nieveen, N. (2006). *Educational design research.* London: Routledge.

Wellington, J. (Ed.) (1989). *Skills and processes in science education. A critical analysis.* London: Routledge.

Wenzel, T. J. (2001). The influence of modern instrumentation on the analytical and general chemistry curriculum at Bates college. *Journal of Chemical Education, 78*, 1164-1165.

Widstrand, C. G., Nordell, K. J., & Ellis, A. B. (2001). Designing and reporting experiments in chemistry classes. Using examples from materials science: Illustrations of the process and communication of scientific research. *Journal of Chemical Education, 78*, 1044-1046.

Practical Work in Higher Level Chemistry Education

STUART W. BENNETT
The Open University, Milton Keynes, United Kingdom

MICHAEL K. SEERY
Dublin Institute of Technology, Ireland

DORIS SÖVEGJARTO-WIGBERS
University of Bremen, Germany

Practical work has an unassailable position in the study of chemistry and, as a consequence, its role, its relevance and most importantly, its nature have rarely been seriously questioned. This chapter seeks to examine what the traditional approach to practical work actually achieves and to expose some of its limitations. A distinction between exercise and experiment is made in the context of an analysis of possible approaches to practical work and ways for optimising the use of costly laboratory resources are suggested. A tighter correspondence between learning outcomes and practical activity can lead to improved and deeper learning as well as to better mapping to assessment.

What is practical work and what is it for?

The literature abounds with statements which can be paraphrased as '*Chemistry is an experimental science and practical work is an essential component of the study of chemistry*'. Such views may seem to be self-evident but that does not mean that they should not be questioned (see e.g. Tobin, 1990; Hodson, 1993; Lunetta, 1998; Hofstein, 2004; Reid & Shah, 2007). In some ways chemistry is little different from many other areas of intellectual endeavour (see Floriano, Reiners, Markic, & Avitabile in this book). A study of history is based on evidence and the interpretation of that evidence. What about philosophy where ideas are explored in a logical manner and tested for validity against a set of structured criteria? The major difference in science is that evidence often comes from the laboratory or the

Chapter consultant: Martin J. Goedhart, University of Groningen, The Netherlands.

I. Eilks and B. Byers (Eds.). Innovative Methods of Teaching and Learning Chemistry in Higher Education, pp. 85-102. © 2009 RSC Publishing.

field so it is generally easier to identify the role of practical work. Even so, theoretical chemistry or physics may often seem to have more in common with history or philosophy in the way in which an investigation is conducted.

In general, the division between theory and practical work in chemistry education is often seen as the physical boundary of the laboratory. What happens in the laboratory is practical work and what occurs outside it is not. This viewpoint is clearly flawed both in the historical context in which chemistry developed and in terms of what happens in research today. In these contexts, there neither was nor is, any clear boundary between 'theory' on the one hand, and 'practical work' on the other; they are intimately entwined. It is only in education, in schools, colleges and universities where the division between theory and practical work tends to be prominent and this is almost certainly as a result of operational considerations. Access to laboratory facilities, timetabling, teacher confidence and ability and cost all have an effect in delineating and enforcing the boundary.

One result of the different environments in which practical work and theory classes are usually conducted is the reinforcement of this separation in the minds of both students and teachers. A report, from a UK House of Commons Science and Technology Select Committee (The Guardian, 2002) referring to science in schools, states that '...*students have to cram in so many facts that they have no time to explore interesting ideas and slog through practical exercises which are completely pointless*'. There has been some progress since then but the integration between theory and practical work both at undergraduate and school level remains poor.

A common response to the question '*What is practical work for?*' is to suggest that it is essential for the training of professional chemists. Perhaps for wholly vocational disciplines, such as medicine or veterinary science, where the aim of almost all students is to go on to practise, such an answer would be reasonable and valid. In the case of chemistry however, it is not (Duckett, Garratt, & Lowe, 1999; RSC, 2007). In the UK fewer than half of all chemistry graduates now go on to use chemistry in their subsequent employment and even fewer become professional chemists. Actual figures may vary from country to country throughout Europe but in general only a minority of students currently taking chemistry laboratory classes in higher education will find the experience of direct relevance to their future employment. Therefore to focus practical work *solely* on the requirements of future professional chemists is to ignore the needs and aspirations of the majority of our students.

Practical work does of course have a role in the consolidation of other learning. It can provide insight into how information and data are obtained (Tobin, 1990). It is a salutary experience for many students to realize that information that appears on a single page in a text book is often the result of weeks, months or even years of painstaking practical work. Practical work can certainly provide the opportunity to develop investigative skills and to apply them in a critical context (Kipnis & Hofstein, 2007).

All undergraduate subjects taught in the UK are mapped to a Benchmark Document which identifies the knowledge, abilities and skills that might reasonably be acquired at the Bachelor level (QAA, 2007). In addition to routine chemistry-related practical skills such as safe handling of materials and an ability to carry out standard laboratory procedures, skills in independent working, design and planning of experiments and interpretation of results are also required.

Current practice

There is evidence that current laboratory teaching practices are over-reliant on traditional teaching methods which have implicit shortcomings (e.g. Tobin 1990; Hofstein, 2004; Hofstein & Lunetta, 2004). An analysis of eleven commercially available undergraduate laboratory manuals found that students were required to operate only in the lower half of Bloom's Taxonomy: knowledge, comprehension and application (Domin, 1999a). An analysis of first year chemistry practicals from thirty-five English universities showed that only two per cent included truly experimental work with the remainder being primarily concerned with the development of investigational techniques or in the verification of known laws and relationships (Bennett, 2000). An aside to this work was the observation that on average each student performed over fifty burette filling operations during the first year at university; surely not the best use of expensive laboratory time. The distinction between experiment and exercise is important and was noted in the work of the UK Commons Committee above. An analysis of undergraduate practicals in the UK produced similar findings (Meester & Maskill, 1995). Domin (1996) contends that there are two primary reasons why traditional 'recipe-style' teaching methods do not reach their full potential: That the students are overly concerned with getting what they perceive to be the 'right answer' and that a process of reflection on the role of the practical work is not facilitated.

A way forward has been suggested by Johnstone and Al-Shuaili (2001):

> '...we might say that the purpose of laboratory work is to teach hand skills and to illustrate theory. But is this the end of the story? If we are going to look at the variety of strategies available for laboratory work, we shall have to be clearer about the purposes of the laboratory to enable us to decide which of these strategies lend themselves best to the achievement of our purposes. Similarly, if we are to try to match the assessment to the outcomes, we will have to be clear about the outcomes we desire to see in our students.'

The key is not only to identify desired learning outcomes for practical work but to ensure that these are directly linked to assessment. It is also important not only to identify the learning outcomes for individual practicals (and to communicate them to the students) but to look at the wider picture of learning outcomes for the whole programme or module. On many occasions such an analysis has shown that some learning outcomes are addressed over and over again while others are neglected. Indeed, Johnstone (1997) convincingly argues that overload of working memory (see Byers & Eilks in this book) in the laboratory, is largely responsible for the lack of engagement and superficial learning displayed by many students.

In considering the goals for practical work, it is important to recognize the differences between practical work and other classroom activities, something that educators often overlook (Hofstein & Lunetta, 2004). The excellent investigation by Millar, Le Marechal, and Buty (1998) considers this issue in some depth. The additional opportunities that a laboratory setting can provide may facilitate learning outcomes that accommodate different learning styles and abilities; facilitate inquiry and engage students in reflection and justification of their work based on evidence (Hofstein & Lunetta, 2004). Furthermore, given the extensive resources that are required for laboratory education, and accepting that chemistry graduates may not become chemists on graduation, it may be beneficial to rethink laboratory teaching methods in order to develop a wider range of transferable skills (Bennett & O'Neale, 1998), as well as to provide greater intellectual stimulation (Carnduff & Reid, 2003).

The way forward

What follows is a description on how a consideration of the learning outcomes for practical work (partly based on Kirschner & Meester, 1988; Domin, 1999a), and alignment of these outcomes with assessment can facilitate the development of both scientific and wider transferable learning skills.

In the *traditional* or *expository* laboratory teaching method, students are required to follow a given procedure to obtain a pre-determined outcome, usually to verify laws or illustrate concepts. The learning outcomes of this type of laboratory practical could include (Bennett & O'Neale, 1999):

· Students should be able to *manipulate* laboratory apparatus and/or instrumentation.
· Students should be able to complete routine *techniques* in the laboratory.
· Students should be able to *collect data* during an experiment and *process data* afterwards.
· Students should be able to *interpret data* after an experiment, although this may depend on the experiment.
· Students should be able to *communicate* their findings in the form of a report.

Examples of these types of laboratory practicals are numerous, and the bulk of laboratory work undertaken by students is of this type. Note that the learning outcomes here are associated largely with lower-level scientific rather than transferable skills. The assessment method for such practicals is usually based on a laboratory report, completed after the practical, while the laboratory skills themselves are often not assessed (see e.g. Bryce & Robertson, 1985). It could therefore be argued that many of the identified learning outcomes are not aligned with the assessment method in this case.

In the *experimental* or *inquiry* laboratory teaching method (e.g. Kipnis & Hofstein, 2007; Hofstein, Navon, Kipnis, & Mamlok-Naaman, 2005), students complete laboratory exercises that are unstructured with no pre-determined outcome, and are required to devise their own procedures. These exercises are usually conducted in small groups. The learning outcomes for this type of practical, in addition to those mentioned above are:

· Students should be able to *problem solve* by applying chemical knowledge to a given problem.
· Students should be able to *design experiments* to test a hypothesis.
· Students should be able to *work in groups* to solve a shared problem.
· Students should be able to explicitly *consider safety* aspects in experimental design.

This method allows for greater freedom in the laboratory as students now take on board the responsibility for experimental design. Notice that the additional learning outcomes are transferable in nature and are skills potentially applicable to a wide range of activities beyond the immediate task. The assessment method here will usually involve consideration of an individual or group report as well as cognizance of the role of group members in the project, through journals or reflective logs. This approach therefore allows for a better alignment of learning outcomes with assessment methods, although it is again unusual for the laboratory techniques themselves to be directly assessed. However, in this case, the experiments chosen by students, and the range/type of experiments carried out, can give some indication of practical ability.

In the *divergent* or *discovery* method, students are usually given some initial information and procedures and on the basis of experiments completed, are required to develop their own experiment in a number of different ways. The outcome is predetermined and the procedure provided. The learning outcomes for this method include both the scientific and transferable sets described above, perhaps with more emphasis on interpretation of results and less on experimental design. The assessment method can be in the form of a report or other communication method (e.g. poster) which can assess the approach students have taken and their reasoning for doing so. The aim of this approach is to assist students to discover a concept or idea for themselves, thus making the process more personalized. It is suggested that this is likely to make the learning more meaningful to the student, although this has been contested by some educationalists. This method differs from the *inquiry* approach only in that in this case, the outcome is known to the instructor.

In the *problem-based* or *investigatory approach*, students are provided with a problem which has a pre-determined outcome. They are required to solve the problem by deciding on an experimental approach and completing the necessary laboratory work, revising their approach as appropriate (see Goedhart, Finlayson, & Lindblom-Ylänne in this book). This approach is becoming increasingly popular, with problems being contextualized to enhance the sense of motivation and "real-world" relevance to students (see Overton, Byers, & Seery in this book). This approach includes all of the learning outcomes listed above and assessment methods align with these through the use of evaluating students' notebooks, considering reports (in written/oral/poster form) and reflective logs/journals. Practical work in the laboratory is again not usually directly assessed.

It is interesting to note that the four approaches described above differ primarily in the type and amount of information that is provided to the students. To put it pragmatically '*to change the experience, you don't need to change the experiment, just what you do with it*' (Carnduff & Reid, 2003). Each has its own benefits and disadvantages (based primarily on Domin 1999a), which are listed in Table 1. However, returning to the arguments presented above: that laboratory time is expensive; that learning outcomes in the laboratory will not necessarily be the same as those in the lecture hall and that laboratory time can be used to address a far wider set of skills than those with direct chemistry applications, it is worth considering the relative advantages and disadvantages of these approaches in more detail.

Table 1: Laboratory teaching methods: advantages and disadvantages (based on Domin, 1999a)

Method	Advantages	Disadvantages
Expository	• Relatively low cost (time, space, personnel) • Can be completed by large numbers simultaneously • Mimics professional environment (following SOP) • Modular Friendly	• Little planning or interpretation required by students • Portrays unrealistic nature of scientific inquiry (short time span, everything "works") • Little meaningful learning • Product over process
Inquiry	• Sense of student ownership • Authentic investigative processes • Fosters critical thinking	• Time-consuming • Loss of instructor 'control' • Not widely adopted • Significant working memory skills required by student • Pedagogical approach unclear: scientific process *vs.* scientific content
Discovery	• Students 'find out for themselves' – personal value • Tests data interpretation effectively	• Time-consuming • Strategies may not be transferable • Pedagogical arguments unsound – true nature of "discovery" is debated
Problem-based	• Emphasis on process as well as/instead of product • Student has opportunities to design experiments in controlled environment • Students must apply their understanding to a problem	• Time-consuming • Loss of instructor 'control' • Deductive approach – students must use *existing* knowledge in new scenarios

Problem-based practical work has its foundations in research in chemistry (see Goedhart, Finlayson, & Lindblom-Ylänne in this book). When one is faced with a problem worthy of investigation, a first step is to try to identify methods and approaches that will yield pertinent information. One might talk with colleagues, draw on one's experience and consult the literature. The outcome of this should be a strategy or approach likely to be modified, of necessity, by the resources, time and facilities available. The investigator only then enters the laboratory with a carefully prepared plan and attempts to follow it through. The process moves on to an analysis of the data acquired before reaching any conclusions and finally disseminating the results obtained as indicated in Figure 1. An important part of the process is to produce a reflective critique of the procedure which should suggest additional work to be done or possible modifications to the procedure. This total process is known as *experimentation* and the laboratory practical work is an important but by no means the only part of it. It is essential to make this distinction between experimentation and practical work - as it is to distinguish between experimentation and simulation (Borrows, 2008).The engagement of a student with the totality of experimentation involves two aspects in addition to the practical work. The student now enters the laboratory having already had to address the problem and has ownership of the 'recipe' which will form the basis for any subsequent laboratory work.

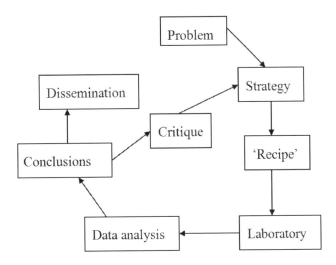

Figure 1. Route through an investigation.

Following the previous discussion on the aims of practical work and current practice, there is a continuing drive for the development of innovative techniques in laboratory education (Hofstein & Mamlok-Naaman, 2007; Moore, 2006; Reid & Shah, 2007), which are described in more detail below.

But, perhaps the single biggest advantage provided by a laboratory environment is that it facilitates inquiry based activities on the part of the student (Hofstein & Lunetta, 2004). Although there is little hard evidence to suggest that student *learning* is increased merely by using one method rather another, there is a growing body of anecdotal evidence to suggest that alternative laboratory education methods ensure greater student interaction, focus more on problem-solving and reflection of process and result in an increased motivation on the part of students. Limited studies do indicate that, where the student has engaged with the experiment design and 'ownership', retention is also significantly improved (see e.g. Reid & Shah, 2007; Kipnis & Hofstein, 2007).

Aligning examples from practice with each of the four teaching methods given above is problematic, as definitions can differ (Fay, Grove, Towns, & Bretz, 2007). For example, the nature of *inquiry* means that it can be inquiry (or enquiry), discovery or problem-based. Attempts have been made to identify and define levels of inquiry by means of a rubric (for example, Fay et al., 2007). The following examples are selected to illustrate particular aspects of innovative teaching.

Considering Overall Process

A range of practicals has been assembled with the associated skills and outcomes identified (Bennett & O'Neale, 1999). This book concentrates in particular on the early stages of undergraduate education across the chemistry disciplines (physical, organic, inorganic and analytical) and considers activities which fit into the four teaching approaches described above, as well as the skills associated with each of them. Student handouts, tutor guides, and technician information are also provided.

Changing from traditional to innovative

As mentioned above, it is often only a change in the type and amount of information that is provided to students that results in a different teaching method and a different learning experience. This can be done by replacing the 'recipe' with a set of clear objectives and useful information to give a practical which changes from traditional to problem-based. This was illustrated effectively by McGarvey (2004) who describes "transformations" from traditional to problem-based for an ionic strength experiment and a kinetics experiment. This work includes appropriate assessment methods to align with the new learning outcomes achieved by the problem-based method.

Contextualisation

Similar work by McGarvey considers the role of *context* in these types of experiments (McGarvey, 2005; McGarvey 2007). This work places activities in an industrial context, using examples of photochromism and the UV absorbing properties of organic molecules as applied to sunscreens. Contextualised chemistry experiments are also included in some textbooks, although these are in the main expository in style (see for example, Hill & Holman, 2001).

Multi-week 'mini-projects'

Several practitioners have considered the use of problem-based or inquiry type mini-projects, which aim to reflect the scientific process by introducing students to experimental design, trial, error and analysis. The emphasis from the instructor's perspective is on the process students take, rather than the results or product that they obtain. Examples of this approach include experiments in analytical chemistry (Dunn & Philips, 1997; Yuzhi, 2003; Arnold, 2003); environmental chemistry (Byers 2002); spectroscopy and analysis (McDonnell, O'Connor & Seery, 2007) and physical chemistry (Tsaparlis & Gorezi, 2007). Assessment of these projects usually includes a component that specifically considers the planning and overall experimental process employed.

Pre-and post-laboratory activities

In addition to the time students spend in the laboratory, there is a significant body of work that demonstrates that student time spent prior to the practical work, in terms of planning/preparing/identifying key concepts and after the practical in terms of analysis of results/reflection on process/prediction of similar concepts have a significant role to play in terms of maximising the student learning from the experimental time (Byers, 2002; Carnduff & Reid, 2003; Reid & Shah, 2007). Twenty pre- and post-lab activities for common experiments across a range of disciplines have been developed by the RSC (Carnduff & Reid, 2003). These outline measures to facilitate students thinking about the concepts and experiments they will conduct in the lab and from their analysis of the work, deduce or make predictions on similar concepts. One interesting concept that is referred to here and expanded on by other workers is the issue of flow diagrams, as a means of helping students conceive the experimental process in their own minds. Three aspects of preparation for laboratories have been identified: (i) an appreciation of the underlying theory of the practical and the procedure to be used; (ii) prerequisite skills and knowledge; (iii) detailed understanding of chemistry and the underlying steps to be carried out (Rollnick, Zwane, Staskun, Lotz, & Green, 2001). It has been suggested that flow diagrams could prove a particularly effective learning strategy with respect to this last point (Davidowitz & Rollnick, 2001). In this study, the authors found that students felt that flow diagrams helped them to "see the bigger picture" and helped them link theory and practice. In a later, more detailed study, the same authors completed a case-study of flow diagrams, and found that the students were encouraged to engage in metacognitive practices as a result of using flow diagrams (Davidowitz & Rollnick, 2003).

Pre-lab activities were also found to increase student motivation before they entered the lab in a quantitative correlational study (Pogačnik & Cigić, 2006). In this study, the emphasis was shifted from post-lab to pre-lab work, and feedback from students was generally positive.

Such exercises go well beyond an individual simply reading the lab manual pre, and writing up the experiment post, the lab activity. In both pre- and post-lab phases, cooperative learning in small groups can help to foster interaction and communication, and thus provide a more effective learning environment (see Eilks, Markic, Bäumer, & Schanze in this book).

Student response to non-traditional methods

Most of the studies mentioned above incorporated some level of evaluation of student engagement and motivation, and in some cases student learning which resulted from the implementation of the new teaching approach. There are several reports which study student response in more detail. A phenomenonographical study of the attitudes of first year students to the implementation of problem-based type laboratories was conducted by Domin (2007), who found that the majority of students believed that the problem-based environment helped them to better understand, or at least understand to an equal extent, the concepts when compared to the previous expository approach. Furthermore, in an interesting analysis, it was suggested that students perceived that conceptual development occurred during their time in the laboratory when using a problem-based approach but *outside* the laboratory after completion of the practical with the expository method.

Deters (2005) surveyed students on their opinions regarding inquiry-type labs (where inquiry was any of the three alternative methods) and noted some interesting observations. Among these were that more effort and thinking are required, and whereas instructors are often worried about losing control in these alternative methods, students are often afraid of having to take control. However, students also referred to a sense of pride in their independent learning and development of skills, and indicated that they became aware of the scientific method, felt their communication skills were enhanced, even believed that they subsequently performed better in expository labs as a result of completing these inquiry labs and significantly, had more fun doing these practicals. Similar findings were expressed in a study on students who completed guided-inquiry experiments (Friel, Albaugh, & Marawi, 2005).

Safety and sustainability in lab instruction

Beside the methodological aspects discussed above, it seems appropriate that this chapter should also focus on some topical content: Safety and sustainability issues in lab instruction. The importance of 'Health and Safety' issues and ecological conscientiousness to all activities conducted in a chemistry laboratory are now well-recognized (see e.g. www.suschem.org). As teachers, we have both a legal and a moral duty to provide a safe and ecologically friendly learning environment for our students. Although there are probably conditions and working practices that we would all feel comfortable with, legal requirements tend to vary from country to country. Statutory provisions however must always be kept in mind when designing or supervising any laboratory activity, and they also need to be made explicit to the students who may need to be aware of them in their subsequent careers.

Good citizenship in general and good chemical practice in particular must surely embrace both acting responsibly with respect to risks and being committed to protecting the environment and this will often go well beyond strict adherence to the 'letter of the law'. Good teaching practice in higher level chemistry education should aim to ensure that our students, the chemists of the future, become familiar with strategies on how to act responsibly with respect to risks to humans and the environment.

Over the last fifteen years, the idea of 'Green chemistry' has increasingly become an integral part of both chemistry and chemical technology, and it should therefore also be seen as part of chemical education at all levels:

> *"Green chemistry is the utilization of a set of principles that reduces or eliminates the use or generation of hazardous substances in the design, manufacture and application of chemical products." (Anastas & Warner, 1998)*

In general, the focus of green chemistry is on minimizing the hazard and maximizing the efficiency of any chemical procedure. One strategy to obtain this goal is to reduce or eliminate hazards through their replacement with less- or non-hazardous compounds. But, green chemistry also addresses long-term environmental issues by dramatically lowering waste production, choosing renewable raw materials, preventing waste by using catalytic reagents, reducing energy consumption, and avoiding the use of persistent compounds, e.g. halogenated solvents (Figure 2) or the generation of toxic by-products whenever possible.

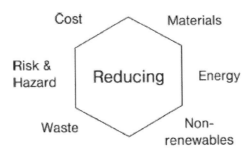

Figure 2. The heart of Green Chemistry – "Reducing"

One example of how to implement the thinking of green chemistry into undergraduate chemistry education is the Sustainable Organic Lab NOP (www.oc-praktikum.de; Ranke, Bahadir, Eissen, & König, 2008). The NOP has been developed in recent years within a cooperative project involving participation several German universities with funding received from the German Environmental Foundation (Deutsche Bundesstiftung Umwelt, DBU). The course is an open lab with a flexible format, acessible via a platform on the Internet (www.oc-praktikum.de).

As an introduction to the course, the platform offers an overview of the essential ideas of green chemistry, the philosophy of sustainability and sustainable development and their increasing relevance to chemistry and chemical engineering. The description encompasses technical guidelines, safety instructions, requirements for waste collection, statutory provisions and a glossary (Figure 3).

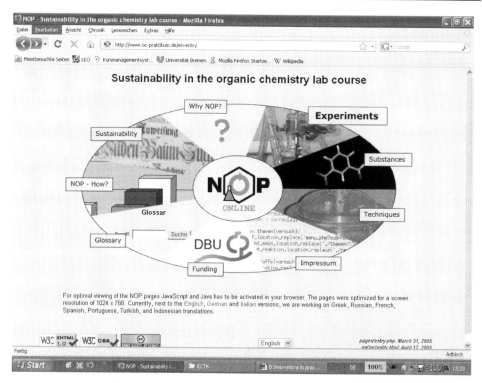

Figure 3. Start screen of the NOP platform

Figure 4. List of Experiments

The main part of the platform consists of 75 experiments at three different levels of complexity. All experiments have been developed around the principles of green chemistry, and descriptions of practical procedures, lab techniques and analytical measures clearly establish the connections between the experiments and green chemistry concepts. Laboratory instructions, operating schemes, lists of required equipment, chemical, physical, biological and toxicological data needed to carry out environmental and risk assessments and user comments are provided for all experiments (Figure 4). Discussion of the persistence of various substances in the environment, details concerning life-cycle assessments, significance with respect to the principle of atomic economy (Trost, 1995) and tools to evaluate chemical substances and reactions, e.g. the Sheldon factor E of environmental acceptability (Sheldon, 1994) are also provided (Figure 5).

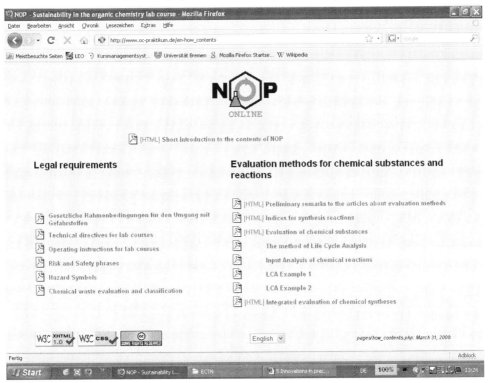

Figure 5. Evaluation of chemical substances and reactions

An integrated evaluation of the experiment is required as part of a student's lab report. This integrated report should contain not only all the experimental results, but also details of the ecological and risk assessments condensed into a short evaluation. This evaluation should include details of yields and purity, the processes' substance efficiency and energy efficiency. On the basis of the data collected the experiment is then labelled with a green, yellow or red light.

Therefore by sing NOP, besides learning basic organic chemistry and laboratory procedures, the students should also learn the important principles of 'green chemistry' listed below:

· Energetically efficient and environmentally friendly pathways for reactions involving the use of catalytic and enzymatic reactions.
· Alternative methods of applying energy to reactions such as photochemical, electrochemical, or microwave techniques.
· Modern chemo-, regio-, and stereo-selective reactions.
· Use of resource-conserving starting materials and intermediates and the use of renewable resources.
· Use of environmentally benign solvents.
· Recycling of reagents and solvents.

NOP is only one example of how to implement issues of safety, ecological consciousness, sustainability and principles of Green Chemistry into lab-work instruction. But, it shows how the traditional aims of practical work in higher level chemistry education can be connected with objectives arising from new challenges, with the aim of educating students to be able to take over a responsible role in their future jobs when dealing with any kind of potential harmful substance. This connection should be thoroughly considered when planning or conducting any courses for students in chemistry. For even those students not aiming for careers as professional chemists are likely to find it useful to know about the risks of potential harmful substances, and the solutions that chemistry can offer to avoid or deal with threats to health, safety, and the environment.

Assessment

Given the time, cost and use of specialist resources that go to providing facilities for practical work in chemistry, it is clearly regarded as an important part of the study experience of chemistry undergraduate. Thus, it can be argued, it should be assessed. Unfortunately there is a tendency for assessment to address only those aspects of learning that are easily assessed and to under-assess (or not assess at all) features where valid assessment proves difficult (see also Bennett & Wilson in this book). Practical work comes right into this category. It is undoubtedly difficult to assess.

The most common method used to assess practical work remains the post-activity 'write-up'. This often involves little more that rewriting a set of instructional notes with the inclusion of some data which may have been self-generated or may have come from another student (possibly even from another class). The basic 'write-up' process can be improved by asking such questions as how the procedure could be improved, what is the weakest part of the procedure, how reliable are the data etc? The question that we need to ask ourselves is what is it that we want to assess? If, for example, the desired learning outcome for a particular laboratory session is that the student should be able to select, assemble and use appropriate equipment to carry out a simple distillation or recrystallization, assessment based only on a write-up is unlikely to tell you what you want to know. One way that such an assessment could be done is by have someone in the laboratory assessing students as they work their way through the various techniques. However, as the presence of an 'overseeing assessor' can have a perturbing effect on the students the validity of the assessment might be compromised.

Learning outcomes are essential for practical work assessment. Exactly what is it that we expect the student to be able *to do* afterwards, as a result of the learning experience? This is where Figure 1, which summarises the totality of experimental work, can help us. It may be that the particular piece of practical work in question relates to few or only one of the components of this diagram, such information should then make it possible to design assessments that will test the appropriate learning outcomes. Of the seven areas involved in experimental work, only one (the laboratory) requires active assessment while the student is working. Assessment of all the other aspects can be achieved by written work or interview, although these other areas are equally important with respect to the need for assessment. It is important to match the assessment method to the task in hand. It might be more appropriate to discuss the strategy that the student has developed for the experiment rather than ask for a written rationale.

There is a danger that, in an attempt to improve the quality of the assessment process, assessment becomes a time burden both on the student and on the teacher. Not everything needs be assessed. Only a proportion of the students' practical sessions should be subject to assessment. Whether the teacher tells the student which ones are to be assessed is a judgement that must depend on the circumstances.

Resources

For further reading on the on the lab in science education see e.g. Hofstein and Lunetta (1982, 2004), Tobin (1990), Hodson (1993), Lazarowitz and Tamir (1994); Lunetta (1998), Johnstone and Al-Shuaili (2001), Hofstein (2004), Lunetta et al. (2007), Hofstein and Mamlok-Naaman (2007), or Reid and Shah (2007).

Acknowledgements

Inputs to this chapter are gratefully acknowledged Christine M. O'Connor, School of Chemical and Pharmaceutical Sciences, Dublin Institute of Technology, Ireland, Hazel Wilkins, School of Life Sciences, Robert Gordon University, United Kingdom, and Antje Siol, Centre for Environmental Research and Sustainable Technologies, University of Bremen, Germany.

References

Anastas, P. T., & Warner, J. C. (1998). *Green Chemistry: Theory and practice*. Oxford University Press.

Arnold, R. J. (2003). The water project: A multi-week laboratory project for undergraduate analytical chemistry. *Journal of Chemical Education, 80*, 58-60.

Bennett, S. W. (2000). University practical work: Why do we do it?. *Education in Chemistry, 37*, 49-50.

Bennett, S. W., & O'Neale, K. (1998). Skills development and practical work in chemistry. *University Chemistry Education, 2*, 58-62.

Bennett, S. W., & O'Neale, K. (1999). *Progressive development of practical skills in chemistry*. London: RSC.

Borrows, P. (2008). What is practical work?. *Education in Chemistry, 45*, 32.

Bryce, T. G. K., & Robertson, I. J. (1985). What can they do? A review of practical assessment in science. *Studies in Science Education, 12*, 1-24.

Byers, W. (2002). Promoting active learning through small group laboratory classes. *University Chemistry Education, 6*, 28-34.

Carnduff, J., & Reid, N. (2003). *Enhancing undergraduate chemistry laboratories: Pre-laboratory and post-laboratory exercises*. London: RSC.

Davidowitz, B., & Rollnick, M. (2001). Effectiveness of flow diagrams as a strategy for learning in laboratories. *Australian Journal of Education in Chemistry, 57*, 18-24.

Davidowitz, B., & Rollnick, M. (2003). Enabling metacognition in the laboratory: A case-study of four second year university chemistry students. *Research in Science Education, 33*, 43-69.

Deters, K. M. (2005). Student opinions regarding inquiry-based labs. *Journal of Chemical Education, 82*, 1178-1180.

Domin, D. S. (1999a). A content analysis of general chemistry laboratory manuals for evidence of higher-order cognitive tasks. *Journal of Chemical Education, 76*, 109-112.

Domin, D. S. (1999b). A review of laboratory instruction styles. *Journal of Chemical*

Education, 76, 543 – 547.

Domin, D. S. (2007). Students' perceptions of when conceptual development occurs during laboratory instruction. *Chemistry Education Research and Practice, 8*, 140-152.

Duckett, S. B., Garratt, J., & Lowe, N. D. (1999). What do chemistry graduates think?. *University Chemistry Education, 3*, 1-7.

Dunn, J. G., & Phillips, D. N. (1997). Introducing second year students to research work through mini-projects. In: R. Pospisil & L. Willcoxson (Eds.), *Learning through teaching, Proceedings of the 6th Annual Teaching Learning Forum* (p. 271-275). Perth: Murdoch University.

Fay, M. E., Grove, N. P., Towns, M. H., & Bretz, S. L. (2007). A rubric to characterize inquiry in the undergraduate chemistry laboratory. *Chemistry Education Research and Practice, 8*, 105 – 107.

Friel, R. F., Albaugh, C. E., & Marawi, I. (2005). Students prefer a guided inquiry format for general chemistry laboratory. *The Chemical Educator, 10*, 176 – 178.

Hill, G., & Holman, J. (2001). *Chemistry in context: Laboratory manual.* Cheltenham Nelson Thornes.

Hodson, D. (1993). Re-thinking old ways: Towards a more critical approach to practical work in school science. *Studies in Science Education, 22*, 85-142.

Hofstein, A. (2004). The laboratory in chemistry education: Thirty years of experience with developments, implementation and evaluation. *Chemistry Education Research and Practice, 5*, 247-264.

Hofstein, A., & Lunetta, V. N. (1982). The role of the laboratory in science teaching: Neglected aspects of research. *Review of Educational Research, 52*, 201-217.

Hofstein, A., & Lunetta, V. N. (2004). The laboratory in science education: Foundations for the twenty-first century. *Science Education, 88*, 28-54.

Hofstein, A., & Mamlok-Naaman, R. (2007). The laboratory in science education: The state of the art. *Chemistry Education Research and Practice, 8*, 105-107.

Hofstein, A., Navon, O., Kipnis, M., & Mamlok-Naaman, R. (2005). Developing students' ability to ask more and better questions resulting from inquiry-type chemistry laboratories. *Journal of Research in Science Teaching, 42*, 791-806.

Johnstone, A. H. (1997). '... And some fell on good ground'. *University Chemistry Education, 1*, 8-13.

Johnstone, A. H., & Al-Shuaili, A. (2001). Learning in the laboratory: Some thoughts from the literature. *University Chemistry Education, 5*, 42-51.

Kirschner, P., & Meester, M. A. M. (1988). The laboratory in higher education: Problems, premises and objectives. *Higher Education, 17*, 81-89.

Kipins, M., & Hofstein, A. (2007). The inquiry laboratory as a source for development of metacognitive skills. *International Journal of Science and Mathematics Education, 6*, 601-627.

Lazarowitz, R., & Tamir, P. (1994). Research on using laboratory instruction in science. In: D. L. Gabel (Ed.), *Handbook of research on science teaching and learning* (pp. 94-130). New York: Macmillan.

Lunetta, V. N. (1998). The school science laboratory: Historical perspectives and contexts for contemporary teaching. In: B. J. Fraser & K. G. Tobin (Eds.), *International Handbook of Science Education* (pp. 249-268). Dordrecht: Kluwer.

Lunetta, V. N., Hofstein, A., & Clough, M. (2007). Learning and teaching in the school science laboratory: An analysis of research, theory and practice. In: N. Lederman and S. Abell (Eds.), *Handbook of research on science education* (pp. 393-441). Mahwah: Lawrence Erlbaum.

McDonnell, C., O'Connor, C., & Seery, M. K. (2007). Developing practical chemistry skills by means of student-driven problem based learning mini-projects. *Chemistry Education Research and Practice, 8*, 130-139.

McGarvey, D. J. (2004). Experimenting with undergraduate practicals. *University Chemistry Education, 8*, 58-65.

McGarvey, D. J. (2005). Industry-supported context-based chemistry practicals, In: *Proceedings of the HEA Science Learning and Teaching Conference, Warwick, United Kingdom*, 149-152.

McGarvey, D. J. (2007). Investigating commercial sunscreens. *Education in Chemistry*, *44*(4), 116-120.

Meester, M. A. M., & Maskill, R. (1995). First-year chemistry practicals at universities in England and Wales: Aims and the scientific level of the experiments. *International Journal of Science Education, 17*, 575-588.

Millar, R., Le Marechal, J.-F., & Buty, C. (1998). *A map of the variety of labwork*. Brussels: European Commission.

Moore, J. W. (2006). Let's go for an A in lab. *Journal of Chemical Education, 83*, 519.

QAA (2007). *Chemistry Benchmark*. Gloucester: Quality Assurance Agency in Higher Education.

Pogačnik, L., & Cigić. B. (2006). How to motivate students to study before they enter the lab. *Journal of Chemical Education, 83*, 1094-1098.

Ranke, J., Bahadir, M., Eissen, M., & Koenig, B. (2008). Developing and disseminating NOP: An online, open-Access, organic chemistry teaching resource to integrate sustainability concepts in the laboratory. *Journal of Chemical Education, 85,* 1000-1005.

Reid, N., & Shah, I. (2007). The role of laboratory work in university chemistry. *Chemistry Education Research and Practice, 8*, 172 – 185.

Rollnick, R., Zwane, S., Staskun, M., Lotz, S., & Green, G. (2001). Improving pre-laboratory preparation of first-year university chemistry students. *International Journal of Science Education, 23*, 1053-1071.

RSC (2007). *Statistics of chemistry education*. Retrieved February 02, 2007, from www.rsc.org/Education/Statistics/index.asp.

Sheldon, R. A. (1994). Consider the environmental quotient: When evaluating alternative routes to a product both the amount and nature of the waste make a difference. *Chemtech,* 25 (3), 38-47.

The Guardian (2002). 12 July 2002. London: Scott Trust.

Tsaparlis, G., & Gorezi, M. (2007). Addition of a project-based component to a conventional expository physical chemistry laboratory. *Journal of Chemical Education, 84*, 668-670.

Tobin, K. G. (1990). Research on science laboratory activities: In pursuit of better questions and answers to improve learning. *School Science and Mathematics, 90*, 403-418.

Trost, B. M. (1995). Atom Economy - A challenge for organic synthesis: Homogeneous catalysis leads the way. *Angewandte Chemie International Edition, 34*, 259-281.

Yuzhi, W. (2003). Using problem-based learning in teaching analytical chemistry. *The China Papers*, July, 28-33.

Cooperative Learning in Higher Level Chemistry Education

INGO EILKS, SILVIJA MARKIC, MARCUS BÄUMER
University of Bremen, Germany

SASCHA SCHANZE
Leibnitz-University Hannover, Germany

Starting with some essential elements from modern learning theory this chapter seeks to justify the use of cooperative learning approaches for teaching chemistry students in higher education. The basic principles of cooperative learning are described, their applications in theoretical and practical courses are discussed and the approach is illustrated using a number of examples taken from higher level chemistry courses. The chapter concludes by considering the potential of computer technology to support cooperative learning environments.

Introduction

Contemporary wisdom regarding the teaching and learning of chemistry identifies a need for teaching methods that will activate the learner (see Byers & Eilks in this book). Such methods should seek to encourage the learner to become cognitively engaged in developing understanding of the topic being taught. This point of view can be justified from the constructivist and socio-constructivist perspective on learning which has became one of the most influential theories of learning in recent years (Bodner, 1986). The potential of cooperative learning, in contrast to the more traditional passive and individualist approach, can be derived and justified from these ideas (Johnson & Johnson, 1999).

The socio-constructivist perspective on learning is usually attributed to the Russian psychologist Lev Vygotsky. Although Vygotsky carried out much of his work in the early part of the 20th century, his ideas were not well-recognized outside the Soviet Union until many years later. However, following the introduction of his ideas into the West in the 1960s and the translation of one of his most important works 'Mind in Society' (Vygotsky,

---

Chapter consultant: Tina L. Overton, University of Hull, United Kingdom.

I. Eilks and B. Byers (Eds.). Innovative Methods of Teaching and Learning Chemistry in Higher Education, pp. 103-122. © 2009 RSC Publishing

1978) into English in 1978, his ideas rapidly became very influential in developing the theory of constructivism all over the world. For a short insight into the importance and ideas of Lev Vygotsky, see Hodson and Hodson (1998).

Vygotsky's ideas concerning the role of communication/social interaction, enculturation and the zone of proximal development provide a framework for reorganizing the learning environment to promote cooperative learning (Johnson & Johnson, 1999; Lazarowitz & Hertz-Lazarowitz, 1998) and this provides the focus for this chapter. The Vygotskyan perspective on learning and instruction puts the emphasis on the importance of communication. From this point of view sustainable learning does not only take place via the contemplation of a content by an individual learner. Learning is rather seen as a process that mainly functions through social mediation about content (Driver & Oldham, 1986). The construction of meaning can be understood in terms of a process of negotiating in discussions with others, an exchange of critical ideas (Prawat, 1989).

Building on the ideas of Johnston and Driver (1990), Lazarowitz and Hertz-Lazarowitz (1998, p. 451) describe the social component of constructivist learning as:

> "...cognitive construction is facilitated through the following activities, all of which are based on peer-interaction: students present their own ideas by explaining them to other group members; they think and talk about their experiences; they suggest and try out new ideas; they reflect on changes in their ideas; they negotiate and aid other students to clarify their thoughts; and they move ideas forward by making sense of new ones. Indeed, constructivist theory brings to light the significance of social-cognitive interaction, cooperation and collaboration to the science teaching-learning context."

Far more than a mere exchange of ideas can take place in such environments. Stahl (2004) stressed the importance of the social dimension within cooperative learning. Instead of studying the mental content of individual minds, social learning focuses on the processes of interaction, discourse, and participation. Scardamalia and Bereiter (1996) described social learning as 'building collaborative knowing', where the group is able to attain a level of understanding that could not have been achieved through the mental processing of any one individual in the group alone.

A further step is provided by the idea of enculturation. A novice in any field needs to be encultured into the expert's world by learning the appropriate language and technical terms and their use. Until the learner becomes encultured into the expert's world, he/she will have problems expressing thoughts on a scientifically reliable base and will experience difficulty in understanding the experts and their media. However, an ability to communicate effectively is not easily developed when communication on the topics is carried out exclusively with the teacher. Teachers and textbooks, being expert resources, tend to operate at a different level and use a language different from the learner's one, as he is still a novice. From a

Vygotskian perspective on learning, an approach where the expert tries to explain the meaning of difficult concepts in a well-articulated manner is unlikely to overcome this invisible barrier between the novice's language and the experts' world. Vygotsky's ideas suggest the need for learning environments where students are rather encouraged to interact and communicate with each other. Such learning environments can help students to discuss scientific phenomena and tasks on their own level, expressing ideas and describing concepts at a level that is comprehensible to their peers. Such environments ask students to explain their thoughts, to develop hypotheses, to find words and explanations for their ideas and to test them in relation to the knowledge (or alternative frameworks) of the others.

Such situations should provoke and encourage a period of free discussion between the students before being interrupted by intervention from the teacher. The discussions should help students to become clear about their own thinking and encourage them to reflect upon their own assumptions, before being required to express them to their teachers, and before being informed what the scientific community considers to be the 'right' answer. Such approaches are likely to help students to become clearer regarding their own thinking about a topic, to be able to recognize cognitive conflicts between their own thinking and the thinking of their peers and also to incorporate more technical terms gradually and incrementally. Learning can be considered successful from the moment that a student becomes able to communicate to others in the group about what has been learned.

Such discussions among students appear to have a high potential to take students into their zones of proximal development. Vygotsky's idea of the zone of proximal development suggests that learning can only take place in a small zone between those steps the student can take alone and those steps he can only take with optimal guidance by a teacher. Unfortunately, this zone is very dependent on the individual learner and is hard for the teacher to identify. This is especially the case when content matter has to be presented in a lecture hall simultaneously to a large group of students. However, settings where students are asked to work on given tasks in groups appear to provide better opportunities for students to operate in their zones of proximal development, because each of the students is now free to decide which learning pathways are best suited to their own personalities, interests and needs.

Of course, just putting students into a group does not necessarily lead to success. Evidence from research on cooperative learning can give some guidance here. Cooperative learning means creating environments where students start learning together, helping and peer tutoring each other and working towards a common goal (Lazarowitz & Hertz-Lazarowitz, 1998). Unfortunately, the smooth working of groups is often disrupted by a lack of structure within the group and differing interests among the group members. The disruptive behaviour of individuals can also often contribute to a lack of success in group work (Renkl, Gruber, & Mandl, 1999). Thus, it is important that the group should have a clear structure, and sometimes it may even be preferable to leave it up to the students themselves to agree on the structure to be adopted. The five criteria proposed by Johnson and Johnson (1999) and listed below, form a useful and well-established basis for reflecting on the success of a cooperative learning experience:

- Positive interdependence
- Face-to-face promotive interaction
- Individual accountability
- Interpersonal and small group skills, and
- Group processing.

Where these quality criteria for cooperative learning are achieved, the learning environments tend to be characterized by high levels of student motivation and the development of non-cognitive skills. Such skills include team working abilities, such as organizing and structuring of projects, and negotiating of consensus following conflict within the group. As Lazarowitz and Hertz-Lazarowitz (1998) have stated, these processes of cooperation and competition are characteristic of many types of human activity including 'doing science'. Cooperative learning methods provide excellent opportunities for the learning and development of these much needed social skills. The use of cooperative learning activities has been found to result in higher cognitive achievement, better development of higher-level thinking skills, increased student self-confidence and satisfaction and better attitudes towards subject matter (e.g. Cooper, 1995; Lazarowitz & Hertz-Lazarowitz, 1998; Doymus, 2008).

For a broader discussion of the theoretical background to cooperative learning and peer-tutoring see, e.g. Johnson, Johnson, and Smith (1991), Goodsell, Maher, and Tinto (1992), Johnson and Johnson (1999), Boud, Cohen, and Sampson (2001), or Falchikov and Blythman (2001). Details of the use of cooperative learning in chemistry and science education settings has also been reviewed, e.g. by Kerns (1996), Lazarowitz and Hertz-Lazarowitz (1998) or Springer, Stanne, and Donovan (1999).

Basic models of cooperative learning

The learning paradigm of cooperative learning redefines the roles of both teachers and students. Strommen and Lincoln (1992) suggest that the teacher becomes just a part of the team rather than the heart of the classroom and refer to him or her as the project manager or tutor. Daniel (2001) characterises the teacher as a collaborator or guide while Javid (2000) adopts the terms coach or facilitator.

These definitions follow collaborative learning practice by indicating new levels of freedom within a classroom. It is assumed that students' individual knowledge and ideas are diverse and that teaching by explaining new concepts (one authority – many listeners) will fail (see Byers & Eilks in this book). Collaborative learning however will be successful where it helps to find a common understanding of the concept to be learned. This model is often misunderstood. Success will not be achieved where only the classroom arrangement changes and the teacher continues to provide the content and sets the learning goals. Cooperative learning settings,

"... to be successful, require students and teachers to change how they understand and assign authority. Students need to assume more authority, assign authority to their peers, and to value their own thoughts and ideas. [...] Students may converge on an understanding that is recognizable as authoritative, rather than an optimal understanding." (Hubscher-Younger & Narayanan, 2003, p. 316).

In recent years a number of different models for structuring cooperative learning environments have been described. Some basic models are reviewed below and connections are made to recent interpretations.

Learning Together

The learning together method can be traced back to Johnson and Johnson (1999). In the learning together model, students form groups of four or five. The students are asked to learn together or to reach a common goal. The activities and aims may include paper-work as well as out of classroom activities or lab-work. In order to achieve the joint aim, the students have to learn together, discuss, exchange and share ideas together and have to prepare each other as a group for achieving the joint goal. While the group is heterogeneous, everyone is expected to help and to be helped. Nevertheless, each of the students is individually responsible for mastering the learning material. Research and classroom experience suggest that it can often be advantageous to involve more structured elements into learning together settings. Because individualism can disturb the smooth functioning of a group activity, it is important that all members of a group accept the joint aim and possibly even negotiate in advance their specific roles and/or contributions. 'Learning together' can be organized in a number of different ways. For example in chemistry education group tasks might be set within a traditional lecture (Cooper, 1995), group building activities can be used in parallel to a traditional course (Hurley, 1993; Kogut, 1997), or students can work in groups in a lab environment, with each member of the group being assigned a specific role and activity by the teacher (Biersmith, Hinton, Nomand, & Raymond, 1975).

The Jigsaw Classroom

The Jigsaw Classroom was suggested by Aronson, Stephan, Sikes, Blaney, and Snapp (1978) as an approach likely to promote structured interdependence between members of a group, while maintaining the need for individual accountability. Within the Jigsaw Classroom method the class is divided into small groups of 4-5 students who must learn about a joint topic. The joint topic is divided into sub-units of similar size and responsibility for each of these is assigned to one of the students. The sub-units have to be independent of each other so that each of the group members can learn about it individually. After becoming familiar with their piece of information the students from all groups with responsibility for the same sub-unit are grouped together (expert round, see Figure 1). These expert groups continue working on their topic as a group with the aim of developing an explanation of their topic that can be shared with others. The students eventually return to their starting groups and teach and learn from each other about the different pieces of the whole picture (teaching round, see Figure 1).

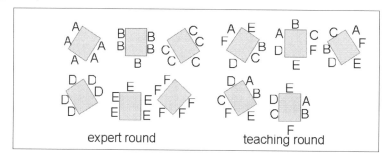

Figure 1. The Jigsaw Classroom

Subsequent developments of the Jigsaw Classroom method have led to different models including its application to laboratory investigations (Sharan & Hertz-Lazarowitz, 1980) and also to the introduction of mechanisms to safe-guard the process in the event that one of the team members experiences difficulties (Eilks & Leerhoff, 2001; Eilks, 2005). The idea of including lab-work in the Jigsaw Classroom were developed with reference to the method of Group Investigation (see below) and named Peer Tutoring in Small Investigative Group (PTSIG). The PTSIG-Method maintains the jigsaw structure as a frame but uses the Group Investigation method as the basis for the work of the expert groups (Lazarowitz & Karsenty, 1990). The Jigsaw Classroom can be safe-guarded, by for example doubling-up in the expert groups or by providing everyone with a basic explanation of each of the topics underlying the joint task (Eilks & Leerhoff, 2001; Eilks, 2005). A successful example of the use of a Jigsaw Classroom for teaching chemical equilibrium in undergraduate general chemistry education was recently described by Doymus (2008).

Student Teams and Achievement Divisions and Teams Games Tournament

The Student Teams and Achievement Divisions (STAD, Slavin, 1978) and the Teams Games Tournament (TGT, De Vries & Slavin, 1978) use competition between groups as a framework to support a cooperative learning experience. After being assigned to a specific set of information or learning objectives, the students start learning as a team in heterogeneous groups. The objective is to prepare each other to be individually successful in a quiz, test or game. Everyone has to participate in the quiz, test or game individually but his or her score is not only registered for him or her as an individual. The scores also contribute to the group performance so everyone has a vested interest in how the teammates perform and is aware that this is dependent on their joint preparation. An interesting example of the use of these ideas in introductory organic chemistry education is described by Dinan and Frydrychowski (1995).

Group Investigation

The Group Investigation (GI) devised by Sharan and Hertz-Lazarowitz (1980) is a six stage model for carrying out a joint project within a group. After considering a common project, the whole class determines appropriate sub-topics and is then split up into respective sub-groups. Within each sub-group students plan their investigations for their part of the project. The groups proceed to conduct investigations within the laboratory. The process is supported by a rich variety of resources which can be searched and analyzed by the students working independently. The teacher acts as a mentor, convener and collaborator for the students' inquiry. Each of the groups gives a presentation, poster, report or some other contribution to the whole class to bring the sub-topics back together. The results of the groups are presented or put together and, finally, evaluated by the students and teachers. An example of an application of the GI in an undergraduate general chemistry course is described by Varco-Shea, Darlington, and Turnbull (1996).

Besides the above models, there is now a large variety of additional cooperative teaching techniques (e.g. Sharan, 1999). Most of these techniques have their origin in primary or secondary education, but can be readily adapted for use in higher education. Many creative ideas on how to reorganize traditional teaching to introduce cooperative teaching methods can be found in a variety of publications or via the Internet.

Examples of cooperative teaching and learning in higher level chemistry education

Cooperative settings in theoretical courses

Cooper (1995) discusses how cooperative learning may be used to overcome the inherent defects associated with the large enrolment *lecture* format in undergraduate chemistry courses. This format is described as leading to passive students and is therefore hardly conducive to learning. In contrast, Cooper (1995) describes four major differences between cooperative learning approaches as compared to a didactic lecture format:

- Students take responsibility for their own learning, become actively involved and have responsibility for the learning process.
- Students develop higher order cognitive skills. For example students start synthesizing and analyzing meaningful concepts better than if they were only listening to a lecturer's distribution of information. The students also learn to explain, listen and negotiate actions and meanings and thus become better prepared for a world outside the lecture hall, where such activities are required on a daily basis.
- Cooperative learning leads to the integration of all students and is thus motivating, especially for disadvantaged minorities. The reason lies in increased participation with a group of non-competitive peers.
- Finally, it is suggested that cooperative learning leads to an increase in students' satisfaction with their overall learning experience, which in turn leads to more positive attitudes towards the subject matter.

Considering his experiences with undergraduate chemistry education, Cooper (1995) described how positive interdependence and individual accountability for group work can be promoted by allocating a small number of marks (10 %) to the results achieved by the group. This was facilitated by introducing breaks into the lecture format where students in their groups were able to take short quizzes or to undertake some group work within the frame of the lecture system.

A more structured approach has been discussed by Kogut (1997). He described the results and experiences on a course of general chemistry which promoted cooperative activities between the students. He asked the students to form groups of 4 to 6 and to meet at least once a week in the chemistry lecture room. He asked the students to share their tasks and to document their results and group discussions as well as the solutions to the problems that they were set. In order to provide additional extrinsic motivation for groups to start collaborating, team assignments contributed 10% to the final course grade, as suggested by Cooper (1995). Kogut (1997) reported that this extrinsic approach was well received and cooperative working time gradually expanded as the course progressed. The culture of learning together was accepted and spread to other courses and the learning results improved in comparison to other groups. The reason is thought to be an increase in on-task activity time among the students due to their group activities and a growing willingness of students to help and tutor each other. Kogut (1997) advises that constant vigilance and clear communication and guidance by the instructor are essential for success in establishing a culture of cooperative learning at the beginning of a programme.

A related example was described by Hurley (1993). Responding to the observation that students frequently become frustrated when they are unable to complete tasks in isolation, the idea of a study-group framework was implemented into a general chemistry course. A large class was divided into groups of 15-18 students, which were then further divided into smaller study-groups of 4-8. The aim of the study-groups was to offer structure and guidance during a small portion of the students' learning time. The study-groups met with a more advanced undergraduate student once a week. The advanced student was asked to monitor problems and attendance and also to act as a peer-tutor to guide explanation. Problems to be solved were assigned to each group, members of the group were each required to accept special responsibility for one of the tasks within the assignment and asked to present their individual solutions in detail at the weekly meetings. Other universities nowadays are also replacing presentations in front of the whole class by presentations to small groups. Towns and Grant (1997) described the introduction of additional sessions to consider conceptual issues rather than algorithmic problem solving in a postgraduate thermodynamics course. They found that cooperative learning activities moved students away from rote learning strategies towards deeper thinking approaches, which allowed them to integrate concepts over the entire semester. Towns and Grant also reported improvements in interpersonal and communication skills which the students perceived as an important component of their learning.

At Bremen and Oldenburg Universities in Germany the *Jigsaw Classroom* technique has been used to exchange solutions for mathematical tasks in the context of undergraduate physical chemistry seminars. To prepare students individually or as a group, to contribute effectively they are constantly encouraged and guided to search for further information and help from books, the instructor or any other source. In addition to the weekly meetings, in an example described by Hurley (1993), quiz sessions were also used. In these quiz sessions the class was divided into teams of 3-4. Each of the groups received a task sheet similar to a traditional examination paper and the groups were then required to solve the problems under examination conditions, with the one exception that they were allowed to work as a team. The only assistance available was provided by a peer-tutor who was allowed to provide encouragement without giving the solutions. For other ideas on combining cooperative activities into chemistry lectures, see e.g. Ross and Fulton (1994) or Felder (1996).

The importance of providing structure to a learning process has been discussed by Hurley (1993) for the specific case of making group work successful in the context of cooperative learning (see also Dougherty et al., 1995). In the feedback all stakeholders (instructor, study-group tutor and quiz section tutors) as well as the students themselves responded very positively to this restructuring. A transfer of the 'working in small groups' culture over into the lab-work part of the programme was observed. A more positive attitude towards chemistry learning was described and better problem-solving skills were also found (see also Cardellini, 2006; Wood, 2006):

> *"Students like the group work activity for several reasons. It helps them organize their study time, and keeps them up to date with the homework. They feel that becoming an expert on one or two homework problems is more feasible than trying to master all the assigned problems alone. The team approach to the worksheets exposes the students to alternative ways of thinking about a concept, and verbalizing a problem-solving strategy crystallizes it in their own minds. Finally, doing the worksheets under examination conditions lessens the anxiety they experience when working on the actual examinations, and being able to work out 'difficult' problems boosts their self-confidence."(Hurley, 1993, p. 652)*

Cooperative learning in the lab environment

Exercise classes, practical work, and lab courses are all considered to be important elements of chemistry teaching. These practical activities focus on how theoretical knowledge can be used to solve both theoretical and practical problems. Ideally, more sophisticated levels of understanding ranging from the ability to employ taught concepts and formulae to solve "simple" problems, to an ability to use the wider knowledge base for solving "complex" problems that require the combination of knowledge from different areas, can be developed in this way. Ultimately, students should reach a position where they are capable of creatively and independently developing or discovering scientific ideas and strategies for themselves on the basis of experimental investigations, e.g. as described in examples from secondary chemistry education by Witteck and Eilks (2006) or Witteck, Most, Kienast, and Eilks (2007). Such an approach should be seen as an essential part of modern higher level chemistry education (see Goedhart, Finlayson, & Lindblom-Ylänne in this book).

Proficiency in laboratory work is considered as an essential competency for future chemists and indeed for anyone wishing to work in a related field of science and technology (see Bennett, Seery, & Sövegjarto-Wigbers in this book). The laboratory provides a unique opportunity to develop the competencies of problem solving and 'hands-on' practical skills. While the latter is likely to be achieved in nearly every lab where students actually undertake practical activities, learning about how to solve problems in the lab is less straight forward. Only labs where students are given the chance to become actively involved in the planning of experiments, to conduct their experiment with some degree of freedom, and to interpret and reflect upon their experimental observations in an open forum are likely to lead to competencies in this respect (Tobin, 1990; Witteck, Most, Kienast, & Eilks, 2007). Of course, conducting an experiment should involve not only 'hands-on activity', but also 'minds-on activity' (Lunetta, 1998).

Asking students merely to follow a recipe is unlikely to actively engage their mental processes with the underlying concepts behind an experiment. On the other hand, open experimental tasks and experiments that provide certain freedom of action will be much more likely to stimulate such mental activity. But, working individually on a problem may lead to frustration and ill-defined approaches. Also, science today is no longer the preserve of individual researchers, but has become more and more dependent on teamwork. People working together need to make and explain suggestions for progress, have to negotiate a common strategy, and to reflect and negotiate about interpretation and meaning. As a result of these developments team-oriented skills are now one of the most useful attributes when starting a professional career, e.g. in industry. Using cooperative learning in the lab therefore introduces authentic working practices into the education system.

A number of approaches on how to use cooperative learning methods in lab environments, varying in the degree of structured cooperation and in the level of 'openness' of the experimental tasks, are now available (e.g. Cooper 1994).

Group work in a lab course

An example of how to include group working practices into an organic chemistry lab-course and comparisons with an individualistic approach has been described, e.g. by Biersmith et al. (1975). In this course design-specific tasks were given to individual students and other students were assigned a specific role in a team of three. For example one of the students was appointed as the project leader whereas the various operative tasks within the project (synthesis, analysis etc.) were shared among the other group members. Although the leader takes responsible for organizing the work schedule and leading the discussions, the overall strategy for solving any given problem must be discussed and agreed upon by the whole group. The roles change from project to project so that everybody has the opportunity to take on different perspectives and to practice different skills. Biersmith et al. (1975) reported a general improvement in the exam performance of students who had participated in the group work compared to those working individually. Interestingly, it was also found that the lower achieving students generally made the most progress. Other examples are e.g. using the Jigsaw Classroom method (see above) to prepare for a laboratory experiment to be conducted in a group. Here, each of the students prepares a specific step, procedure or aspect for the experimental task. Again, this approach was found to have a positive effect on students' achievement, especially for the lower achievers (e.g. Smith, Huckley, & Volk, 1991).

Challenging tasks to allow for a research experience

Coppola and Lawton (1995) report on a modification to their course on structure and reactivity. The re-design of this course was aimed at capturing a research experience through the implementation and evaluation of an experiment with uncertain outcomes to overcome the limitations associated with traditional cook-book recipe style of lab work and to promote cooperative learning in the lab. Students' tasks focused on the identification of unknown materials. The cooperative set-up was introduced and justified by providing information about the way most chemists now work, stressing the importance and preponderance of teamwork. The students were each given one solid sample chosen from a large number of different organic substances. The task given to the students was to find peers with the same substance they had. They were told to compare reactivity, physical properties and/or analytical data and to spot their samples side-by-side on a TLC plate. The final proof of whether the two substances were identical or not was based on a comparison of the melting point for the two samples and that for a mixture of them. This approach is easily expanded to include other examples including liquids or solutions. Coppola and Lawton (1995, p. 1122) conclude:

> *"This activity gives a way for instructors to demonstrate the relationship between collecting experimental data and drawing conclusions, as well as how to make and evaluate comparisons. Students also are required to create procedural standards and to communicate within the context of a scientific problem in a natural and need-based manner. Collaborative identification is an honest inquiry that encourages students to combine technical and social skills, a goal of many reform-minded educators."*

Involvement in research projects

Buono and Fasching (1973) described an approach which includes small, open-ended projects on authentic problems into their analytical chemistry course. After having learned the basics ideas and standard procedures in analytical chemistry during the first half of the course, the students together with an instructor, were asked to choose an authentic problem with limited complexity. Such projects included e.g. the determination of lead in pottery or the determination of urea in urine and blood. The students in small groups were asked to evaluate two potential procedures for each of their problems while working together in the library. Having selected the procedures the group was then required to negotiate their laboratory plan with regard to the experimental set-up, the availability of equipment, time, etc., with the instructor. Students were required to conduct their analysis alone, with the instructor functioning to troubleshoot problems and to give advice if needed. At the end of the project the groups had to prepare a report outlining both the problem and their solution. From their experiences and evaluation Buono and Fasching (1973, p. 617) concluded:

> *"Special projects and conventional experiments promote different aspects of students' capability. Conventional experiments test a student's ability to follow established procedures while special projects test a student's initiative, ingenuity, creativity, scientific curiosity, and ability to work with others. These are traits which a student will find useful in a scientific career but which are not usually developed or tested in a conventional laboratory scheme. [...] The undertaking of special projects gives a student a real understanding of how science is applied to problems in today's world."*

For other reports on the project approach to cooperative learning in the chemistry lab see e.g. Bishop (1995) or Varco-Shea, Darlington, and Turnbull (1996).

Peer tutoring in lab courses

An interesting way to implement cooperative learning between students from different levels, involves the use of programmes where older students take over the peer-tutoring of younger students in a lab, as an element of their own education. Whereas they learn to act as a coach and guide, the younger students benefit from their experience in dealing with experimental problems. In this way, a new dimension of cooperative learning is achieved: student-student interactions do not only take place horizontally (within one cohort) but also vertically (between students across different levels of their education). The tutors also profit from their experience of guiding a group of beginners. They have to learn how to supervise and guide, they learn reciprocally by explaining their recently acquired knowledge to others, and they have to develop their social skills to successfully take on the role of the instructor. At the University of Bremen, Germany, it is now a requirement that third year chemistry students supervise freshman students on the introductory general chemistry course for chemists, biologists and others. Experiences with this approach have shown that both groups feel highly motivated to work and learn together. The advanced students not only provide very effective supervision in the laboratory but they also have the opportunity to reflect about what they have already learned.

The advantages of these approaches to lab work are obvious. Students learn that many problems in research are not solved merely by following established recipes (cook-book), but rather as a result of creative new ideas, often developed by combining different expertise and negotiated within a team. It is not surprising that such an environment creates a more stimulating atmosphere for learners, and is thus more motivation than traditionally organised courses where provided recipes are followed step-by-step.

However, is the cooperative approach really more effective regarding cognitive and non-cognitive achievement than other methodologies? There are currently an insufficient number of detailed studies to allow this question to be answered unambiguously. Setting up identical conditions when comparing approaches and providing a statistical relevant data set using a high enough number of students is a difficult task. Available reports in the literature, do however, indicate that cooperative learning offers distinct advantages at least with respect to cognitive and collaborative skills (e.g. Burron, James, & Ambrosio, 1992), while practical skills appear to be better developed on an individual basis (Okebukola & Ogunniyi, 1984). Furthermore, several studies come to the conclusion that the benefits of cooperative learning are greater for the weaker students than for the best students in a class, who appear to perform well regardless of the method used. In any event, all studies report higher levels of motivation and more positive attitudes for students exposed to cooperative methods of teaching (e.g. Okebukola, 1986).

Even so, elements of cooperative learning in higher level chemistry lab courses remain rather sparse. This is probably at least partially due to reservations that university teachers feel about assuming a new role as a coach rather than a supervisor. Also, it is often believed that the poorer students within a group will try to hide behind the more skilled group members. Even where teachers are willing to introduce cooperative learning methods into their modules, a lack of resources to (re)organise courses and to set up a flexible lab environment will be likely to prevent its realisation. The non-standardised sequence of experiments – students do not follow the same rigid procedures and schedule as in a traditional course – leads to a higher demand for individual support and hence for staff time.

Computer supported cooperative learning (CSCL)

Information and communication technology (ICT) has emerged as an important tool for supporting communication between students and between students and their teachers. Computer-supported collaborative learning (CSCL) now provides an additional dimension to cooperative or collaborative learning. Its development has spawned a large field of educational design and research over the past decade (see Laganà et al. or Brouwer & McDonnell both in this book).

In the brief history of CSCL a number of different interpretations of the acronym for the second 'C-word' are to be found; these include collective, coordinated, cooperative and collaborative (Lipponen, Hakkarainen, & Paavola, 2004). It has been suggested that CSCL was formed by combining the terms, computer supported collaborative work (CSCW) and collaborative learning (Hung, 2005), though others define the method as computer-supported collaboration *and* learning (Lipponen et al., 2004). To stress that collaborative learning might better be understood as a theory of pedagogy rather than as a particular type of learning, Koschmann (1999) expands the acronym to computer support *for* collaborative learning. This multiple usage of the acronym symbolizes the variety of research taking place in this field. Fortunately, the majority of current research groups now shows consensus by using the term computer-supported collaborative learning (e.g. Lehtinen, Hakkarainen, Lipponen, Rahikainen, & Muukkonen, 1999; Strijbos, Kirschner, & Martens, 2004).

The primary aim of CSCL is to provide an environment that supports and enhances collaboration between students, in order to enhance students' learning processes (Kreijns, Kirschner, & Jochems, 2002). In CSCL the use of computers and ICT, such as the World Wide Web, is aimed at supporting the acquisition of knowledge in collaborative settings. Therefore, the terms cooperative and coordinated work, where tasks are initially divided up so that knowledge is build on an individual basis, are now rarely used in the context of CSCL.

CSCL settings can be divided into situations where group members interact either *around* or *through* computers (Crook, 1994). In the first situation, students are learning in one place and face-to-face communication is possible or supported, while in the second situation group members are spatially separated and communicate via networks. Common CSCL learning environments are able to provide tools to support communication for either scenario. Most of them are textual, forcing the group members to externalise their ideas, knowledge and arguments, making these propositions debatable and so contributing to the building of collaborative knowing. Computer mediated communication (CMC) tools can support synchronous communication, such as 'chat rooms' and video or audio conferencing, and asynchronous communication, such as email, Wikis and forums or both, such as shared whiteboards.

Interaction through computers suffers from the same debilitating effects as face-to-face collaboration, like social loafing or the free-rider effect (Janssen, Erkens, Kanselaar, & Jaspers, 2007). Particularly with (asynchronous) distance learning scenarios, the lack of any sense of direct contact can adversely affect the communication and therefore the group results. CSCL needs additional strategies to encourage high levels of involvement and equal participation. Besides incorporating positive interdependence and individual accountability into the group tasks (Johnson & Johnson, 1999; O'Donnell & O'Kelly, 1994), a system of monitoring participation in terms of how much each group member relatively contributes to group discussions or to providing external feedback, are possible strategies (Janssen et al., 2007).

Unlike face-to-face communication, the whole discourse in a collaboration-through-computers-setting takes place through computer based representations (see Laganà et al. in this book). Common tools already mentioned above are able to support this communication using mainly textual representations; moreover, in science education they are important in encouraging participants to use domain specific terminology. Science disciplines, especially chemistry, however, also need to communicate ideas based on diagrams such as graphical representations, structure or process models, designed artefacts, symbolic representations, and animations and simulations. Besides supporting communication, all representations constructed in CSCL settings are also resources of shared knowledge.

Some examples may illustrate these thoughts and also give an overview about the variety of tools nowadays available.

Complex knowledge structures often require tools, supporting cross-linked representations, such as mind or concept maps. Common CSCL environments for science education use combinations of graphical and textual representation tools. *ChemSense* (chemsense.org) is an example of a knowledge-building environment which

> *"... allows students and instructors to collaborate in the investigation of chemical phenomena, collect data, build representations of these phenomena, and participate in scaffolded discourse to explain these phenomena in terms of underlying chemical mechanisms"* (Schank & Kozma, 2002, p. 253).

The *ChemSense Animator* will also allow students to create animations which represent chemical processes at the molecular level.

While learning with *Co-Lab - Collaborative Laboratories for Europe* (www.co-lab.nl) in an area of applied science, such as water management or climate control, students integrate the knowledge they gain step-by-step into a graphic model, starting with a sketch or a concept map on a whiteboard they work up through a qualitative or semi-quantitative model to finally produce a quantitative stock-and-flow model. The finished model should be runnable and able to reproduce experimental data that can be obtained from simulations, datasets or remote experiments (Bell et al., 2007).

Stochasmos (Kyza & Constantinou, 2007) is a web-based platform for supporting reflective learning and teaching (www.stochasmos.org). It integrates activities such as data organization, evidence identification, articulation, and reflection from the beginning of the students' inquiry, through an area called reflective workspace. This workspace builds on work around the *Progress Portfolio* (Loh et al., 1998), a stand-alone, inquiry-support software tool that provides a separate space where students can organize data, like text, graphs or pictures, and are prompted to explain their reasoning while making connections to the data they can use as evidence in support of their ideas. These examples illustrate the variety of tools, supporting the creation of external representations and describe how they can be implemented within collaborative learning in higher level chemistry education.

This list could be extended with numerous others including *Molecular Workbench* (workbench.concord.org), *NetLogo* (ccl.northwestern. edu/netlogo), or *WISE* (wise.berkeley.edu).

Although CSCL is a relatively new and rapidly changing field of education, there is already evidence about its effects. This evidence covers two perspectives on learning outcomes, the researcher and the practitioner perspective. Assessment of learning should focus on a certain model of learning (Chan & Van Aalst, 2004). The paradigm shift from supporting individual learning to developing collaborative knowledge requires at least two models, represented by Anna Sfard's two learning metaphors: acquisition and participation (Sfard, 1998). The acquisition metaphor focuses on traditional learning as something in an individual's mind and knowledge in terms of property and possession, whereas in collaborative learning settings it is not even meaningful to talk about well-structured individual knowledge. The participation metaphor deals with learning as becoming a participant and with knowledge as an aspect of practice, discourse and activity. Many studies focussing on learning results (acquisition metaphor) tend to favour a particular CSCL tool and report educational benefits.

It is difficult to generalise about the effectiveness of CSCL on learning because of the diversity of technologies, contexts and research methods used in the studies. However, Lethinen et al. (1999) advise that the statement "... *that it is possible to improve the quality of learning by using CSCL methods*" (p. 28) should be treated with caution. Concerning social goals, CMC groups engage in more complex, broader, and cognitively challenging discussions (Benbunan-Fich, Hiltz, & Turoff, 2003), and group members participate more equally (Fjermestad, 2004), compared to face-to-face groups. CSCL environments like CSILE (now *Knowledge Forum*, www.knowledgeforum.com) and *Belvedere* (belvedere.sourceforge.net) are helpful for encouraging higher order social interaction (Scardamalia & Lamon, 1994). Fjermestad (2004) found positive motivational outcomes with students who collaborated in CMC groups, reporting higher levels of satisfaction. It must be acknowledged that a number of studies have also shown results that are in contrast with the studies mentioned above. For instance, students working in CMC groups sometimes perceive their discussions as more confusing (Thompson & Coovert, 2003) or time consuming when compared to face-to-face groups.

However, for the practitioner these studies show that while integrating CSCL into their teaching may be beneficial, there is no guarantee that collaborating with computers will automatically lead to improvements in learning. Chan and Van Aalst (2004) describe a mismatch between assessment and collaborative learning when achievement is measured at the end of the course by traditional written tests evaluating factual knowledge. This validity problem could be compared to using oral or written examinations instead of testing process-orientated competencies at the end of a laboratory course. Their view is that assessment in CSCL learning environments should focus on both, individual and collaborative learning. Besides a summative assessment *of* learning there should also be formative assessment *for* learning that gives feedback "... *to enable students to understand and improve their own learning*" (Chan & Van Aalst, 2004, p. 93).

In learning environments, such as *WISE* or *Stochasmos*, it is possible for the tutor to monitor students' progress by looking at their submitted work and providing feedback to them. *Stochasmos* also enables two groups to connect and collaborate on a shared workspace, providing the opportunity for *peer-evaluation*. These social-constructivist forms of assessment *for* learning offer great promise but examples of its use are still quite limited:

> *"A different culture needs to be developed shifting from an emphasis of individual, competitive assessment to one that emphasis collaboration and contribution to others' learning (e.g., peer assessments, collaborative knowledge products). ... Nevertheless, it needs to be pointed out that the focus on collaboration does not exclude the need for individual assessment; the key idea is that the overemphasis on individual performance needs to be reconsidered."* (Chan & Van Aalst, 2004, p. 107)

Conclusions

Higher education is characterised by self-organized learning, often misunderstood as individual acquisition of knowledge. Other important skills, like sharing or monitoring a discussion, debating, negotiation skills, or working in a team are disregarded but they are nonetheless essential social and communications skills that will be needed in the future world of work. The tradition of cooperative learning stemming mainly from primary and secondary education, but soundly based on educational theory, offers a number of tools to promote those skills mentioned above in higher level chemistry education, too. There is considerable evidence that cooperative learning methods are at least as effective as more traditional approaches to instruction. Where used cooperative learning can help to develop social skills, communication abilities, and even the development of independent learning skills. Many studies also suggest that cooperative learning helps to raise motivation and promotes learning in the cognitive domain.

References

Aronson, E., Stephan, C., Sikes, J., Blaney, N., & Snapp, M. (1978). *The jigsaw classroom.* Beverly Hills: Sage.

Baltes, B. B., Dickson, M. W., Sherman, M. P., Bauer, C. C., & LaGanke, J. (2002). Computer-mediated communication and group decision making: A meta-analysis. *Organizational Behavior and Human Decision Processes, 87,* 156-179.

Bell, T., Schanze, S., Gräber, W., Slotta, J., Jorde, D., Berg, H., Strömme, T., Neumann, A., Tergan, S.-O., & Evans, R. (2007). Technology-enhanced collaborative inquiry learning: Four approaches under common aspects. In: R. Pintó & D. Couso (Eds.), *Contributions from science education research* (pp. 451-463). Dordrecht: Springer.

Benbunan-Fich, R., Hiltz, S. R., & Turoff, M. (2003). A comparative content analysis of face-to-face vs. asynchronous group decision making. *Decision Support Systems, 34,* 457-469.

Biersmith, E. L., III, Hinton, J., Normand, R., & Raymond, G. (1975). Group organic chemistry. *Journal of Chemical Education, 52,* 593-596.

Bishop, E. O. (1995). Group work for undergraduates. *Education in Chemistry, 32,* 131-132.

Bodner, G. M. (1986). Constructivism: A Theory of Knowledge. *Journal of Chemical Education, 63,* 873-878.

Boud, D., Cohen, R., & Sampson, J. (2001). *Peer learning in higher education: Learning from & with each other.* Sterling: Stylus.

Buono. J. S., & Fasching, J. L. (1973). Initiative, ingenuity, creativity and chemistry, too?. *Journal of Chemical Education, 50,* 616-617.

Burron, B., James, M. L., & Ambrosio, A. L. (1992). The effects of cooperative learning in a physical science course for elementary/middle level preservice teachers. *Journal of Research in Science Teaching, 30,* 697-707.

Cardellini, L. (2006). Fostering creative problem solving in chemistry through group work. *Chemistry Education Research and Practice, 7,* 131-140.

Chan, C. K. K., & Van Aalst, J. (2004). Learning, assessment and collaboration in computer-supported environments. In: J.-W. Strijbos, P. A. Kirschner & R. L. Martens (Eds.), *What we know about CSCL. And implementing it in higher education* (pp. 87-112). Boston: Kluwer.

Cooper, M. M. (1994). Cooperative chemistry laboratories. *Journal of Chemical Education, 71,* 307.

Cooper, M. M. (1995). Cooperative Learning: An approach for large enrollment courses. *Journal of Chemical Education, 72,* 162-164.

Coppola, B. P., & Lawton, R. G. (1995). Who has the same substance I have?. *Journal of Chemical Education, 72,* 1120-1122.

Crook, C. (1994). *Computers and the collaborative experience of learning.* London: Routledge.

Daniel, E. G. S. (2001). Participant interaction models and roles in a computer supported collaborative learning (CSCL) environment: A Malaysian case study. *Proceedings of the 13th World Conference on Educational Multimedia, Hypermedia & Telecommunications,* Tampere, Finland.

De Vries, D. L., & Slavin, R. E. (1978). Teams-Games-Tournament: Review of ten classroom experiments. *Journal of Research and Development in Education, 12*(4), 28-38.

Dinan, F. J., & Frydrychowski, V. A. (1995). A team learning method for organic chemistry. *Journal of Chemical Education, 72,* 429-431.

Dougherty, R. C., Bowen, C. W., Berger, T., Rees, W., Mellon, E. K., & Pulliam, E. (1995). Cooperative learning and attitudes in general chemistry. *Journal of Chemical Education, 72,* 793.

Doymus, K. (2008). Teaching chemical equilibrium with the jigsaw technique. *Research in Science Education, 38,* 249-260.

Driver, R., & Oldham, V. (1986). A constructivist approach to curriculum development. *Studies in Science Education, 13,* 22-105.

Eilks, I. (2005). Experiences and reflections about teaching atomic structure in a jigsaw classroom in lower secondary school chemistry lessons. *Journal of Chemical Education, 82,* 313-320.

Eilks, I., & Leerhoff, G. (2001). A jigsaw classroom - Illustrated by the teaching of atomic structure. *Science Education International, 12*(3), 15-20.

Falchikov, N., & Blythman, M. (2001). *Learning together peer tutoring in higher education.* London: Routledge.

Felder, R. M. (1996). Active-inductive-cooperative learning: An instructional model for chemistry?. *Journal of Chemical Education, 73,* 832.

Fjermestad, J. (2004). An analysis of communication mode in group support systems research. *Decision Support Systems, 37*(2), 239.

Goodsell, A., Maher, M., & Tinto, V. (1992). *Collaborative learning: A sourcebook for higher education.* University Park, National Center on Postsecondary Teaching, Learning, and Assessment.

Hodson, D., & Hodson, J. (1998). From constructivism to social constructivism: A Vygotskyan perspective on teaching and learning science. *School Science Review, 79* (289), 33-41.

Hubscher-Younger, T., & Narayanan, N. H. (2003). Authority and convergence in collaborative learning. *Computers & Education, 41,* 313-334.

Hung, D. (2005). Preserving authenticity in CoLs and CoPs: proposing an agenda for

CSCL. *Proceedings of the 2005 conference on computer support for collaborative learning.* Taipei: International Society of the Learning Sciences.

Hurley, C. N. (1993). Study groups in general chemistry. *Journal of Chemical Education, 70*, 651-652.

Janssen, J., Erkens, G., Kanselaar, G., & Jaspers, J. (2007). Visualization of participation: Does it contribute to successful computer-supported collaborative learning?. *Computers & Education, 49*, 1037-1065.

Javid, M. A. (2000). A suggested model for a working cyberschool. *Educational Technology, 40*, 61-63.

Johnson, D. W., & Johnson, R. T. (1999). *Learning together and alone: Cooperative, competitive, and individualistic learning* (5th ed.). Boston: Allyn & Bacon.

Johnson, D. W., Johnson, R. T., & Smith K. A. (1991). *Active learning: Cooperation in the college classroom.* Edina: Interaction Book Company.

Johnston, K., & Driver, R. G. (1990). *Children's learning in science projects: Interactive teaching in science-workshop for training courses.* Leeds: Centre for Studies in Science and Mathematics Education, University of Leeds.

Kerns, T. (1996). Should we use cooperative learning in college chemistry?. *Journal of College Science Teaching, 25*, 435-438.

Kogut, L. S. (1997). Using cooperative learning to enhance performance in general chemistry. *Journal of Chemical Education, 74*, 724.

Koschmann, T. (1999). Toward a dialogic theory of learning: Bakhtin's contribution to understanding learning in settings of collaboration. *Proceedings of the 1999 conference on Computer support for collaborative learning.* Palo Alto: International Society of the Learning Sciences.

Kreijns, K., Kirschner, P. A., & Jochems, W. (2002). The sociability of computer-supported collaborative learning environments. *Educational Technology & Society, 5*(1), 8-22.

Kyza, E. A., & Constantinou, C. P. (2007). *Stochasmos: A web-based platform for reflective, inquiry-based teaching and learning.* Cyprus: Learning in Science Group.

Lazarowitz, R., & Hertz-Lazarowitz, R. (1998). Cooperative learning in the science curriculum. In: B. J. Fraser & K. G. Tobin (Eds.), *International Handbook of Science Education* (pp. 623-640). Dordrecht: Kluwer.

Lazarowitz, R., & Karsenty, G. (1990). Cooperative learning and student academic achievement, process skills, learning environment and self-esteem in 10th grade biology. In: S. Sharan (Ed.), *Cooperative learning, theory and research* (pp. 123–149). New York: Praeger.

Lehtinen, E., Hakkarainen, K., Lipponen, L., Rahikainen, M., & Muukkonen, H. (1999). Computer supported collaborative learning: A review. *The J.H.G.I. Giesbers Reports on Education* (pp. 1-58). Nijmegen: University of Nijmegen.

Lipponen, L., Hakkarainen, K., & Paavola, S. (2004). Practices and orientations of CSCL. In: J.-W. Strijbos, P. A. Kirschner & R. L. Martens (Eds.), *What we know about CSCL. And implementing it in higher education* (pp. 31-50). Boston: Kluwer.

Loh, B., Radinsky, J., Russell, E., Gomez, L. M., Reiser, B. J., & Edelson, D. C. (1998). The progress portfolio: designing reflective tools for a classroom context. *Paper presented at the SIGCHI conference on Human factors in computing systems.* Los Angeles, United States.

Lunetta, V. N. (1998). The school science laboratory: Historical perspectives and contexts for contemporary teaching. In: B. J. Fraser & K. G. Tobin (Eds.), *International Handbook of Science Education* (pp. 249-268). Dordrecht: Kluwer.

O'Donnell, A. M., & O'Kelly, J. (1994). Learning from peers: Beyond the rhetoric of positive results. *Educational Psychology Review, 6*, 321-349.

Okebukola, P. A. (1986). Cooperative learning and students attitudes to laboratory work. *School Science and Mathematics, 86*, 582-590.

Okebukola, P. A., & Ogunniyi, M. B. (1984). Cooperative, competitive, and individualistic science laboratory interaction patterns - Effects on students' achievement and acquisition of practical skills. *Journal of Research in Science Teaching, 21*, 875-884.

Prawat, R. S. (1989). Teaching for understanding: Three key attributes. *Teaching & Teacher Education, 5*, 315-328.

Renkl, A., Gruber, H., & Mandl, H. (1995). *Kooperatives Lernen in der Hochschule. Forschungsbericht Nr. 46.* Munich: Ludwig-Maximilians-Universität.

Ross, M. R., & Fulton, R. B. (1991). Active learning strategies in the analytical chemistry classroom. *Journal of Chemical Education, 71,* 141.

Scardamalia, M., B., K., & Lamon, M. (1994). The CSILE project: Trying to bring the classroom into world 3. In: K. McGilly (Ed.), *Classroom lessons:Integrating cognitive theory and classroom practice* (pp. 201-227). Cambridge: Bradford Books/MIT Press.

Scardamalia, M. B. K & Bereiter, C. (1996). Computer support for knowledge-building communities. In: T. Koschmann (Ed.), *CSCL: Theory and practice of an emerging paradigm* (pp. 249-268). Mahwah: Lawrence Erlbaum.

Schank, P., & Kozma, R. (2002). Learning chemistry through the use of a representation-based knowledge building environment. *Journal of Computers in Mathematics and Science Teaching, 21,* 253-279.

Sfard, A. (1998). On two metaphors for learning and the dangers of choosing just one. *Educational Researcher, 27*(2), 4-13.

Sharan, S. (Ed.) (1999). *Handbook of cooperative learning methods.* Westport: Praeger.

Sharan, S., & Hertz-Lazarowitz, R. (1980). A group investigation method of cooperative learning in the classroom. In: S. Sharan, P. Hare, C. Webb & R. Hertz-Lazarowitz (Eds.), *Cooperation in education* (pp. 14-46). Provo: BYU Press.

Slavin, R. E. (1978). Student Teams and Achievement Divisions. *Journal of Research and Development in Education, 12,* 39-49.

Smith, M. E., Hinckley, C. C., & Volk, G. L. (1991). Cooperative learning in the undergraduate laboratory. *Journal of Chemical Education, 68,* 413-415.

Springer, L., Stanne, M. E., & Donovan, S. (1999). Effects of cooperative learning on undergraduates in Science, Mathematics, Engineering, and Technology: A meta-analysis. *Review of Educational Research, 69,* 21-51.

Stahl, G. (2004). Building collaborative knowing. In: J.-W. Strijbos, P. A. Kirschner & R. L. Martens (Eds.), *What we know about CSCL. And implementing it in higher education* (pp. 53-85). Boston: Kluwer.

Strijbos, J.-W., Kirschner, P. A., & Martens, R. L. (2004). What we know about CSCL. In: J.-W. Strijbos, P. A. Kirschner & R. L. Martens (Eds.), *What we know about CSCL and implementing it in higher education* (pp. 245-259). Boston: Kluwer.

Strommen, E. F., & Lincoln, B. (1992). Constructivism, technology, and the future of classroom learning. *Education and Urban Society, 24,* 466.

Thompson, L. F., & Coovert, M. D. (2003). Teamwork online: The effects of computer conferencing on perceived confusion, satisfaction and postdiscussion accuracy. *Group Dynamics, 7*(2), 135-151.

Tobin, K. G. (1990). Research on science laboratory activities: In pursuit of better questions and answers to improve learning. *School Science and Mathematics, 90,* 403-418.

Towns, M. H., & Grant, E. R. (1997). I believe I will go out of this class actually knowing something: Cooperative learning activities in physical chemistry. *Journal of Research in Science Teaching, 34,* 819-835.

Varco-Shea, T. C., Darlington, J., & Turnbull, M. (1996). Group project format in first-semester general chemistry lab. *Journal of Chemical Education, 73,* 536-538.

Vygotsky, L. S. (1978). *Mind in society: the development of higher psychological processes.* Cambridge: Harvard University Press.

Witteck, T., & Eilks, I. (2006). Max Sour Ltd. – Open experimentation and problem solving in a cooperative learning company. *School Science Review, 88* (323), 95-102.

Witteck, T., Most, B., Kienast, S., & Eilks, I. (2007). A lesson plan on separating matter based on the learning company approach – A motivating frame for self-regulated and open lab-work in introductory chemistry lessons. *Chemistry Education Research and Practice, 7,* 108-119.

Wood, C. (2006). The development of creative problem solving in chemistry. *Chemistry Education Research and Practice, 7,* 96-113.

Online Support and Online Assessment for Teaching and Learning Chemistry

NATASA BROUWER
University of Amsterdam, The Netherlands

CLAIRE McDONNELL
Dublin Institute of Technology, Ireland

*In this chapter, examples of innovative approaches that use
educational technology to support active learning in chemistry
lectures, tutorials and laboratory sessions are considered. The
scope of the chapter is limited to blended learning. The
strengths and weaknesses of e-learning are examined and the
options available for online assessment using electronic tests
and e-portfolios are discussed. In addition to the literature
references provided in the chapter, several examples of good
practice involving the implementation of information and
communication technology for chemistry teaching in higher
education are incorporated. A list of online resources for
lecturers is also included.*

Introduction

*"Learning how to learn has become the most fundamental skill
that an educated person needs to master, and the instrument that
enables learning in almost every field is the computer."*
*(Dr. Peshe Kauriloff, Adjunct Associate Professor of English, University of
Pennsylvania, retrieved from e-Learning Centre website at www.e-
learningcentre.co.uk/eclipse/Resources/quotations.htm)*

Students today use communication technology extensively. They chat online
daily with their friends, they use e-mail and social networking sites and
many children already have a mobile phone by the age of ten (Schüz, 2005).
Young students are already accustomed to retrieving information they
require rapidly and at any time using the Internet and to viewing, generating
and sharing video clips on a wide range of topics using websites such as
YouTube. In addition, they often keep weblogs or contribute to discussion
boards or forums that interest them. Thus, this should make it easy and

Chapter consultant: Ron Cole, University of Ulster, United Kingdom.

*I. Eilks and B. Byers (Eds.). Innovative Methods of Teaching and Learning Chemistry in
Higher Education, pp. 123-152. © 2009 RSC Publishing*

125

natural for them to use similar technologies in education such as electronic learning environments, discussion boards and chat rooms.

The aim of this chapter is to examine innovative teaching and learning methods in which learning technology is applied to facilitate learning, as well as web-based assessment for undergraduate chemistry students in both practical sessions and lectures. The scope of this chapter is limited to blended learning. Distance learning is not considered. The strengths and weaknesses of online learning are examined initially and then a brief overview of the relevant educational theories is presented. Examples of how online resources have been used to support the learning of chemistry undergraduate students in laboratory practicals and in lectures are discussed. This is followed by an examination of approaches used that involve online assessment. In addition to online multiple choice tests and quizzes, e-portfolios and online collaborative group assessment are also discussed. The online resources provided to lecturers and to students are then considered and several lists of those available appear at the end of the chapter. The chapter closes with a brief review of developing and future trends.

Blended learning

The examples discussed here involve blended learning rather than web-based learning alone. The term blended learning is usually understood to describe course delivery in which a combination of face-to-face and online teaching and learning takes place, but the "mix" of the two components can vary considerably (Williams, Bland, & Christie, 2008). There are several alternative interpretations of what blended learning involves, including one that views it as a blend of different types of web-based tools and media only (Whitelock & Jelfs, 2003). In their review, Sharpe, Benfield, Roberts, and Francis (2006) acknowledged that blended learning is not easy to define but they came to the conclusion that the use of the term should be continued because this lack of clarity allows teaching staff the flexibility to develop their own meaning appropriate to their context. They also suggested that academic staff feel reassured by the implication that face-to-face contact with students is preserved in a blended learning approach. The rationale that is recommended is that online learning be used to complement other methods, not replace them, and that it should only be incorporated if it enriches and enhances learning (Charlesworth & Vician, 2003).

Implementation of educational technology in higher education institutions

There is no doubt that the introduction of technology in teaching costs money. Laurillard (2002) analysed the methods of online communication used for teaching and learning in higher education and discussed their implementation. She found that the relationship between benefits and costs is complex. Laurillard (2007) later developed a modelling tool to allow developers to construct a plan on how to improve learning benefits while controlling the associated teaching costs. She determined that there are four factors that help to bring costs down: Substitution, rather than duplication of online services, greater reuse and sharing of e-learning resources, increased peer learning, and more standardised production of materials. Systems that are well-managed and mature are necessary to make these factors work and, in many countries, governments have prepared strategic plans to improve the quality of learning using technology (DfES, 2003).

Collaborative organizations such as the *SURFfoundation* in the Netherlands (www.surffoundation.nl) or *JISC* (www.jisc.ac.uk) and the Higher Education Academy (www.heacademy.ac.uk/) in the United Kingdom play a significant role in introducing technology into higher education in their respective countries. Initiatives that have been undertaken include funding of renovation projects to develop, improve and implement e-learning, provision of support from experts and the formation of special interest groups.

Almost every higher education institution has now incorporated an online element (often referred to as e-learning) into their courses. To be able to use this technology, academic staff need to modernize their teaching and it is important that their attitude towards their teaching is as progressive as their approach towards carrying out research. Michael (2001) makes this point and recommends that, just as academics will keep up to date with and evaluate novel methods and technology in their field of research, they should also ensure that they are aware of new teaching and learning technology and methodologies.

The way in which learning technology is used for teaching and learning can vary significantly. In the United Kingdom, Sharpe et al. (2006) carried out a wide ranging review of literature and practice on the undergraduate experience of blended learning. They classified two main approaches adopted in higher education institutions. The first is the provision of additional support material online. The second, less common, one involves course redesign to promote learner communication and interaction using information and communication technology (ICT). A third approach that uses technology in education aims to bring learning closer to research practice. Research-oriented learning activities stimulate the development of independent learners (Brouwer, Byers, & McDonnell, 2006; see Goedhart, Lindblom-Ylänne, & Finlayson in this book). In many fields in chemical research, computers are essential and applications often use data online. In addition, collaboration of research groups, learners or individuals is now often web-based (see Eilks, Markic, Bäumer, & Schanze in this book). Most computer applications for research have become sufficiently user-friendly to enable them to be used by students in research-oriented learning activities to solve realistic chemistry problems. To perform research, students need access to the latest literature and this is facilitated by using electronic scientific literature resources such as *Google Scholar* (scholar.google.nl), *ISI Web of Knowledge* (apps.isiknowledge.com), *SciFinder Scholar* (www.cas.org/SCIFINDER/SCHOLAR/) and *Beilstein CrossFire* (www.beilstein.com). These resources, with the exception of *Google Scholar*, are not open access although many institutions offer them as a facility for their students and staff.

Evaluation of the strengths and weaknesses of e-learning

The benefits

The use of ICT can support the learning process and enhance communication. It facilitates the transformation from the classical teacher-centred process characterized by teacher-to-student communication flow, separated working forms, guided tutorials and closed experiments (Figure 1) to a flexible student-centred learning process in which the student constructs his or her knowledge using different sources (Figure 2) (Brouwer, 2006).

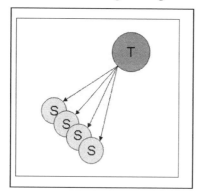 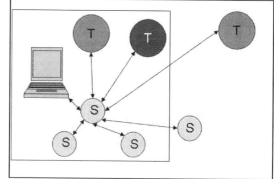

Figure 1: Teacher-centred process   *Figure 2: Student-centred process*

Communication online can be synchronous (chat room) or asynchronous (discussion board). These options can accommodate situations where the students and the teachers are not in the same location and where they may or may not be online at the same time. Also, others can become involved in the educational process, e.g. lecturers from other courses and students and lecturers from other institutions or experts in the field (Figure 2). Students can readily collaborate online by working in groups sharing online space and discussion boards (see Eilks, Markic, Bäumer, & Schanze in this book).

Face-to-face interaction differs significantly to online and it is important to recognize this. Gilly Salmon (2004) has developed an excellent five-stage model for e-tutors to provide a framework within which they can assist learners with this change and support them sufficiently during their initial online experiences.

Flexibility of access to online resources and communication tools is a significant benefit of web-based learning. By means of electronic learning platforms, students can access teaching materials and resources at any time and use a range of communication tools and online quizzes or tests on any networked computer. Computers can also be very useful tools for diagnosing students' pre-knowledge. Adaptive electronic tests can be used and learners receive feedback individually so that they know where they have any knowledge gaps they need to address. A learning support to facilitate refreshing students' pre-knowledge can also be provided within the virtual learning environment (VLE) for a particular course. This approach has helped students to get better results when studying chemistry and to improve their performance in exams (Lovatt, Finlayson, & James, 2007) or to brush up on gaps in mathematical knowledge before studying courses such as quantum chemistry (Koopman, Brouwer, Heck, & Burna, 2008).

Simulations can be used to develop understanding of chemical concepts in different contexts and, in inquiry-based courses, computers can be used as research tools to help solve more complex and realistic problems.

Barak and Dori (2005) showed that integrating information technology (IT)-supported project-based learning into a chemistry course had a positive effect on students' learning outcomes and their level of understanding. Web-based inquiry activities in combination with the construction of 3D molecular models on a computer enhanced the learners' ability to operate on four levels of chemistry understanding: Macroscopic, microscopic, symbolic and process. Another development is the use of online resources and freeware programmes to redesign teaching laboratories so that they replicate the situation in a research laboratory. This approach produces situations that mimick real-life and can improve the development of students' problem solving skills (Cox et al., 2008; Tsai, 2007).

The Internet provides an excellent means of providing learner support and resources. However, in order to make full use of its potential, web-based learning can also be employed as a framework for learner activities, particularly collaborative group activities. An important advantage of web-based information is that it provides the opportunity to work in groups to produce and edit web materials using wikis. The wiki functionality can thus be used in education to provide a space in which students work and learn collaboratively. The additional flexibility afforded by web-based learning as well as its suitability for collaborative group learning through the use of discussion boards, chat rooms and wikis has the benefit of providing a new means of developing independent learners. Chickering and Ehrmann (1996) emphasised the benefits of using online group projects as assessment methods as they incorporate several of their seven principles of good practice in undergraduate education, including active learning, student-student interaction and the requirement for time on task. They also reported that it is often observed that learners perform to higher levels when they know that their peers will be able to view their assignments and correspondence online. Another advantage of e-learning is that it assists the development of information technology, collaborative work and communication skills which are all very important in a working environment. It is interesting to note that several studies have shown that female students benefit more from web-based learning activities than male students and that they opt more often for voluntary activities than male students (Herman et al., 2005; Botch et al., 2007).

Common problems

There are several common difficulties associated with online learning The initial induction and access stage is critical and requires careful planning and support (Salmon, 2004; Laurillard, 2002; Holmes & Gardner, 2006; Sharpe et al., 2006). Other issues include the challenge of keeping learners motivated and engaged, access to networked computers, technical problems, anxiety over time management and the difficulty with developing social interaction online. There are also a number of barriers to the successful implementation of online learning that are often encountered at an institutional level such as the provision of the necessary support structures and development of a clear e-learning strategy. Thus, institutional and financial support, sufficient time allocation, appropriate professional development courses for academic staff to learn new technologies and ongoing support from experts and peers are important requirements. Holmes and Gardner (2006) emphasise that structures and resources need to be put in place to facilitate web-based learning innovations without excessive preparation and time commitments and Mason (2001) observes that ways of reducing the time demands on online tutors need to be found as 'interaction fatigue' can set in. The introduction of technology in education has had a significant impact on time resources, both of the student and of the lecturer (Laurillard, 2007). On one hand, technology can save a lot of the time required to evaluate students' work. On the other hand, it diminishes the border between time and space and students expect instant feedback from their lecturers 24 hours a day.

The observation has also been made that students can find the change from traditional teaching practices difficult because they are now required to work continuously over the entire academic year. Lovatt et al. (2007) report that the first year undergraduates they studied engaged with the teaching material provided online in the weeks before exams but did not tend to engage during the rest of the semester. Related to this is the problem of the extent of part-time work that students are currently undertaking. Concannon, Flynn, and Campbell (2005) identify 'full time part time students' as a recent phenomenon in higher education institutions. These learners are enrolled on full time courses but also spend significant amounts of their time working in part time jobs.

Problems with online learning can also arise due to a lack of permanence of the links to the resources provided. Markwell and Brooks (2008) analyzed a "link rot" phenomenon in chemistry web courses. They followed the URLs of 515 web courses. About 100 disappeared after one year and, after 78 months, only 181 were still accessible. Possible causes were also discussed by the authors. Another issue is that information online can contain errors and misinformation. This was reported in a study published in Nature (Giles, 2005), however, reliability seems to be improving as science entries in *Wikipedia* contain approximately four inaccuracies on average and entries in *Encyclopaedia Britannica* about three.

In technology-enhanced learning, special attention must be given to providing guidelines about plagiarism, especially when students are working on projects or writing reports and essays. Students can often be tempted to use the copy and paste function when reporting on the work of others. Educational software such as *Ephorus* (www.ephorus.com/higher-education) and *Turnitin* (www.turnitin.com) is available to detect plagiarism and assignments submitted using the *Blackboard* electronic learning environment can be scanned automatically for plagiarism. Cheating is also considered to be a potential problem in e-learning, however, Charlesworth, Charlesworth, and Vician (2006) showed that students' perception of the effect of using an electronic course management system on the level of cheating is not significant. In addition, clear guidelines on "netiquette" (internet etiquette) are required when students will be engaged in communicating by electronic means (Shea, 1997).

Knowledge for all

We would like to end this section by emphasising the potential of ICT to bring educational resources to every citizen of the world for the cost of an internet connection. For example, Massachusetts Institute of Technology has opened its course materials to the whole world with their *MIT Open Courseware* (ocw.mit.edu/OcwWeb/web/home/home/index.htm). This decision was made based on the argument that educational resources should be accessible according to non-proprietary, peer-to-peer, and open-source software principles (Malloy, Jensen, & Regan, 2002). Sharing of material and the resultant exchange of ideas among lecturers also has an important role to play in improving the quality of teaching in higher education. Initiatives such as the *Open Educational Resources Commons* (www.oercommons.org) (Mittal, Krishnan, & Altman, 2006), *MERLOT* (Multimedia Educational Recourse for Learning and On Line Teaching, www.merlot.org/merlot/index.htm), the European learning objects repository *Ariadne* (www.ariadne-eu.org), and the ECTN chemistry tests database EChemTest (www.cpe.fr/ectn-assoc/echemtest/index.htm) offer lecturers access to educational material and hopefully motivate them to share their own materials. Issues relating to intellectual property and copyrights for open access teaching material in higher education are regulated according to the *Creative Commons Licence* (creativecommons.org).

Relevant learning theories

There are a number of learning theories underpinning e-learning methods. These are cognitivism (relates to online tutor support and teaching materials), learner differences theory (multiple representations of a topic e.g. animations, text, video and audio clips, graphs) and constructivism (online learning activities, e.g. quizzes, crosswords, wiki construction, problem solving). Where online collaboration is involved, this incorporates a social constructivist approach. A brief summary of the main principles of each educational theory follows (see also Byers & Eilks, or Eilks, Markic, Bäumer, & Schanze both in this book).

Cognitivism focuses on the means by which the learner processes information. Knowledge is considered to be absolute and fixed and links to existing knowledge are encouraged. The goal is to develop critical thinking and problem-solving abilities (Toohey, 1999). Information is structured and sequenced to facilitate processing and the tutor organises practice and feedback to ensure that new knowledge is assimilated. Use of learner support resources such as notes and summaries, practice problems, useful links and online tutor support reflect a contribution from the cognitivist approach. The variation in style and approach that exists among learners is the basis for the learner differences theory (Beetham, 2002). Multiple representations of learning content are required to accommodate the range of learner types (graphs, simulations, animations, text, video) and it is recommended that a number of routes (linear and networked / cross-linked) to navigate through material or an activity be provided (Chickering & Ehrmann, 1996).

Constructivism holds that knowledge arises from our engagement with the realities around us and that meaning is constructed. This leads to the assumption that it is possible that different people will construct knowledge in varying ways and will construct their own interpretations of the knowledge provided to them. Thus, each individual learner will have their own perspective and experiences (Crotty, 1998). Providing learners with online activities should keep the learner motivated and encourage them to take charge of their learning. Active learning is considered necessary to the constructivist approach and so the use of online learning activities shows the influence of constructivism on course design.

The social constructivist theory of learning, which originated with Vygotsky (1962), claims that learning centres on social interaction and shared tasks in which individuals build their learning by interacting with the environment, particularly teachers and fellow students (Beetham, 2002). Collaboration on meaningful and challenging activity-based programmes promotes exploratory learning and is regarded as a highly effective means of encouraging learning (Bigge & Shermis, 2004). The advantages of this approach are that learners can capitalize on their strengths and overcome their weaknesses while working on a collaborative task. They also get the opportunity to encounter alternative methods adopted by other learners. A number of authors point out that interactive, collaborative learners can be well-supported in a web-based environment and remark that asynchronous online communication encourages significant peer interaction to take place (Roberts, 1995; McMahon, 1997; Oliver, 2001; Gagné, Wagner, Golas, & Keller, 2005).

Effects of e-learning activities on students' learning progress

Online self-directed learning to construct knowledge and skills

Among the significant benefits of online learning identified by students are the opportunity to work at a suitable pace and the accessibility afforded. Provision of a range of online learning materials, activities and self-tests with instant feedback allows learners to determine how well they understand and can apply material introduced in their lectures (Adams, Byers, Cole, & Ruddick, 2003). This type of support has been found very useful for teaching chemistry to large groups of first year undergraduates, particularly those who have not studied chemistry at secondary level.

Examples of this approach include development of online self-study quizzes with instant and detailed feedback to allow first year students at Dublin Institute of Technology, Ireland, to determine how well they understand and can apply the topics they are being taught (O'Connor & McDonnell, 2005). In order to encourage use of these quizzes, an online assessment test that used a selection of the self-study quiz questions was introduced towards the end of the academic year. Another example at Plantijn University College, Belgium, involves the provision of online courses and exercises for self-directed study and related exercises (e.g., stoichiometry problems) online. The purpose of the courses and exercises is to allow learners to fill any gaps between their secondary school science knowledge level and the initial knowledge level required for higher education. Extensive feedback is provided online to students who have attempted the exercises. In addition, staff and each student can track the activities they have undertaken and thus monitor learning progress. Based on their work at Dublin City University, Ireland, Lovatt et al. (2007) have reported that there is some evidence that first year students will only interact with quizzes and other support material if they form part of the assessment for the course. Also, they found that if quizzes are considered too difficult, then generally, if they are not assessed, they will not even be attempted. A description of the online support provided at Robert Gordon University in Scotland follows:

Online help for on-campus and off-campus students at the Robert Gordon University

Several years ago, the Robert Gordon University in Scotland developed its own VLE called the *Virtual Campus*. It provided a comprehensive infrastructure and facilitates interaction between staff and students supporting course delivery, tutoring, and discussions. The Virtual Campus was used by two distinct groups of students; full-time on-campus students and the off-campus students who study by distance and on-line learning. This latter group of students was particularly dependent on the material posted on the Virtual Campus. The university recently made a strategic decision to change their VLE to *Moodle* (www.moodle.com) and, since September 2008, the VLE has been called *Campus Moodle* (campusmoodle.rgu.ac.uk). Course materials are posted up by module, but there are also general information modules. Material posted varies with each lecturer but, typically, not only will the lecture materials be posted up for downloading, but other support materials such as useful website addresses, computer quizzes and sample exam questions are also included. For first year students, revision materials and self-study materials are also posted to help fill in any gaps in their knowledge and understanding from the various courses they have studied prior to entering the university. It has been suggested that posting up lecture materials can result in students stopping attending the lectures, but this has not been found to be the case here and indeed the extra materials can help students to take charge of their own learning.

122 first year science students (forensic science, biomedical science and nutritional science) who all took the same introductory science module were asked to fill in a questionnaire about how they used the support materials on the Virtual Campus. 64 replies were received. 100% of these downloaded the lecture notes. When asked, however, if they downloaded the answers to tutorials or tried the mole calculation quiz the "yes" response dropped to 56% and 58% respectively showing that there is still some work to be done to encourage students to become more independent. The responses then

dropped to only 24% with regard to using the recommended text book. The drop in use of the support materials could however also be attributed to the fact that this was an introductory science module. Therefore, some of the students would be very familiar with the materials and knowledge and would not have felt the need to complete the extra work.

For the off-campus students studying the diploma in applied chemistry by distance-learning, the Virtual Campus provides a comprehensive infrastructure with the flexibility for study in the students' own time. The learning materials are accessed using the Internet. The Virtual Campus further facilitates interaction between staff and students to support the course delivery by the use of discussion forums, community groups and email. A large part of the learning experience is delivered by online tutorials or by email. In a similar way to the on-campus students, quizzes, crossword puzzles and other support materials have also been devised in addition to the main course content. Students are also directed to suitable websites. This use of the VLE is becoming more and more attractive to students wishing to study part-time whilst pursuing full-time employment.

In the first years in which they study chemistry, students are required to learn quite a lot of information. For example, to understand organic chemistry at an advanced level, it is recommended that the learner is familiar with a certain number of important reactions. Study aids such as the "Reaction Rolodex" have been developed to help students to remember important information about these essential organic reactions. It has been shown that students who used this tool responded positively to it and their performance on the reactions section in their first year organic chemistry exam was better than in the group not using it (Mahan, 2006). Koopman et al. (2008) have shown that students were better able to comprehend lectures in quantum chemistry when they had brushed up on their mathematics pre-knowledge gaps systematically using the computer algebra test tool *MapleT.A.* (www.maplesoft.com/Products/MapleTA/index.aspx). The software provided instant feedback and the quantum chemistry lecturer reflected on this feedback in the lectures. The study carried out showed that good mathematical skills are essential, but were not sufficient for studying quantum chemistry as abstract thinking skills were also required. This approach, combined with interactive teaching activities implemented to improve abstract thinking, resulted in a substantial improvement in the percentage of students who passed the quantum chemistry course.

Development of information literacy skills is very important, as the ability to find relevant information quickly and efficiently is one of the key factors that can promote lifelong and self-directed learning (Sormunen, 2006). Ambrose and Gillespie (2003) are among several authors who have made the case for integration of information literacy skills into curricula. It is recommended that during their first semester, undergraduates are introduced to library resources and are encouraged to develop library research skills to enable them to make effective use of library resources, both paper and electronic, and to evaluate their usefulness and relevance. This process can be readily supported by means of online activities and materials, such as the

Internet Chemist Tutorial (www.vts.intute.ac.uk/he/tutorial/chemistry). These skills need to be developed on an ongoing basis and Walczak and Jackson (2007) discuss the implementation of an information literacy skills component into a third year analytical chemistry course. In addition, the analytical chemistry programme involves the use of role-play. Each student gets an opportunity to have a manager, chemist, hardware or software role in a four person group called a "company" with much of the communication among the group being carried out online.

Preventing misconceptions

Chemistry is challenging to learners because a chemist needs to think on several levels: The observational level (macro level), the molecular level (sub-micro level) and the symbolic and process level (Johnstone, 1982, see Fiorano, Markic, Reiners, & Avitabile in this book). This can lead to misconceptions which are often very difficult to overcome and can even prevent any further learning. Visualization of chemical structures and reactions on a molecular level is introduced to develop a deeper understanding of chemistry in learners. Computer animations, simulations and 3-D molecular modelling can be used to improve learning and understanding of chemistry, not only by students at the beginning of their study, but throughout. In addition, experts in the field now often also make use of these techniques in their research.

In the *VisChem* project, all levels of chemistry are combined and taught together using computer animations and molecular models (Tasker & Dalton, 2006, 2008). The *VisChem* learning design helps students to deal with their misconceptions in four steps: (1) explain the observation using the prior mental model, (2) recognize the failures of the prior model, (3) use computer animations to reconcile the discrepancies in the model and (4) apply the new model to a new chemical topic. This constructivist learning design makes it possible to construct better mental models however it must be noted that, by using molecular models and animations, the students can also develop different misconceptions.

Limniou, Roberts, and Papdopoulis (2008) compared the effects of using computer-based 2-D chemical animations with using 3-D ones. It was found that the students who used the 3-D animations had a better understanding of molecular structures and changes that occur during a chemical reaction than those who were using the 2-D animations. In addition, an increased level of enthusiasm was noted among the students who had access to the 3-D option.

Project-based learning

Project-based learning (PBL) requires students to solve real life problems and information technology provides a very effective support for this teaching and learning method. Barak and Dori (2005) researched the effect of IT-enhanced PBL on students' achievements and on their ability to traverse various chemistry understanding levels in three undergraduate chemistry courses. The student projects included three assignments: Molecules in daily life, elements in the periodic table, and scientific theories. To solve these problems, students used a range of IT tools for modelling and visualization of molecular structure as well as internet resources. The qualitative and quantitative results indicated that incorporating IT-rich PBL into chemistry courses can enhance students' understanding of chemical concepts, theories and molecular structures.

Online collaboration

Slocum, Towns, and Zielinski (2004) have devised a method for analyzing electronic communication by means of discussion board diagrams which show the effect the tutor/facilitator is having and identify all interactions that have occurred. Their analysis has allowed them to formulate useful guidelines for effective facilitation of online collaboration in chemistry courses. Glaser and Poole (1999) describe the development of collaborative learning communities in organic chemistry facilitated by online communication. Students worked in groups of 5 to 6 and researched a range of topics. The students were only required to format their reports so that they could later be easily published on the module website but half of the groups were sufficiently motivated to build their own websites. Peer assessment of reports by other groups was also incorporated (see also Eilks, Markic, Bäumer, and Schanze in this book).

Keller and Cox (2004) developed an innovative cross-disciplinary collaboration between business and chemistry students studying a Biochemistry module that involved a significant amount of online communication. The chemistry students investigated the type of research and product lines for a number of companies who had a mission statement that mentioned proteomics. Business students, who were enrolled on an online course, then analyzed the business model, marketing plan and industry growth potential of these companies and 1000 dollars of virtual money was invested in a company. Towns, Sauder, Whisnant, and Zielinski (2001) have developed a number of online physical chemistry modules that are used across several American third level institutions and allow collaboration between their students.

Activation of students during lectures and tutorials

In a lecture environment, incorporation of online methods can be achieved by using simulations, animations and computer-generated molecular models to demonstrate and explain difficult concepts. Some lecturers opt to develop this type of material themselves using the scientific software employed for their own research but it is also possible to search for this material online in a range of repositories (see the lists of resources at the end of this chapter).

A good explanation by the lecturer is not enough to achieve deep learning by students. The learners need to be actively involved (Stanley & Porter, 2002). Plenary or group discussions and an exchange of opinion with a neighbouring student as well as asking questions are common methods employed to make lectures active and interactive. Electronic voting systems (also often called student response systems, personal response systems, audience response systems, audience paced feedback, classroom communication systems, voting-machines, zappers or clickers) have been used since the early 1960s. Initially, these systems were built in but nowadays the personal response systems are wireless and portable and are relatively inexpensive. In some cases, web-based public response systems are used which involve students using their mobile phones to vote (Prensky, 2005). MacArthur and Jones (2008) have published a comprehensive review of the implementation of clickers in third level chemistry courses in which they report that students have invariably been found to react positively to use of this technology and that, in cases where some type of student collaboration was also incorporated, measured improvement in student learning was observed. Niyadurupola and Read (2008) reported similar findings when they piloted the use of clickers in two English universities.

A teaching method called peer-instruction was introduced very successfully in physics courses for new undergraduates at Harvard University and has been extended to a number of other colleges (Mazur, 1997). In his introductory physics lectures, Mazur asked each student to provide a response to multiple choice questions using a clicker. Students were then required to discuss their chosen answer with their neighbours and then vote again. This approach was shown to dramatically increase pre-to-post test gains (Crouch & Mazur, 2001). It should be noted that careful selection of questions is an important factor in implementing this approach successfully. Wieman and Perkins (2005) also discuss how educational technology can be used effectively to improve learning by physics students and, in particular, the role of clickers and online interactive simulations.

Christie (2008) has used commercially available technology (Mimio hardware and software; www.mimio.com) to capture pen strokes made on a white board during a lecture and save them to video files that can be played by students anywhere. He has used this system to allow conventional organic reaction mechanisms to be stored, played, paused and rewound as necessary. Since the diagrams are hand-drawn, there is no learning curve for lecturers that involves complex computer software and, because the pen-strokes are recorded in real time, the diagram evolves on the computer screen as it did on the whiteboard in the lecture.

Enhancing learning during lab sessions

There is no need to emphasize how important it is for chemistry students to obtain effective laboratory experience (see Bennett, Seery, & Sövegjarto-Wibers in this book). The quality of the learning process can be enhanced by ICT during pre-lab or post-lab activities. For example, computer simulations can support learning about particular experimental techniques and may, in certain cases, replace working in the laboratory if there are safety or ethical reasons (e.g., live animal experiments) which preclude this (Wang, 2001).

Pre-lab activities have been shown to be important in improving learning in chemistry across all levels. For example, in a simple operation such as extraction, many students find it difficult to visualize what is happening at a molecular level. An interactive simulation of this process used in a pre-lab session has helped students to understand it better at the macroscopic and at the molecular level (Supasorn, Suits, Jones, & Vibuljanc, 2008). Interactive multimedia exercises (IMMEX), were developed at the University of California Los Angeles medical school. The problems can be used as a pre-lab session to enable learners to become acquainted with a particular technique, or as an assessment tool. The IMMEX problems are based on real life situations which students might encounter involving organic separations and TLC, qualitative organic analysis, and spectroscopic analysis. The online software used makes it possible to interpret students' problem solving strategies (Cox et al., 2008).

Chittleborough, Mocerino, and Treagust (2007) studied the impact of online pre-laboratory exercises and resources on students' learning in an introductory chemistry course. The online pre-laboratory exercises were designed to make students identify the aim of the weekly experiments. Pictures and diagrams of unfamiliar equipment were provided to introduce the methods and the procedures and students could use a range of resources (online and the manual) to solve the problems they were asked to complete. Immediate electronic feedback on the student's solution was provided and multiple attempts were allowed. The results show that the majority of students appreciated the flexibility in time and place provided by this system and most of the students stated that they felt that this system prepared them better for the laboratory activities than the classical approach previously used. Burewicz and Miranowicz (2006) report that students who used interactive multimedia in their pre-lab sessions completed the experiments in a shorter time and with less problems than the students who used the printed or video instruction.

Josephsen and Kosminska Kristensen (2006) gave their students on an introductory inorganic chemistry lab course a computer simulation of the laboratory assignment in addition to the laboratory assignment and a written problem. In all three types of learning resources, the information was given at the macroscopic level only. The students had to transform this information into chemical conclusions. The computer simulation used (*SimuLab*) is also a cognitive tool and it was found to develop the learners' experimental and analytical skills and to improve their interpretation of experimental results. It facilitated students' knowledge construction by engaging them in cognitive activities which would not be possible during the laboratory session because of their cognitive load. It has been shown that lower cognitive processes in the lab are not performed automatically by novices and, for this reason, they cannot use their higher cognitive skills optimally during the early stages in the lab (Sweller, 1988; Sweller & Chandler, 1991).

Educational technology has also been applied to improve writing skills in larger groups of students. *Calibrated Peer Review* (CPR, cpr.molsci.ucla.edu) software is a browser-based tool which enables academic staff to create writing assignments that incorporate a requirement for students to review examples (calibration assignments) and, after they submit their work, review assignments submitted by their peers. The tool is universal as the lecturer determines the structure of the assignment using different templates with criteria such as learning goals and can calibrate source materials, questions, answers and examples. Margerum, Gulsrud, Manlapez, Rebong, and Love (2007) used the CPR tool in a large introductory chemistry lab course for pre-lab and post-lab writing assignments. They implemented a series of CPR assignments aimed at improving technical reading and writing and found that students responded that the "writing to learn" approach adopted was achieving its aims and, in general, they were engaged and motivated by this teaching method. In addition, it is reported that the students who worked with CPR could better apply their knowledge in the following year compared to students who did not complete these writing assignments. Morris (2007) also reports an improvement in learning as a result of using online self and peer-assessment tools in an introductory chemistry course.

Limniou, Papadopoulos, Giannkoudakis, Roberts, and Otto (2007) discuss the introduction of an interactive viscosity simulator into pre-laboratory sessions. It was shown that the students who were allowed to use the simulator in advance found that the approach was useful, that they had a better grasp of the underlying theory and that they were more confident during the laboratory session. The incorporation of an interactive UV-Vis spectrophotometer simulator into a course on chemical instrumentation is described by Limniou, Papadopoulos, and Roberts (2007). Students were asked to share measurements, observations and conclusions from their virtual experiments on the simulator by communicating online. It was found that the students valued that opportunity to collaborate with their colleagues and that they felt more confident about operating a real instrument and had a better understanding of the function and technical principles of a UV-Vis spectrophotometer than the control group of students studied.

Online assessment

It is important to ensure that both online assessment and "classical" assessments fit the didactic structure and learning objectives of the course in which they are used (Biggs, 2003). When online assessment is mentioned, we often think only of multiple choice tests. This type of assessment can be very useful for evaluating students' knowledge or pre-knowledge, particularly in the early stages of a chemistry degree. Third level institutions use electronic tests in a range of ways such as self-study quizzes, diagnostic tests or summative assessments. A range of software tools are available for designing online quizzes. Some are available free of charge, such as *Hot Potatoes* provided by the University of Victoria (hotpot.uvic.ca) and others, such as *Questionmark Perception* and *Respondus* are available commercially. In addition, most of the institutional electronic learning platforms (*Blackboard, Moodle, and Sakai*) offer online assessment tools.

However, electronic tools can deliver much more than multiple choice tests and it is possible to assess students' knowledge across a range of cognitive levels. Lecturers can set online assignments that require students to submit their work to be reviewed or peer-reviewed online. This approach was discussed at the end of the previous section on enhancing learning during lab sessions in relation to pre- and post-lab writing assignments (Margerum et al., 2007) In addition, for competence-oriented modules or programmes, electronic portfolios can be used to assess students.

There are many benefits to online assessment, which include;

- Flexibility of time and place.
- After an electronic test is submitted, instant results and tailored feedback can be provided.
- Improved chance for personal development due to automatic feedback and/or online feedback from teachers and peers.
- Time savings on assessing students' work for academic staff.
- Sharing of complete student assessment results by all lecturers on a course.
- Sharing of approved tests and test items among colleagues.
- Statistical analysis of results provides information that facilitates improvement of test questions and of the course as a whole.

There are also some disadvantages:

- Initial development of online test assignments takes more time than for paper-based exams.
- Cheating by students taking tests at locations outside the college can be difficult to prevent.
- Sharing of tests and test items among lecturers who use different operating systems and/or different learning platforms is not possible if the test tools do not correspond to the same technical standards.

Effective learning support for first year undergraduates

The online self-study quizzes described in the previous section on online self-directed learning to construct knowledge and skills are often one of a series of measures implemented to support first year undergraduate chemistry students and to scaffold their learning. Lovatt et al. (2007) describe how a VLE was used in conjunction with a drop-in science clinic to provide additional learning support to first year students. Several other authors already mentioned have described similar initiatives (O'Connor & McDonnell, 2005, Charlesworth & Vician, 2003) in which a coordinated approach is undertaken that involves online support, quizzes and/or assessment as a central feature. It has been shown that students appreciate the flexibility and easy access to learning materials and that this approach results in an improvement in their confidence in relation to the subject. In addition, an improvement in exam success rates was observed when a VLE and several other changes in teaching methods were introduced in Dublin Institute of Technology, Ireland (McDonnell & O'Connor, 2005).

A recent example of an approach to improving retention and exam success rates that made use of the technology available while coping with a reduction in teaching staff resources was implemented in the University of Dundee, United Kingdom (Morris, 2007). *Questionmark Perception* tests were used to provide formative feedback and unlimited attempts were allowed. A *Blackboard* VLE was made available and the discussion board and e-mail, online group work tools and test exercise self and peer assessment tools were utilized. In-class tests using personal response systems (PRS or clickers) were also introduced and, for certain topics, just an introductory lecture was provided and this was followed by self-directed study supported online and assessed using the clickers and an online assessment. This new approach has shown a significant increase in exam pass rates and in student satisfaction.

Bunce, Van den Plas, and Havanki (2006) report on the impact on student achievement of using electronic student response systems (SRS or clickers) to deliver tests to pairs of chemistry students in class compared to that of daily online quizzes delivered outside of class using a VLE. Both systems provide immediate feedback but the VLE quizzes were available for review coming up to end of semester exams while the clicker questions were not and this use of the WebCT quizzes to reflect on and review learning was found to improve student achievement. These results showed also that the way in which lecturers use clickers has a large effect on the learning success of students.

In a situation where students need to remediate their knowledge gaps to start a new programme or to follow the next course, it is very convenient to use an online preparatory course. Botch et al. (2007) described their application of *ChemPrep*, a stand-alone short course which helps students to fill the gaps in knowledge needed to begin to study general chemistry. The students who worked with *ChemPrep* were found to perform much better on the General Chemistry course than those who did not. However, use of *ChemPrep* was voluntary and it was found that it was the stronger and more motivated students who opted to do so. It is often difficult to reach less motivated and weaker students when using online applications. However, an example in which this problem was tackled is provided by Koopman et al. (2008) in relation to the first year quantum chemistry course at the University of Amsterdam, The Netherlands, as students were only allowed to sit the final exam in this course if they had completed all of the *MapleT.A.* electronic mathematics pre-knowledge tests (see above). The students could sit these electronic tests as often as they wanted and, on each attempt, a different test was generated. Instant feedback was provided and the lecturer discussed the problems during tutorials. There was no minimum electronic test result required in order to be allowed to sit the quantum chemistry exam, but it was specified that no student could submit blank or nonsensical answers in the online tests.

Online support for first year undergraduates has recently been successfully implemented at Genoa University, Italy, for a group of 300 students undertaking an inorganic chemistry module (Cardinale, 2008). As is often the case, these students have a diverse range of previous knowledge and a series of online exercises allowing them to practice stoichiometry and chemical reactions was provided which were supplemented by several face-to-face tutorials. Completion of these exercises was not compulsory but students were required to complete the other online component, a pre-lab online activity incorporating an explanatory video produced in both DVD and streaming formats using *Studio Pro 1.02* and *Cleaner 5.1* with

QuickTime 5.1 software respectively. This development is part of the web-enhanced learning project in collaboration with the CNR-ITD, an Italian research group which examines educational innovation brought about through the use of ICT.

EChemTest

The EChemTest is a project undertaken by the European Chemistry Thematic Network (ECTN, ectn-assoc.cpe.fr/echemtest/). The project involved identification of common core content in chemistry first cycle (bachelor) courses in all EU member states in physical chemistry, organic chemistry, inorganic chemistry, biological chemistry and analytical chemistry followed by the design of computer-based tests which are available in many languages to evaluate competence in these areas. Tests have also been designed to evaluate competence in general chemistry at two levels - a level equivalent to that of a person at the end of compulsory education (level 1, generally at 16 years of age) and a level equivalent to that of a student about to commence a third level course in chemistry (level 2, generally 18 years old). Students can attend a testing centre to take the test in their chosen areas and receive a certificate on successful completion. A typical EChemTest has thirty questions; 15 easy, 10 intermediate and 5 difficult. Demonstration tests can be accessed from the EChemTest website to allow students to practice. These demonstration tests can also be used as a teaching resource by academic staff. Tests at masters level are being developed and when these tests are completed, they could be used to test PhD students (see also Laganà et al. in this book).

Physical sciences question bank

This resource has been developed by the Physical Sciences Centre in the Higher Education Academy in the United Kingdom. The *Question Bank* (www.heacademy.ac.uk/physsci/home/projects/jisc_del/questionbank)   is searchable according to topic, keywords, difficulty and pedagogic style. Selected questions can be downloaded in a form that can be immediately imported into a VLE or assessment tool. At present, *WebCT, Blackboard, Moodle, StoMP and Questionmark Perception* are supported. In addition, the questions can be downloaded into *Powerpoint* for use with clickers (Bacon, 2008). Many of the questions available have feedback incorporated. All users are encouraged to contact the Physical Sciences Centre with questions that they are willing to share.

Diagnostic tests

Online diagnostic tests have many applications. They can be used to advise incoming students of the probability of their success in higher education chemistry courses (Legg, Legg, & Greenbowe, 2001) and are often also used to identify and address common misconceptions that students encounter and to evaluate the impact of a change in teaching method on students' understanding (Tan, Goh, Chia, & Treagust, 2002). In addition, as discussed previously, they can allow students to identify areas where they have knowledge gaps that need to be addressed (Koopman et al., 2008).

Collaborative group assessment

The suitability of online learning for use in collaborative group activities has already been discussed and examples of activities that involve online collaboration were provided. Assessment of this collaborative group work often incorporates online peer review and grades are usually criterion referenced (Glaser & Poole, 1999). Self and peer assessment of a students' contribution to the group are also often used (Hinde & Kovac, 2001; Towns et al., 2001). These assessments may be circulated electronically or can be paper-based. The facility to view the history of all revisions of a wiki page prepared by students allows teaching staff to track the contributions made by each student and makes this aspect of assessment of collaborative assignments considerably easier.

e-Portfolios

An e-portfolio can be defined as *"an archive of material, relating to an individual, held in a digital format"* (Madden, 2008). e-Portfolio software provides an electronic content management system that can be used by an individual to collect, reflect on, select and present learning outcomes as well as other professional achievements (Jafari, 2004). The content can include podcasts, emails, discussion threads, blogs, written work, and journals. In some higher education institutions, customisable e-portfolios tools have now been implemented across the entire college (Lambert & Corrin, 2007). Jafari (2004) has examined the attributes needed for a successful e-portfolio system in higher education and they include ease of use, lifelong support and interoperability. He advises that it has been found to reduce confusion over what is expected if the main purpose of the e-portfolio is included in the name (*e.g.* student learning e-portfolio, career e-portfolio). Herman and Kirkup (2008) discuss a case study in which a set of structured and guided online activities were used to good effect to develop an e-portfolio on a course for women returning to employment in the science, engineering and technology (SET) sector after a break. A description of the e-portfolio system used with chemistry students in the University of Amsterdam follows:

e-Portfolios to support development of academic skills

During the three years of the chemistry bachelor degree at the University of Amsterdam, The Netherlands, special attention is paid to the development of academic competences within the compulsory modules (also called framework courses). The competences are developed to an increasing level as the students progress through their degree (Figure 3).

In 2003, in order to make the students more aware of their academic development, an electronic portfolio system was implemented which made it possible for them to collect evidence material, to reflect on the skills development process and to get feedback online. For example, within the writing skills line in first year, the students reflect on keeping a laboratory notebook during one of their lab courses and they relate this to the quality of their report on the experiments. In second year, the portfolio assignment is about writing a report on a short research project and in third year, when they have written their bachelor research thesis, they reflect on the whole process and prepare a development plan for the future. The students get feedback from the lecturers and, in some assignments, from their peers also.

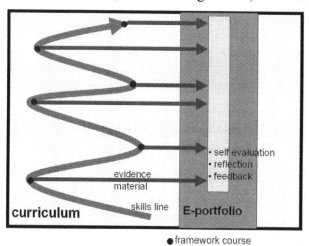

Figure 3: Skills development approach for the chemistry bachelor degree at the University of Amsterdam

In 2007, an e-portfolio matrix was introduced and this integrated reflection on development of skills with the content of the framework chemistry courses. In the cells of the matrix, students archive the evidence material about their level of academic skills and reflect on the learning process. Having the facility to look back on previous reflective assignments in their electronic portfolio allows students to recognize more readily the improvements they have made and to ascertain the areas where they still need to improve. The students can also use the matrix for material about the non-compulsory courses or extracurricular activities which they find important for their academic development. In this way, the matrix represents a mirror of their profile as a professional scientist.

The e-portfolio tool that the University of Amsterdam uses is called OSP (Open Source Portfolio) and was developed by *Sakai. Sakai* is a worldwide community of academic institutions and the software they develop is open access and open source. More information about the *Sakai* project can be accessed online at: sakaiproject.org/portal

Training and support for academic staff

Earlier in the chapter, the importance of academic staff maintaining an awareness of new developments in teaching methods was discussed (see also Yates & Maciejowska in this book), as was the necessity for effective online tutoring, particularly in the early stages of a course that has an online component. Both of these issues are impacted on by the extent to which adequate training of academic staff is provided so that they have developed the skills to interact effectively with learners online. Munro and Walsh (2005) discuss the development and delivery of an online tutoring course for tutors on distance education programmes. They make the point that, because web-based tutoring is a recent development, many academic staff did not experience it themselves as students and this means that they tend to feel uncomfortable about this teaching method. In order to overcome this problem, they applied the approach recommended by Salmon (2004) which is that experiencing being a student in an online environment is the most effective way to acquire the skills required to manage and facilitate online synchronous and asynchronous communication. Cunningham, McDonnell, McIntyre, and McKenna (2008) provide a detailed case study of a course of this type which is run for academic staff in Dublin Institution of Technology, Ireland. They also comment on the barriers that are often encountered at an institutional level which include lack of provision of the necessary support structures and no clear e-learning strategy.

Donnelly and O'Rourke (2007) warn of the danger that adoption of web-based learning can be undertaken in a superficial way by third level institutions if the metric used is the quantity instead of the quality of the learning. Thus, if it is perceived that information repository and course management aspects are all that are involved in online learning, then there is little incentive to develop interactive activities and assessments (individual and/or collaborative). Donnelly and O'Rourke also emphasise the need for professional development of academic staff in the area of e-learning coupled with ongoing support from experts and peers. Butler and Sellbom (2002) report that there are three main barriers to adoption of internet and web technology that they identified. They are a lack of financial support, lack of institutional support and a lack of time to learn new technologies.

The role of virtual learning environments in chemistry education

Virtual Learning Environments (VLEs), also referred to as electronic learning platforms, electronic learning environments or course management systems, are now in use in practically every European higher level institution to support flexible learning (see Laganà et al. in this book). They are software tools that provide a framework within which students can access teaching materials, resources and tests and use different communication tools at any time using a networked computer. They also facilitate course management by providing academic staff with the means to communicate assessment criteria and deadlines and other information to groups of students. Most of the innovative e-learning approaches that we describe are supported within the framework of a VLE. Some institutions use open source software such as *Moodle* to develop VLEs while others use a commercially available alternative such as *Blackboard*, *WebCT* or *Sakai* and some use customized systems that were developed in-house.

The extent to which a VLE is used as a teaching tool varies widely. In some institutions, the main functions it serves are for course management and the communication tools are used only by staff to communicate course information to the students. In others, the assessment and learning support tools available are used and, in some, students undertake online collaborative assignments and use asynchronous and synchronous communication tools. Ball et al. (2007) report that there is a great deal of anecdotal evidence claiming that use of a VLE can improve student performance and decrease failure rates.

Several authors have discussed the use of VLEs for chemistry in higher education. Chin (2003) has produced guidelines for using VLEs in the physical sciences. Charlesworth and Vician (2003) described their introduction of a *WebCT* VLE to attempt to improve motivation and learning on a first year chemistry programme. Students appreciated the flexibility that the system allowed and, as a result of the online tests and tutor communication tools introduced, they reported having less anxiety about exams and improved confidence and perceived learning.

Lovatt et al. (2007) examined the interaction of first year undergraduates with the *Moodle* VLE available to them. The VLE provided self-test quizzes, lecture notes, tutorial questions, links to relevant websites and discussion forums. Students reported that they liked the accessibility and ease of use of the VLE. It was found that the learners who accessed resources (mainly self-test quizzes and notes) performed better in the summative exam than those who did not and this was interpreted to show that students who were motivated to use all available resources did better in their examination. The authors intend to implement online continuous assessment to provide additional motivation for accessing and practicing the online quizzes. Williams et al. (2008) report using a blended learning approach to teaching inorganic chemistry. Study packs were prepared based on lecture notes and included learning activities. Paper copies were made available and they were also accessible on the Blackboard VLE, as was a formative online assessment quiz for each study pack. Evaluation showed that student achievement and satisfaction increased and the authors were of the opinion that this was attributable in some part to the variety and extra support provided by blended learning.

Resources for lecturers

A great deal of material useful to teaching and learning is available online to lecturers. Many chemistry textbooks have an accompanying website which often allows lecturers to download the schemes published in the book as well as *PowerPoint* presentations that relate to the material in the book and sample answers to questions. Many publishers offer a *Blackboard* cartridge which can be opened as a *Blackboard* course site and adapted by the lecturer. Lecturers are usually required to register with the publisher to access these resources. In addition, online material such as 3D animations and simulations and electronic tests is frequently provided for students.

At the end of this chapter, we list some of the useful free resources available online at present. However, the rate of development is such that many links on this list may well become obsolete within a relatively short time as improved resources become available. Where possible, the name of the organization providing the resources and their main webpage has also been provided as it is hoped that this approach will prolong the usefulness of the list.

Emerging and future developments

Some of the relevant emerging and future trends in online learning in higher education will now be examined briefly. Online roleplay is a teaching and learning method that has been applied in a number of disciplines to date. This approach allows learners to become aware of multiple perspectives surrounding an issue and has recently been used to teach the concept of sustainability to engineering students (Maier, Baron, & McLaughlan, 2007).

An emerging trend of particular interest and relevance is online problem-based learning (PBL). There have been a number of recent developments in this area. Savin-Baden (2007) emphasises that the aim of online PBL is to develop and supplement what has already been achieved rather than replace it. Another development is podcasting. This approach essentially involves making audio files available to download (Campbell, 2005). Learners have reported that audio file contributions were much more memorable than written discussion threads posted and facilitated a humanisation of the interaction. Holmes and Gardner (2006) have remarked on the potential benefits of recording feedback while assessing work and posting the audio file to the student immediately afterwards. However, they identify that there are problems associated with this rapid feedback approach if comments are made that have not been considered fully.

Mobile learning or m-learning is another emerging trend. At present, many institutions have a texting software package to keep students up to date with announcements such as exam deadlines and cancelled lectures and Conole, Dillon, Dart, and Darby (2006) have found that students use mobile phones extensively to communicate with peers and tutors. Sharples (2007) has described the *MyArtSpace* project, in which multimedia mobile phones were supplied to second level students when they arrived at a museum. They were given several tasks to perform that required them to interact with the exhibits. These included taking photographs and video clips and collecting other relevant material which they then edited back at their schools to produce an online gallery. It was found that the students spent significantly more time interacting with the exhibits and gathering information when this approach was used compared to the traditional visit format.

Greenbowe (2008) has recently proposed that a new publication to communicate the best practices for teaching chemistry be designed and developed. He suggested that magazines that teach people to learn to play the guitar be used as a model. The new publication would include "master" teachers explaining chemistry education techniques and current technologies (an associated DVD and website) would be used to ensure effective and timely dissemination.

Conclusions

The extent to which web-based technology can be used to support and assess learning in chemistry at third level has been explored in this chapter. A very broad range of applications have been discussed, including learning activities such as simulations of laboratory equipment, 3-D animations for visualization at a molecular level and cross-disciplinary online collaboration to research which biotechnology company has best potential for attracting investment. The variety of online assessment methods examined included peer review, pre-knowledge and knowledge testing with instant feedback and e-portfolios.

The approach used has been to provide references to and descriptions of good practice in this area as well as links to useful resources within the chapter. It is hoped that this will facilitate adoption of any suitable learning and teaching strategies discussed.

Resources

Assessment tools

- EChemTest website: www.echemtest.com
- Eclipse crossword software: www.eclipsecrossword.com/
- Hot Potatoes assessment software: website with free download hotpot.uvic.ca/
- PBworks software (formerly Pbwiki, allows generation of wikis accessible only to specified group members): PBworks.com/
- Physical Sciences Question Bank:
  www.heacademy.ac.uk/physsci/home/projects/jisc_del/questionbank

Chemistry drawing and modelling software

- ChemSketch: www.acdlabs.com/download
- SymyxDraw (formerly IsisDraw): www.symyx.com/downloads/index.jsp

Educational resources for lecturers (can be also used by students)

- Higher Education Academy Physical Sciences Centre:
  www.heacademy.ac.uk/physsci/home
- Higher Education Academy: www.heacademy.ac.uk/
- Intute Chemistry Gateway: www.intute.ac.uk/sciences/chemistry/
- MERLOT (Multimedia Educational Resource for Learning and Online Teaching): www.merlot.org/merlot/index.htm
- MERLOT Chemistry: chemistry.merlot.org/
- List of learning materials for different chemistry subjects:
  chemistry.merlot.org/materials.html
- Mind Map Generation Software: www.bubbl.us/
- MIT Open courseware: Chemistry: ocw.mit.edu/OcwWeb/Chemistry/index.htm
- Open Educational Resources Commons: www.oercommons.org/
- Protein Explorer (macromolecular visualisation database):
  www.umass.edu/microbio/chime/pe_beta/pe/protexpl/
- Royal Society of Chemistry Learnnet:
  www.rsc.org/education/teachers/learnnet/about-learnnet.htm
- Royal Society of Chemistry: www.rsc.org/

Specific video resources and taped experiments

- Chemistry animations and movies on the world wide web: www.klte.hu/~lenteg/animate.html
- JCE Digi Demos: www.jce.divched.org/JCEDLib/DigiDemos/about.html
- Laboratory techniques. digital lab techniques manual (MIT Open courseware): ocw.mit.edu/ans7870/resources/chemvideo/index.htm (it can be used as a teaching resource but primarily this is a student resource)
- Organic chemistry demonstration experiments on video chemistry Visualized: www.uniregensburg.de/Fakultaeten/nat_Fak_IV/Organische_Chemie/Didaktik/Keusch/D-Video-e.htm
- Science-tube.com: www.science-tube.com/, a translation of the German site www.netexperimente.de
- YouTube: nl.youtube.com, uk.youtube.com , de.youtube.com

Acknowledgements

Inputs to this chapter are gratefully acknowledged from Hazel Wilkins, School of Life Sciences, Robert Gordon University, United Kingdom, and Pita Vandervelde, Plantijn Hogeschool, Antwerpen, Belgium.

References

Adams, K., Byers, W., Cole, R., & Ruddick, J. (2003). *Computer aided assessment in chemistry: LTSN Physical Sciences development project final report.* Retrieved March 6, 2007, from www.heacademy.ac.uk/assets/ps/documents/downloads/downloads/computer_aided_assessment_in_Chemistry_1.pdf

Ambrose, A., & Gillespie, B. (2003). *Information-literacy programmes and programme curricula:The case for integration. Level 3, 1.* Retrieved February 18, 2008, from level3.dit.ie/html/issue1_ambrose1.html.

Bacon, R. (2008). *The physical sciences question bank - What next?. Presentation at Variety in Chemistry Education conference.* Retrieved September 19, 2008, from www.heacademy.ac.uk/assets/ps/documents/events/variety_2008/bacon.pdf.

Ball S., Leonard L., Littlejohn A., Kelly J., McAteer E., McCulloch M., & Peacock, S., (2007). *Effective use of virtual learning environments. Online infokit.* Retrieved May 12, 2008, from www.jiscinfonet.ac.uk/InfoKits/effective-use-of-VLEs.

Barak, M., & Dori, Y. J. (2005). Enhancing undergraduate students' chemistry understanding through project-based learning in an IT environment. *Science Education*, *89*, 117-139.

Beetham, H. (2002). *Developing e-Tutor skills: Understanding e-learning. Higher Education Academy resource.* Retrieved April 3, 2007 from http://www.ics.heacademy.ac.uk/events/displayevent.php?id=22.

Bigge, M. L., & Shermis, S. S. (2004). *Learning theories for teachers* (6th ed.). Boston: Pearson.

Biggs, J. (2003). *Aligning teaching for constructing learning.* Higher Education Academy resource. Retrieved September 25, 2008 from www.heacademy.ac.uk/resources/detail/id477_aligning_teaching_for_constructing_learning.

Botch, B., Day, R., Vining, W., Stewart, B., Rath, K., Peterfreund, A., & Hard, D. (2007). Effects on student achievement in general chemistry following participation in an online preparatory course - ChemPrep, a voluntary, self-paced, online introduction to chemistry. *Journal of Chemical Education*, *84*, 547-553.

Brouwer, N. (2006). ECTN working group on developing independent learners in chemistry. Presentation at ECTN Annual Conference. Retrieved May 26, 2007, from

ectn2006.book-of-abstracts.com/presentations/
ECTN2006_WGIndepLearners_ Brouwers.ppt.

Brouwer, N., Byers, B., & McDonnell, C. (2006). *Report from ECTN working group, "Developing Independent Learners in Chemistry".* Retrieved May 26, 2007, from ectn2006.book-of-bstracts.com/presentations/ECTN2006_WGIndepLearners _final_report.pdf.

Bunce, D. M., Van den Plas, J. R., & Havanki, K. (2006). Comparing the effectiveness on student achievement of a student response system versus online WebCT quizzes. *Journal of Chemical Education, 83*, 488-493.

Burewicz, A., & Miranowicz, N. (2006). Effectiveness of multimedia laboratory instruction. *Chemistry Education Research and Practice, 7*, 1-12.

Butler, D., & Sellbom, M. (2002). Barriers for adopting technology for teaching and learning. *Educause Quarterly*, 25(2) 22-28. Retrieved May 25, 2007 from www.educause.edu/ir/library/pdf/eqm0223.pdf.

Campbell, G. (2005). There's something in the air: Podcasting in education. *Educause Review*, 40(6), 32–47. Retrieved January 16, 2008, from www.educause.edu/ apps/er/erm05/erm056.asp.

Cardinale, A. M. (2008). A way to improve undergraduate engagement when learning chemistry: An online support for exercises and pre-lab activities. Message posted to online workspace for this chapter, retrieved July 17, 2008, from www.surfgroepen.nl/sites/ECTN/default.aspx.

Charlesworth, P., Charlesworth D. D., & Vician, C. (2006). Students' perspectives of the influence of web-enhanced coursework on incidences of cheating. *Journal of Chemical Education, 83*, 1368-1375.

Charlesworth, P., & Vician, C. (2003). Leveraging technology for chemical sciences education: an early assessment of WebCT usage in first-year chemistry courses. *Journal of Chemical Education, 80*, 1333-1337.

Chickering, A., & Ehrmann, S. (1996). Implementing the seven principles: Technology as lever. *American Association for Higher Education Bulletin*, October, 3-6. Retrieved February 24, 2008, from www.clt.astate.edu/clthome/Implementing%20the%20 Seven%20 Principles,%20Ehrmann%20and%20Chickering.pdf.

Chin, P. (2003). *LTSN physical sciences practice guide on virtual learning environments.* Retrieved April 28, 2008, from www.heacademy.ac.uk/assets/ps/documents/ practice_guides/practice_guides/ps0081_virtual_learning_environments_sept_2003.pdf.

Chittleborough, G. D., Mocerino, M., & Treagust, D. F. (2007) Achieving greater feedback and flexibility using online pre-laboratory exercises with non-major chemistry students. *Journal of Chemical Education, 84*, 884-888.

Christie, S. (2008). Development of animated hand-drawn reaction mechanisms. Proceedings from Variety in Chemistry Education Conference. Retrieved September 19, 2008, from www.heacademy.ac.uk/assets/ps/documents/events/variety_2008/variety _proceedings_2008.doc.

Concannon, F., Flynn, A., & Campbell, M. (2005). What campus-based students think about the quality and benefits of e-learning. *British Journal of Educational Technology, 36*, 501-512.

Conole, G., De Laat, M., Dillon, T., & Darby, J. (2006, December). An in-depth case study of students' experiences of e-Learning – how is learning changing?. Proceedings from Australian Society for Computers in Learning and in Tertiary Education conference. Retrieved August 8, 2007, from www.ascilite.org.au/conferences/sydney06/ proceeding/pdf_papers/p127.pdf.

Cox Jr., C. T., Cooper, M. M., Pease, R., Buchanan, K., Hernandez-Cruz, L., Stevens, R., Picione, J., & Holme, T. (2008). Advancements in curriculum and assessment by the use of IMMEX technology in the organic laboratory. *Chemistry Education Research and Practice, 9*, 163 - 168.

Crotty, M. (1998). *The foundations of social research.* London: Sage.

Crouch C. H., & Mazur E., (2001). Peer instruction: Ten years of experience and results. *American Journal of Physics, 69*, 970–977.

Cunningham, T., McDonnell, C., McIntyre, B., & McKenna, T. (2008). A reflection on teachers' experience as e-learners. In: R. Donnelly and F. Mc Sweeney (Eds.), *Applied e-learning and e-teaching in higher education* (pp. 56-83). Pennsylvania: Information Science Reference.

DfES (Department for Education and Skills) (2003). *Five year strategy for children and learners.* Retrieved 23 November 2007, from www.dfes.gov.uk/publications/ 5yearstrategy/.

Donnelly, R., & O'Rourke, K. (2007). What now?. Evaluating e-learning CPD practice in Irish third-level education. *Journal of Further and Higher Education, 31,* 31-40.

Gagné, R. M., Wager, W. W., Golas, K. C., & Keller, J. M. (2005). *Principles of instructional design* (5th ed.). Belmont: Thomson Wadsworth.

Giles, J. (2005). Internet encyclopaedias go head to head. *Nature, 438,* 900–901.

Glaser, R., & Poole, M. (1999). Organic chemistry online: Building collaborative learning communities through electronic communication tools. *Journal of Chemical Education, 76,* 699-703.

Greenbowe, T. (2008). We'll make you a better teacher: Learning from guitar techniques. *Journal of Chemical Education, 85,* 191-192.

Herman, C., Casiday, R. E., Deppe, R. K., Gilbertson, M., Spees, W. M., Holten, D., & Frey, R. F. (2005). Interdisciplinary, application-oriented tutorials: Design, implementation, and evaluation. *Journal of Chemical Education, 82,* 1871-1879.

Herman, C., & Kirkup, G. (2008). Learners in transition: The use of e-portfolios for women returners to science, engineering and technology. *Innovations in Education and Teaching International, 45,* 67-76.

Hinde, R., & Kovac, J. (2001). Student active learning methods in physical chemistry. *Journal of Chemical Education, 78,* 93-99.

Holmes, B., & Gardner, J. (2006). *e-Learning concepts and practice.* London: Sage.

Jafari, A. (2004). The "sticky" e-portfolio system: tackling challenges and identifying attributes. *Educause Review, 39*(4), 38–48. Retrieved May 16, 2008, from www.educause.edu/apps/er/erm05/erm056.asp.

Johnstone, A. H. (1982). Macro and microchemistry. *School Science Review, 64,* 377-379.

Josephsen, J., & Kosminska Kristensen, A. (2006). Simulation of laboratory assignments to support students' learning of introductory inorganic chemistry. *Chemistry Education Research and Practice, 7,* 266-279.

Keller, H., & Cox, J. (2004), A cross-disciplinary collaboration in biochemistry and business education. *Journal of Chemical Education, 81,* 519-522.

Koopman, L., Brouwer, N., Heck, A., & Burna, W. (2008). Remedial Mathematics for quantum chemistry. *Journal of Chemical Education, 85,* 1233-1236.

Lambert, S., & Corrin, L. (2007). Moving toward a university wide implementation of an e-portfolio tool. *Australasian Journal of Educational Technology, 23,* 1-16.

Laurillard, D. (2002 (reprinted 2006)). *Rethinking university teaching, A framework for the effective use of learning technologies.* London: RoutledgeFalmer.

Laurillard, D. (2007). Modelling benefits-oriented costs for technology enhanced learning. *Higher Education, 54,* 21-39.

Legg, M., Legg, J., & Greenebowe, T. (2001). Analysis of success in general chemistry based on diagnostic testing using logistic regression. *Journal of Chemical Education, 78,* 1117-1121.

Limniou, M., Papadopoulos, N., Giannakoudakis, A., Roberts, D., & Otto, O. (2007). The integration of a viscosity simulator in a chemistry laboratory. *Chemistry Education Research and Practice, 8,* 220-231.

Limniou, M., Papadopoulos, N., & Roberts, D. (2007). An integrated lecture, virtual instrumentation lab approach to teaching UV-Vis spectroscopy. *Education and Information Technologies, 12,* 229-244.

Limniou, M., Roberts, D., & Papadopoulos, N. (2008). Full immersive virtual environment CAVE in chemistry education. *Computers & Education, 51,* 584-593.

Lovatt, J., Finlayson, O. E., & James, P. (2007). Evaluation of student engagement with two learning supports in the teaching of 1st year undergraduate chemistry. *Chemistry Education Research and Practice, 8,* 390-402.

MacArtur, J. R., & Jones, L. L. (2008). A review of literature reports of clickers applicable to college chemistry classrooms. *Chemistry Education Research and Practice, 9,* 187-195.

Madden, T. (2008). e-Portfolio framework for physical sciences [electronic version]. *Wavelength,* 4(2), 6-7.

Mahan, E. (2006). The "Reaction Rolodex": A web-based system for learning reactions in organic chemistry. *Journal of Chemical Education, 83,* 672-672.

Maier, H., Baron, J., & McLaughlan, R. (2007). Using online roleplay simulations for teaching sustainability principles to engineering students. *International Journal of Engineering Education, 23,* 1162-1171.

Malloy, T. E., Jensen, G. C., & Regan, A. (2002). Open courseware and shared knowledge in higher education. *Behavior Research Methods, 34,* 200-203.

Margerum, L. D., Gulsrud, M., Manlapez, R., Rebong, R., & Love, A. (2007). Application of calibrated peer review (CPR) writing assignments to enhance experiments with an environmental chemistry focus. *Journal of Chemical Education, 84,* 292-295.

Markwell, J., & D. W. Brooks (2008). Evaluating web-based information: Access and accuracy. *Journal of Chemical Education, 85,* 458-459.

Mason, R. (2001). The Open University experience. In: J. Stephenson. (Ed.), *Teaching and learning online: Pedagogies for new technologies* (pp. 67-75). London: Kogan Page.

Mazur, E. (1997). *Peer instruction - A user's manual.* New York: Prentice Hall.

McDonnell, C., & O'Connor, C. (2005). Teaching and learning strategies developed to support learning and improve retention of chemistry students in higher education. Proceedings of the European Variety in Chemistry Education conference. Retrieved February 22, 2007, from www.chemia.uj.edu.pl/~eurovariety/html/index.html.

McMahon, M. (1997). Social constructivism and the World Wide Web – a paradigm for learning. Proceedings from Australian Society for Computers in Learning and in Tertiary Education conference. Retrieved March 12, 2008, from www.ascilite.org.au/conferences/perth97/papers/Mcmahon/Mcmahon.html.

Michael, J. (2001). The Claude Bernard distinguished lecture: In pursuit of meaningful learning. *Advances in Physiology Education, 25,* 145-158.

Mittal, A., Krishnan, P. V., & Altman, E. (2006). Content classification and context-based retrieval system for e-learning. *Educational Technology & Society, 9,* 349-358.

Morris, L. (2007). Pick and mix - Getting the blend right. Presentation at the Variety in Chemistry Education Conference. Retrieved 8 February 2008, from www.heacademy.ac.uk/assets/ps/documents/vce07presentations/morris.pdf.

Munro, M., & Walsh, E. (2005). Online tutors as online students: preparing tutors to teach online. Proceedings from Sixth Annual Irish Educational Technology Users' Conference. Retrieved March 2, 2007, from www.lta.learnonline.ie/course/view.php?id=18.

Niyadurupola, G., & Read, D. (2008). Personal response systems: Enhancing communication and feedback. Presentation at the Variety in Chemistry Education conference. Retrieved September 19, 2008, from www.heacademy.ac.uk/assets/ps/documents/events/variety_2008/niyadurupola_read.pdf.

O'Connor, C., & McDonnell, C. (2005). IT-supported learning and assessment for first year undergraduate students. Proceedings of the European Variety in Chemistry Education conference. Retrieved October 18, 2007, from www.chemia.uj.edu.pl/~eurovariety/html/index.html.

Oliver, R. (2001). Developing online learning environments that support knowledge construction. In: L S. Stoney & J. Burns (Eds.), *Working for Excellence in the e-conomy* (pp.407-416). Churchlands Australia: we-B centre.

Prensky, M. (2005). What can you learn from a cell phone? Almost anything!. *Innovate,* 1(5). Retrieved September 3, 2008, from www.innovateonline.info/index.php?view=article&id=83.

Roberts, L. (1995). *A template for converting classrooms to distributed, asynchronous courses.* Retrieved February 4, 2008, from www.unc.edu/cit/iat-archive/publications/roberts/template.html.

Salmon, G. (2004). *E-moderating: The key to teaching and learning online* (2nd ed.). London: Taylor and Francis.

Savin-Baden, M. (2007). *A practical guide to problem-based learning online.* Oxford: Routledge.

Schüz, J. (2005). Mobile phone use and exposures in children. *Bioelectromagnetics, 26*(7), 45-50.

Sharpe, R, Benfield, G., Roberts, G., & Francis, R. (2006). *The undergraduate experience of blended e-learning: A review of UK literature and practice.* York, UK: The Higher Education Academy. Retrieved August 20, 2007, from www.heacademy.ac.uk/ assets/York/documents/ourwork/research/literature_reviews/blended_e-learning_full_ review.pdf.

Sharples, M. (2007). Mobile learning: Small devices, big issues. In: N. Balacheff, S. Ludvigsen & T. De Jong (Eds.), *Technology enhanced learning: Principles and products* (pp. 233-250). New York: Springer.

Shea, V. (1997). *Netiquette.* San Francisco: Albion Books. Retrieved May 01, 2001, from www.albion.com/netiquette/book/index.html.

Slocum, L., Towns, M., & Zielinski, T. (2004). Online chemistry modules: Interaction and effective faculty facilitation. *Journal of Chemical Education, 81,* 1058-1065.

Sormunen, E. (2006). *Web searching, information literacy and learning – Web-SeaL. Research plan.* Retrieved February 15, 2007, from www.ceris.cnr.it/Basili/EnIL/ gateway/finland/Web_Seal.htm.

Stanley, C., & Porter, M. (2002). *Engaging large classes: Strategies and techniques for college faculty.* Massachussetts: Anker.

Supasorn, S., Suits, J. P., Jones, L. L., & Vibuljanc, S. (2008). Impact of a pre-laboratory organic-extraction simulation on comprehension and attitudes of undergraduate chemistry students. *Chemistry Education Research and Practice, 9,* 169 - 181.

Sweller J., (1988). Cognitive load during problem solving: Effects on learning. *Cognitive Science, 12,* 257-285.

Sweller J., & Chandler P. (1991). Cognitive load theory and the format of instruction. *Cognition and Instruction, 8,* 292-332.

Tan, K., Goh, N., Chia, L., & Treagust, D. (2002). Development and application of a two-tier multiple choice diagnostic instrument to assess high school students' understanding of inorganic chemistry qualitative analysis. *Journal of Research in Science Teaching, 39,* 283-301.

Tasker, R., & Dalton, R. (2006). Research into practice: Visualization of the molecular world using animations. *Chemistry Education Research and Practice, 7,* 141-159.

Tasker, R., & Dalton, R. (2008). Visualizing the molecular world – Design, evaluation, and use of animations. In: J. K. Gilbert, M. Reiner & M. Nakhleh (Eds.), *Visualization: Theory and practice in science education* (pp. 103–131). New York: Springer.

Toohey, S. (1999). *Designing courses for higher education.* Buckingham: The Society for Research into Higher Education & Open University Press.

Towns, M., Sauder, D., Whisnant, D., & Zielinski, T. (2001). Physical chemistry on line: Interinstitutional collaboration at a distance. *Journal of Chemical Education, 78,* 414-415.

Tsai, C. S. (2007). Using computer applications and online resources to teach and learn pharmaceutical chemistry. *Journal of Chemical Education, 84,* 2019-2023.

Vygotsky, L. S. (1962). *Thought and language.* Cambridge: M.I.T. Press.

Walczak, M., & Jackson, P. (2007). Incorporating information literacy skills into analytical chemistry: An evolutionary step. *Journal of Chemical Education, 84,* 1385-1390.

Wang, L. (2001). Computer-simulated pharmacology experiments for undergraduate pharmacy students: Experience from an Australian university. *Indian Journal of Pharmacology, 33,* 280-282.

Wieman, C., & Perkins, K. (2005). Tranforming physics education. *Physics Today, 58*(11), 36-41.

Whitelock, D., & Jelfs, A. (2003). Editorial: Educational media special issue on blended learning. *Journal of Educational Media, 28*(2-3), 99-100.

Williams, N. A., Bland, W., & Christie, G. (2008). Improving student achievement and satisfaction by adopting a blended learning approach to inorganic chemistry. *Chemistry Education Research and Practice, 9,* 43-50.

154

From Computer Assisted to Grid Empowered Teaching and Learning Activities in Higher Level Chemistry Education

ANTONIO LAGANÀ, CARLO MANUALI, NOELIA FAGINAS LAGO, OSVALDO GERVASI, STEFANO CROCCHIANTI
University of Perugia, Italy

ANTONIO RIGANELLI
Dow Europe GmbH, Zürich, Switzerland

SASCHA SCHANZE
Leibnitz-University Hannover, Germany

This chapter deals with the development and implementation of innovative methods of teaching and learning chemistry based on information and communication technologies (ICT) carried out as part of the activities of the ECTN, and its Association, ECTNA. The chapter starts with some basic methodological considerations on the impact of ICT on teaching and learning chemistry through student-centred cooperative efforts and analyzes in this perspective the evolution from computer- to net-assisted approaches. The analysis of these approaches focuses on their exploitation both to assist students and teachers in making the learning process ubiquitous and continuous and to develop virtual and abstract level networked methodologies specific of the management and the acquisition of scientific knowledge. To this end virtual reality and learning management systems, which are already enabling new ways of representing and handling chemical concepts and categories, are discussed in detail on the base of some case studies. Further implementations of ICT for broadband transmissions and grid networking are discussed in order to highlight the resulting empowering of data high availability and cooperative concurrent computing. The related discussion lends itself to the

Chapter consultant: Johannes Fröhlich, Vienna University of Technology, Austria

I. Eilks and B. Byers (Eds.). Innovative Methods in Teaching and Learning Chemistry in Higher Education, pp. 153-190. © 2009 RSC Publishing.

formulation of a proposal for establishing a grid-based virtual organization aimed at ferrying European higher education institutions into the telematic era.

Introduction

During the last 10 years we have witnessed an exponential increase in the use of information and communication technologies (ICT) in teaching and learning activities. Developments and any related problems are now regularly discussed at specific conferences and are subject to lively debate by leading educational institutions.

To confine the size of this chapter within reasonable limits and base it on realistic (as opposed to futuristic) applications we focus our attention here on ICT aspects involved in the teaching and learning activities developed by the working group MUTALC[10] of the European Chemistry Thematic Network (ECTN) and its Association (ECTNA).

For this reason, we limit the first section of this chapter to a brief outline of the pedagogical motivation for teaching and learning to evolve towards electronic formats. This is followed by an outline of the reasons why this is believed to improve learning and mastering of basic skills by fostering more student-centred education and we then consider the impact of this on the rendering and cooperative forming of chemical knowledge.

In the remainder of the chapter, we start by examining computer-assisted teaching and learning (CATL) activities in which the use of the computer is driven by the need to support local human assistance to the students (that is how to use instruments, what materials to access, where to find them and when checkpoints are required). We also examine how this activity (that has led to innovative educational options in carrying out laboratory sessions of wet chemistry and telematic sessions of self evaluation for various levels of knowledge in ECTN) has naturally led to net-assisted teaching and learning (NATL) that builds into the teaching and learning process a great deal of self and distance learning (Harasim, Hiltz, Teles, & Turoff, 1995). Furthermore, we discuss how the management of scientific knowledge at a virtual or an abstract level on the net, through virtual reality (VR) and learning management systems (LMSs), has induced innovative educational options by enabling new ways of representing and handling chemical concepts and categories, as is typical of non standard textual information and symbolic representations. In the same sections we also discuss some activities carried out along these lines by ECTN using virtual reality at the macro- and nano-levels for chemistry, or virtual laboratories and semantic web for LMS purposes.

The new prospects opened to LMS by the emerging "Web of the future" (grid) technologies, which can provide data high availability and initiate a

---

[10] MUTALC (MUltimedia in Teaching And Learning Chemistry) is the ECTN Working Group that has coordinated the activities of the network in the field of ICT application in teaching and learning for Chemistry and has worked in tight contact with the ELCHEM Working Group of the COST D23 Action (see section 7).

new era in distance and networked learning activities, are analysed in the last sections by making particular reference to an ECTN supported project exploiting satellite technology. The grid has also fostered the institution of grid-based virtual organizations (VOs) and the birth, as part of the Enabling Grid for E-sciencE (EGEE, www.eu-egee.org) European project, of a specific chemistry virtual organization named COMPCHEM whose possible impact on teaching and learning activities are discussed. This part ends with a discussion of the implementation of a VO aimed at definitely ferrying European higher education institutions into the telematic era as a suitable mission for ECTN over the next 10 years.

Pedagogical background

The level of information technology equipment in universities has continually increased in recent years. Computers and the World Wide Web are now essential in research and imparting computer literacy is also fundamental in higher education. But not only the learning *how* to use ICT is important. Also the learning *through* or *with* ICT is crucial. The opportunities that are connected with the more and more powerful computer assisted teaching and learning technology lead to new models of education (e.g. Barak, 2007). Using ICT in chemistry education is not only driven by the technological potential but has also pedagogical justifications. The support of self-organized learning strategies enhances students' inquiry abilities and prepares them for future work.

The learning and understanding of chemistry at a university level is very demanding due to the complex and abstract nature of chemical concepts (Solsona, Izquierdo, & De Jong, 2003; Floriano, Markic, Reiners, & Avitabile in this book). Models as representations of abstractions can help to overcome such difficulties. Kozma and Russell (2005) described developing representational competence as essential if students are to become chemists and formulate two types of goals: Students' participation in the investigative practice of chemistry and students' acquisition of important chemical concepts and principles.

Supporting student-centred learning strategies in chemistry learning

Based on constructivist principles learning should be student-centred with an emphasis on active learning and interactive structures (Eilks, Markic, Bäumer, & Schanze in this book) as well as making connections to students' previous concepts (Byers & Eilks in this book). Research evidence shows that ICT-enhanced learning can have a positive effect on students' chemistry achievements, provided the students actively engage (Dori & Barak, 2003; Dori et al., 2003). This paradigm shift from a traditional teacher-centred instructional model supports the idea of a more inquiry-based model with students acting like real scientists is an essential part of LMSs. It requires that students make sense of observations and corresponding concepts rather than merely accepting them in a passive manner, when demonstrated by the lecturer or a textbook.

These learning environments can encourage students to ask questions and test their own hypotheses by identifying and controlling variables (e.g. Van Joolingen, De Jong, & Dimitrakopoulout, 2007). NATL also supports asynchronous/synchronous communication and the process of creating information (e.g. Linn, 2003; Schellens & Valcke, 2006; Eilks, Markic, Bäumer, & Schanze in this book). This fosters a more widespread circulation of teaching and learning products and discussions.

In the context of multicultural classes ICT can enhance teaching and learning in a student-centred model as mediation systems, supporting the formulation and exchange of ideas, reflection and meaning-making (Jonassen, Hernandez-Serrano, & Choi, 2000). Several studies have indicated that information processing, inquiry-based learning, and exploring resources via networks, are beneficial for science education (e.g. Edelson, Gordin, & Pea, 1999; Linn, 2003).

Using representations in chemistry learning

The wide range of approaches using representations in chemistry education is documented in Wu and Shah (2004) or Gilbert (2005b). According to Gilbert (2005b) each model of a phenomenon is placed in one or more of five modes of representations: The concrete (or material) mode, the verbal mode, the symbolic mode, the visual mode, and the gestural mode. All of them have sub-modes with their own 'codes of interpretation' (Gilbert, 2005a). To understand and communicate chemical concepts, students should be able to change between these codes fluently and also between the three levels of representation, the macroscopic, the sub-microscopic and the symbolic level (Johnstone, 1991).

Many chemical concepts can best be understood by using visual representation of the phenomenon (Habraken, 1996; Russell et al., 1997). ICT has options of providing visualizations of the sub-microscopic and macroscopic world using different modes of representation. In chemistry education, different forms of graphical representations exist to support the understanding of chemical structures like structural or stereo-chemical formulas, wire, ball-and-stick, or space-filling models. In addition to graphical representations, computer technology also allows depiction of the dynamic and interactive nature of chemistry, supporting the understanding of process-related concepts like bonding, chemical equilibrium, or stereo-selective reactions. The use of these representations offers opportunities to overcome existing difficulties in imagining chemical structures. For example, Williamson and Abraham (1995) found that first-year university students who viewed molecular animations achieved higher test scores than students who had only viewed still images of the same structures.

In other studies with high school students, computer-generated simulations helped to overcome misconceptions about chemical structures (Hakerem, Dobrynina, & Shore, 1993) and to gain better understanding of the nature of scientific models (Dori & Barak, 2001; Urhahne, Nick, & Schanze, in press). Also in laboratory investigations, representations of the actual activities or nanoscale simulations help students to understand and better to accomplish the required tasks (Kozma & Russell, 2005).

Exploiting semantic ICT and virtual communities

Although ICT shows high promise for higher chemistry education and the technology is being more and more integrated in universities, the change from traditional to more student-oriented teaching remains challenging for teachers and students alike. Recent research has identified variables in the learning environment as well as characteristics of teachers' beliefs, attitudes, and skills as potential factors for the successful integration of ICT into higher education (e.g. Mueller, Wood, Willoughby, Ross, & Specht, 2008).

Fortunately, the evolution of NATL towards semantic approaches is making the use of ICT in teaching and learning activities increasingly natural. At the same time, the evolution of networking technologies makes collaborative work on the Internet more user-friendly. This paradigm shift fosters the build up of an intuitive network infrastructure for a large teaching and learning community based upon constructivist learning theories. The more advanced learning environments now provide opportunities for having access to a wide range of information resources, creating one's own representations and discussion, reasoning, interpretation, and reflection to support knowledge building.

Computer-assisted and net-assisted teaching and learning

From computer-assisted to net-assisted teaching and learning

Computer-assisted teaching and learning activities which are concerned with the use of computers to create an environment designed to facilitate and make higher education more effective are increasingly becoming a component of higher education. Sometimes this may only involve the use of computers in a laboratory or classroom to help and better motivate the students by providing illustrations of difficult practices and non-intuitive concepts. More broadly the term can refer to any use of a structured environment based on computers and various other hardware and software technologies and tools for general teaching and learning purposes.

The use of CATL for carrying out practical laboratory sessions does not differ much from that for classroom activities (like computer-based illustration of procedures, apparatuses, concepts, bibliography, planning of operations, checkpoints, and reports). However, its impact on the organization of practical laboratories is much more dramatic not only for some specific technical features (like the possible interfacing of the computers with the scientific instrumentation) but also for the overall design and implementation of the experiments, for the role played by the teachers and technicians, and for the management of the educational process.

As an example, in a traditional practical laboratory the key role is played by the tutor. The presence of a tutor to guide students on how to apply the procedures, how to proceed step-by-step along the learning path, how to handle collected information and how to report on activities and results obtained is in fact essential. In CATL, on the other hand, tutoring support is largely provided by electronic means (see e.g. Bennett, Seery, & Sövegjarto-Wigbers in this book). Moreover, the CATL software is becoming increasingly modular, portable, self explanatory and user friendly. As a matter of fact, the effort needed to implement and become familiar with CATL software is now more than compensated by the shareability and reusability of related programs and data. Moreover, the use of CATL can also be beneficial in several other ways, including the evaluation of a learning path that builds up across sessions and time, as we shall discuss in detail in the remainder of this chapter.

All this has fostered the evolution of CATL into NATL, a net-assisted teaching and learning environment that incorporates the benefits associated with enhanced networking. NATL is the foundation for efficient ubiquitous and continuous learning. The key features of NATL are:

· Accessibility: Learners have permanent access (unless the outcome of their work is purposefully deleted) to their documents, data, videos and results from anywhere upon request.
· Immediacy: Learners can get in real time, whenever they wish, the information needed to solve their problems.
· Interactivity: Learners can easily get in contact with experts, teachers or other students in a synchronous or asynchronous way.
· Adaptability: Learners can get the information they need in the most appropriate format.
· Integrity: Information is neither lost nor corrupted, providing the storage devices are well maintained, and can be retrieved and used at any time.

In other words, NATL guarantees a permanent two-way interaction between knowledge and people. This can take place in either a formal or an informal setting. In a formal setting the learning procedures and the learning achievements are supported and accredited by an educational organization. In an informal setting, the learning process is left completely with the learner and is carried out on a personal basis.

In both cases, however, NATL is meant to implement complex automated open-access systems where a user can improve his/her own knowledge regardless of the physical location of the resources. In this way NATL fosters multi-language availability of knowledge, data integrity and, at the same time, the standardization of the tools used and the classification of levels of skill and expertise.

ECTN NATL tools: IChemEdu and EChemTest

Within ECTN two main NATL tools have been developed: IChemEdu (www.zid.tuwien.ac.at/zidline/zl12/ichemedu.html) and EChemTest (www.echemtest.net).

IChemEdu is a suite of software based within the Institute of Applied Synthetic Chemistry (Organic Chemistry division) of the Vienna University of Technology, Austria, that has been in collaboration with several other higher education institutions. The main aim of the project was to provide students with a basic web tool, IChemLab, to practise on synthetic organic chemistry. Experimental procedures and theoretical backgrounds are mostly taken from printed literature and have been adapted to site specific conditions. In this way a database containing several hundred detailed synthetic experimental protocols has been developed by extracting and revising information from about ten thousand work reports collected over a number of years.

To enable students to access the system from anywhere at any time IChemLab is designed as a web-based Internet application using Java applets. Acquired data is collected in a MS SQL database server, giving the student the option to get ready for the experiment, submit obtained data, or write the report outside the laboratory course hours using any available networked PC. Experiments, procedures and data stored in the web-accessible database are regularly improved by the feedback entered by students and assistants during laboratory sessions. Any problems encountered can be notified immediately and improvements made in real time.

Since all results and data obtained (such as chemical yields, physical properties, NMR spectra, IR spectra and chromatographic data) are also recorded and stored, the achievement of a single student, which is the basis for assessment, can be objectively compared with those of other students attending the same session (and not, as previously, only with data from the literature).

All chemistry students have to use IChemLab to complete their courses, as their synthetic programs are listed on an electronic file card. They obtain the information relevant to the session from the system, including all the details of the procedures (like material safety data sheets and hints for waste disposal). Students are required to enter relevant data and results into IChemLab during and after performing an experiment for a session to be considered successful.

A second NATL tool of IChemEdu is IChemExam, a self-assessment tool allowing students to check their understanding of the knowledge that will be required to perform the experiments. IChemExam besides using the most popular answering methods, such as multiple choice selection and checks for numeric values, utilizes a tool developed in-house named SEICO (Spherical Environment-based Integer COde) to allow students to predict chemical structures.

A third NATL tool of IChemEdu is IChemLecture which comprises an "e-collection" of textbooks and texts relevant to the practice laboratory that have been converted from printed material by optical character recognition and full text indexing or generated by creating specific contents using an appropriate authoring system.

Direct linking and input of queries among IChemLab, IChemExam and IChemLecture are possible via bidirectional software interfaces.

A second example from ECTN is EChemTest. EChemTest consists of assessment software that can be used to test the skills and knowledge of students in various fields of chemistry. The tests are not designed to confer skills, but rather can be used to evaluate the skills and knowledge possessed by students at various levels and for various purposes. As an example, tests are used by some universities as an integrated assessment component in their courses to assign European credits. EChemTest can also be used to monitor students on exchange programmes, career progression of professionals (e.g. for industrial mobility) and to manage life long learning processes.

An EChemTest session consists of a one hour test made of up to 30 questions of different types, taken at random from a large bank, covering the European core chemistry program at three different levels equivalent to:

1. Ending of compulsory education (General Chemistry 1);
2. Beginning of university studies (General Chemistry 2);
3. Ending of the core chemistry syllabus at university level as defined in the Chemistry Eurobachelor (Analytical, Inorganic, Organic and Physical Chemistry level 3) of ECTNA.

Question banks of more specialized chemical knowledge (like the one associated with a Euromaster in Chemistry) are also under preparation.

Several types of questions are available for EChemTest sessions: multiple choice, multiple response, numeric, selection, text, graphical "hot-spot", and problem solving. The software used also permits a detailed analysis of collected responses to the questions.

If a student successfully passes the EChemTest examination in one of the authorized testing centres, he/she becomes eligible for being awarded the corresponding certificate. Each testing centre is supervised by an educational manager supported by a laboratory technician and assisted by an educational supervisor.

Tests require a computer with a high-speed Internet connection and a modern browser equipped with a Virtual Java Machine running all the interactive sections of the tests. No computing skills are required for the test, apart from being able to use the mouse to point and click, or to use the keyboard to type-in single-word or numeric answers.

The tests, available in several European languages, evaluate recall and understanding of facts, applications of knowledge, evaluation and synthesis of information in chemistry related subjects. They are produced using the commercially available software Question Mark Perception (www.questionmark.com). The text encoding used is UTF-8 for a wider language and character compatibility (so as, for example, to display non-Latin characters correctly).

Tests can be conducted either in a demo or in a certification mode. In the demo mode the platform can be used to carry out sample sessions of tests to see "how it looks", to trial evaluations to understand whether the test is suitable for fostering educational progression or for evaluating differences between the knowledge and understanding before and after a particular sequence of teaching. In the certification mode tests are used to carry out dynamic sessions leading to a final mark for the issuing of European chemistry certificates by ECTNA, for the delivering of credits to students at member institutions and even for awarding professional recognition. In this case the sessions are monitored and the tests are taken under controlled conditions at EChemTest testing centres officially recognized by the ECTNA which have to comply with strict requisites related to:

·   Context and Logistic (computer room, maintenance, etc.);
·   Examination conditions (secure network, bandwidth availability, etc.);
·   Examination procedure (monitoring, ID control, etc.).

The MS Windows Server of the system, located at the testing centre of the University of Perugia, Italy (www.ectn-assoc.org/echemtest/tc/IT_ UPerugia.htm), has been equipped with the Perception software and related data are stored in a MS SQL server database.

Security is implemented at different levels: At data level use is made of a Raid-1 system to guarantee the backup and retrieval of data. An additional level of security is also provided by a local firewall (to protect the server) and by a perimetric firewall (to protect the entire net of the unipg.it domain). The perimetric firewall is configured in a way that allows a personalization on the basis of the IP source/destination address, and service/protocol parameters for each subnet.

EChemTest closely fits the NATL features described above and drives the user step by step from the beginning right to the end of the test session. In addition, the entire process, certification included, is completely paperless, self explanatory, self sufficient and is complemented by demo tests. Up to date EChemTest has registered more than 5000 users and relies on eight official testing centres located in different countries throughout Europe[11].

Learning and virtual environments

Virtual environments for teaching and learning chemistry

CATL and NATL learning environments have gradually evolved with computer technology to the point of becoming virtual learning environments (VLEs). VLEs can be either simplified graphic representations of real environments or sophisticated virtual reality (VR) applications which allow the user to interact with a realistic computer-simulated environment.

Most of the currently accessible virtual reality environments consist primarily of visual experiences, displayed either on a computer screen (ranging from standard to immersive) or using special devices. Some

---

[10] As from ECTNA Official Documents, the recognized Testing Centres are: CPE Lyon (A. Smith, P. Mimero) in France, University of Perugia (A. Laganà, C. Manuali, N. Faginas Lago) in Italy, Technical University of Vienna (J. Fröhlich, C. Hametner, H. Krebs) in Austria, University of Helsinki (K. Wähälä, T. Hase, J. Koskimies, N. Aremo) in Finland, Aristotle University of Thessaloniki (E. Varella, I. Kozaris, E. Koliarmou) in Greece, Jagiellonian University of Krakow (A. Michalak, A. Kolasa, K. Szczeponek) in Poland, University Complutense of Madrid (F. Gavilanes, J. Alcaraz) in Spain, University of Reading (D. Cardin, C. Cardin, C. Covell) in United Kingdom.

simulations include additional sensory information such as sound (through speakers or headphones) and haptic systems (at present including tactile information generally known as force feedback) helpful in medical and scientific applications.

Interaction with virtual environments or virtual artefacts can be achieved using multimodal devices such as wired gloves. However, in practice, it is still quite difficult to create high-fidelity VR experiences in chemistry, not only because of technical limitations on processing power, image resolution and communication bandwidth, but also because related tools are still in their infancy. These limitations, however, are expected to be overcome as processor, imaging and data communication technologies become more powerful and cost-effective over time, thus facilitating development of the necessary computational engines needed to deal with chemical parameters.

As a matter of fact we have recently seen increasing interest in the potential social impact of virtual reality which has been identified as a key cause in a number of important changes both to everyday life and various other activities. In fact, the integration of virtual reality into our daily lives and activities can dramatically influence personal behaviour, interpersonal communication and scientific approaches and learning schemes in all fields of knowledge. As we spend more and more time in virtual space, there is a gradual "migration to virtual space" of our operations, resulting in important changes in economics, worldview, and culture. From the educational point of view, active and experiential (even if virtual) learning (learning by doing) has been recognized as extremely important in natural sciences, in general, and in chemistry in particular. It is possible, in fact, to couple human-size VR (HVR) with molecular-size VR (MVR) when carrying out experiments and virtual laboratory sessions. This makes the acquisition of scientific knowledge not only a personally scheduled, ubiquitous and continuously accessible process (particularly suited also for lifelong education and training) but also a process based on replicable and reversible actions: Users' actions can be reversed (which is often impossible in a real environment) and can be driven to run otherwise unfeasible experiments. Furthermore, virtual experiential learning properly structured with the help of pedagogy experts increases the motivation and the pleasure of learning.

All these elements can be assembled in VLEs. The VLE is a software system designed to help teachers by facilitating the management of educational courses, including their administration, and students, by preparing their access to real facilities and rationalizing related outcomes. Accordingly VLEs, while frequently thought of as tools for distance education, can also provide an invaluable supplement with face to face teaching.

Examples of virtual laboratories

Within ECTN two main examples of VLE applications to chemistry laboratories have been developed: *Network for Education-Chemistry: Chemgapedia* (www.chemgapedia.de) and *VMSLab-G* (Riganelli, Gervasi, Laganà, & Fröhlich, 2005).

The *Network for Education - Chemistry* is an extended cluster of chemistry departments which combined their efforts in developing an e-learning distributed system. The teachers of the networked departments have designed and implemented on the web a large bank of teaching units in the various branches of chemistry. Those concerned with analytical laboratories were coordinated by the Institute of Analytical Chemistry of the Dresden University of Technology, Germany, and have resulted in the assemblage of an Internet-based system of multimedia learning materials called "Digital *Pre*Lab".

In Digital *Pre*Lab users can find a broad range of educational material about the most important chemical methods of analysis in a clear structured form on the web. The theoretical background, as well as typical application areas for each analytical method (e.g. chromatography, spectroscopy), are illustrated with the support of simple multimedia animations. Students are driven to learn by playing with problems and undertaking attractive practice session exercises. Both problems and exercises enable the learner to apply their previous knowledge to new problems and to assessment tests, and to use virtual instruments to receive a specific educational input rather than to replace real laboratory experiments. For example, the virtual analytical laboratory offers training on virtual instruments for the most common analytical methods: Gas chromatography, infrared spectroscopy, Raman spectroscopy, NMR spectroscopy and mass spectroscopy. However in Digital *Pre*Lab emphasis is given to functional relationships rather than to providing a realistic visual appearance. The virtual instruments are introduced by emphasizing their basic features without reproducing the actual components of commercially available apparatuses produced by any particular manufacturer. This allows the virtual instruments not to be modified for a number of years, despite the unavoidable evolution of the real apparatuses. The aim of Digital *Pre*Lab, as indicated by its name, is more to integrate, rather than VR simulate, the actual laboratory before embarking on the real laboratory experience.

A significant step towards constructing a truly VR laboratory has been made by *VMSLab-G*. *VMSLab-G* is a project that utilises virtual reality approaches to offer a realistic virtual experiencing environment for education and training both in academic and industrial contexts. To this end the homonymous portal (www.vmslab.org) has been developed to exploit virtual reality at both HVR and MVR levels so as to facilitate ubiquitous laboratory practice and stimulate insight into scientific research. Examples of combined HVR and MVR approaches (the HVR has been used to build up a chemistry practical virtual laboratory in which the user can walk through the various rooms and play with some practice laboratory apparatuses typical of introductory molecular science courses while the MVR has been used to represent the relevant molecular processes) are given in (Laganà et al., 2005; Riganelli et al., 2005; Laganà, 2007).

As a matter of fact, two distinct features characterize the *VMSLab-G* application:

1. The possibility of treating molecules as real objects undergoing realistic processes in the MVR world;
2. The possibility of running virtual experiments and practice sessions as realistic events from real-life contexts in the HVR world.

The first feature of *VMSLab-G* is the possibility of operating at the already mentioned nano-level by making use of both a molecular simulator (acting as a computational engine for determining molecular structures, dynamics and kinetics) and a set of molecular virtual reality tools allowing the visualization, the walk-through, the composition and the decomposition of molecular aggregates. The second feature introduces the possibility of operating at a macro-level to carry out virtual laboratory experiments either as a pre-lab, to familiarize oneself with apparatus and procedures before actually entering the laboratory or, as a post-lab, to replay the experience and rationalize the results obtained levels. This provides users with an environment able to assist them not only when running step by step chemistry protocols, but also when facing safety and security issues when dealing with potentially hazardous environments (see also Bennett, Seery, & Sövegjarto-Wigbers in this book).

It is important to point out here that VR finds significant applications also for complex experimental research especially when coupled with grid computing technologies. An interesting example of these applications is SIMBEX (SImulation of Molecular Beam EXperiments) (Gervasi & Laganà, 2004b) developed by the Working Groups D23/003/01 and D23/005/01 of the COST in chemistry action D23 (Metachem: Metalaboratories for complex computational applications in chemistry). SIMBEX is also the molecular simulator of reference for *VMSLab-G* when exploiting the Grid to the end of combining the computational resources of the cooperating laboratories.

VMSLab-G makes extensive use of VRML (Ames, Nadeau, & Moreland, 1997), X3D (web3d.org) and Java (java.sun.com) languages. The first two languages are used for the modelling of virtual objects whereas Java is used to elaborate data and to drive the interactions among virtual objects. For this purpose other standard Web technologies might also be used. In particular open-source technologies such as PHP (www.php.net) to make programming work transparent and MySQL (www.mysql.com) to manage the underlying database can be used.

Knowledge management

Ontologies

To cope more in general with the complex objectives of teaching and learning it is necessary to climb to a higher level of abstraction and deal with knowledge management (KM). KM is, in fact, the conceptual platform necessary to support intelligent process automation and collaborative problem solving in large-scale science over the Internet. KM comprises a range of practices able to represent, identify, create, elaborate and distribute knowledge over multiple environments and relies on the possibility of defining and handling ontologies.

"Ontology" is a term inherited from philosophy to indicate the "nature of being". This term began to be used in artificial intelligence in the '80s, and is at present very popular within the information science community (Wilson, 2004) usually bearing the meaning of an explicit specification of a conceptualization. Ontology is currently a buzzword in many other communities, hailed as a mechanism for making better use of the web. Ontologies offer a shared definition of a domain that can be understood by computers, enabling them to complete more meaningful tasks. Considering their potential in this field, most current efforts in dealing with ontologies have focused on developing languages and tools. This is the case with the Web Ontology Language (OWL, www.w3.org/TR/owl-features/) that is a standard language working on top of other existing web languages such as XML (www.w3.org/XML/) and RDF (www.w3.org/RDF/) to offer a high degree of expressiveness. Moreover, a variety of tools are emerging for creating, editing and managing ontologies in OWL.

Ontologies have a range of potential benefits and applications in further and higher education, including the sharing of information across educational systems, providing frameworks for the reuse of learning-objects, and enabling intelligent and personalised student support. Moreover, they offer a shared and common understanding of a knowledge domain to be communicated between people and application systems. Ontologies also attempt to formulate a thorough and rigorous representation of a knowledge domain by specifying all of its concepts, relationships and related conditions and regulations (Davies, Fensel, & Van Harmelen, 2003). They offer also possibilities for organizing and visualizing teaching and learning knowledge and it's sharing and reusing by different educational applications. Furthermore ontologies enable learners to interact with web-based courses and other educational systems in new, better articulated and personalised ways. Finally, ontologies enable complex and dynamic learning requirements to be met automatically, and assist learners in comprehending the domain contents and in building their own concept map. This means that the ontologies empowered web (semantic web) is a good candidate to become a truly effective resource for teachers and learners alike.

Although ontologies of various descriptions have been in development and use for some time, it is their potential as a key technology in the semantic web that is mainly responsible for the current tide of interest. Accordingly, the difficulties inherent in creating a model of a knowledge domain are at present being actively tackled, and the communities involved in the development of various ontologies are cooperating to implement their vision of the Semantic Web.

As a matter of fact, as will be discussed in detail in the following subsections, semantic web-based approaches and new markup languages for science, derived from ontological concepts will now allow us to tackle important challenges of the knowledge lifecycle and in particular those concerned with the acquiring, modelling, retrieving, reusing, publishing and maintaining knowledge.

Markup languages for science

Indeed, the key tools required to build knowledge inside textual information is at present the eXtensible Markup Language (www.w3.org/XML/) in conjunction with the Hyper Text Markup Language (HTML). Domain-specific markup languages, like the Chemistry Markup Language (CML, cml.sourceforge.net) and the Mathematical Markup Language (MathML, www.w3.org/Math/) have been developed for certain disciplines.

CML is an innovative approach to the managing of molecular information. It has an extensive scope as it covers subjects ranging from macromolecular sequencing to the study of the properties of small molecules and quantum phenomena. In other words CML is the "HTML for molecules", though there is much more to it than this. In fact, it is quite obvious that it would be almost meaningless to represent chemical structures simply using the (text-based) HTML environment. In this context molecular structures are merely represented by a single piece of graphic information with no detail on structural data.

Chemical Markup Languages, like CML and associated tools, allow for the conversion of current files (with no loss of the semantics) into structured documents (including bibliographical information) and provide indications on the precise location of the information within files. A similar situation occurs when expressing chemical processes in term of equations and formulae. We should also stress the general unsuitability of HTML representations for visually impaired users.

Similarly, MathML is intended to facilitate the use and re-use of mathematical and scientific content on the web, and for other applications such as computer algebra systems and print typesetting. It can be used to encode both the presentation of mathematical notation for high-quality visual display, and mathematical content, for applications where the semantics plays a key role (such as scientific software or voice synthesis). Several implementations of MathML are available (e.g. browsers and authoring tools), many of which are open-source software.

Research efforts are now being focused on the implementation of the semantic environments and on the definition of the ontologies for various classes of problems regarding, at the same time, chemical structural forms and mathematical formalisms.

Semantic web for scientific knowledge

The management of scientific knowledge in a distributed environment is a key challenge facing web technologies. This is particularly true for domains such as chemistry, physics and mathematics, in which the knowledge is not only widely spread over the network but is also represented by non standard textual information and symbolic representation. Furthermore, there is also a huge potential user base in other domains like life sciences, health care, materials, and nanotechnology.

The proper technology for dealing with this type of scientific knowledge is the semantic web. Most of the information dispersed on the web is, in fact, written in natural languages meant for humans to read yet not for the computer to understand. On the contrary, the semantic web technologies use formal ontologies and structure web information in a way that also makes it understandable and reusable by machines.

To spell out the difference, a search of information on the web usually involves targeting a set of keywords and then filtering and analysing a list of retrieved items. A semantic web search on the other hand implies that software agents can deal with a set of complex queries, targeting the meaning of the electronic data as requested by the user and returning a direct response. It is a common belief that such reasoning services will become so integrated into everyday life that they will be "as necessary to us as access to electric power". In this respect, when analyzing the nature of grid computing and its status and requirements for knowledge support, we find in the related platforms the ideal characteristics and challenges for knowledge management.

A more specific use of semantic web technologies for teaching and learning that has clearly emerged recently is the creation of standards for the management and delivery of learning units in a web environment incorporating semantic technologies. Examples of this include the use of metadata to describe scientific information such as chemistry and molecular science knowledge, rather than the use of web technologies such as *Resource Description Framework* (RDF, www.w3.org/RDF/) to build intelligent assessment tools.

Content and learning management systems

Existing software systems allowing distributed management of knowledge quite often belong, in practice, to the category of content management systems (CMSs). CMSs allow, at least partially, the management of knowledge containers (computer files, image media, audio files, electronic documents and Web semantic or not, objects) on the network. The idea behind CMSs is to make these files available inter-office, as well as over the web, with the first consequences being the web substituting the archive and the workflow replacing document transfer.

This allows a collaborative creation and adaptation of documents and facilitates the organization, control, and publication of a large body of documents and other contents, such as images and multimedia Web resources. A CMS in fact is usually able to support the following tasks:

· Management of documents and multimedia material;
· Identification of all the key users, their profiles and their content management roles;
· Assignment of roles and responsibilities to different content categories or types;
· Definition of the various content workflow tasks, often coupled with event messaging so that content managers are alerted about changes in content;

- Monitoring and management of the evolution of a single or group of instances of content;
- Publish the content into a repository to support user access to related information and make the repository an increasingly inherent part of the system.

CMSs more specifically tailored for educational purposes are the learning management systems (LMSs) which are designed to manage teaching and learning activities. The added value of LMSs over conventional training records management and reporting is provided by the extensive range of functionalities they offer: Learner self-service (e.g. self-registration on teacher-led training), training workflow (e.g. user notification, manager approval, waitlist management), the provision of on-line learning (e.g. computer and net-based training), online assessment, management of continuous professional education (CPE), collaborative learning (e.g. application sharing, discussion threads) and training resource management (e.g. allocation of teaching and learning units, personnel, devices).

Most LMSs are, indeed, already exploiting (or built to exploit) the web in order to foster "anytime, any place, any pace" features to access learning contents and administration. This allows LMSs to enhance different educational, administrative and deployment characteristics. For this reason LMSs are based on a variety of advanced development platforms like *Java Enterprise Edition (EE)* (java.sun.com/javaee/) architectures or Microsoft .NET (2009), and in general make use of robust database back-ends. Moreover, in order to manage the administrative functions of on-line teaching and learning, some systems also provide tools to simplify instructor-led synchronous and asynchronous on-line training in any case founded on learning object methodology.

Accordingly, LMSs are a high-level, strategic solution for planning, delivering and managing most learning events within an organization (including on-line virtual classrooms and instructor-led courses) in which isolated and fragmented learning programs are replaced by systematic means of assessing and raising competence and performance levels throughout a learning pathway. For example, an LMS can simplify global certification efforts, enable entities to align learning initiatives with strategic goals, and provide a viable means of enterprise-level skills management.

A way to promote the use of CMSs and LMSs is to provide authors, instructional designers and subject experts with the means to create, exchange and re-use e-learning contents in an efficient way. A policy often adopted is to create an amount of educational content just sufficient and timely to meet the needs of individuals or groups of learners rather than design and develop entire courses conceived for multiple audiences. These basic knowledge skeletons can then be made available to course developers and content experts throughout the same or other organizations to avoid duplicating development efforts and allow for rapid assembly of customized contents. Sometimes actual (web-based) VLSs are designed in a way that will enable students to complete their preparation at home before carrying out practical work in distributed ad-hoc centres. This gives to a teaching community the connotation of a virtual organization embryo for which teaching and learning is a cooperative task involving a team of remote geographically dispersed educational sites.

SELE: A semantic web application to e-learning

Within the ECTN LMS activities a web-integrated prototype called SELE (SEmantic LEarning) has been developed (Gervasi, Catanzani, Riganelli, & Laganà, 2005). SELE can be seen as an abstract container of teaching and learning units. The proposed architecture is suitable for the implementation of a blended learning system where face to face teaching can be reinforced with e-learning modules.

By making use of suitable ontologies SELE allows the implementation not only of learning objects (through either a local content management subsystem or an acquired one via a URI pointing to external resources) but also of an intelligent assessment tool which is able to take into account the learning path being followed by the student. In SELE the semantic web technologies are used to define and describe the various teaching and learning units introduced by teachers, to make these units reusable and retrievable, and to follow the student during his "walk around" them. The adoption of semantic web technologies for e-learning paves the way for interoperability between LMSs and the various learning facilities and on-line assessment systems. SELE has been developed in a Linux environment making use of free-software and open-source components. It is articulated into three main sub-systems: The user interface, a content management system and the on-line assessment system EoL (Gervasi & Laganà, 2004a).

SELE starts by offering the student the possibility of selecting via a user interface the courses he/she wants to follow by entering a personal code (previously assigned by the teacher or by the system administrator). After accessing the course materials the student can make use of the various teaching and learning units.

A critical point in the process occurs when the student declares, after having gone through all the teaching and learning units, that he/she is ready to carry out a self-assessment session. This is the moment for the teacher to decide whether the test to be taken by the student needs to take into account a specific learning path that he/she has followed. If this is the case, the system will tailor the selected set of operations on the specific optional arguments taken by the student during the preparation. SELE has an ad-hoc designed environment devoted to the production of teaching and learning units; the content management sub-system. This component allows teachers to produce and maintain the teaching and learning units. The insertion of learning material stored in different Web servers is carried out by specifying the corresponding URI and by defining the fields needed to issue RDF statements. The RDF statements are used in this context to classify the teaching and learning units, to indicate its possible use in other courses, to offer the user the possibility of introducing personal annotations and to associate each unit with relevant learning material. This means that the teacher has the possibility of linking a set of questions allowing the student to check the level of acquired knowledge and competences to the various pages of the teaching and learning units.

It is also possible to include questions that deal with related teaching and learning units that a student has also studied. This respect of the possibility of setting sequences of interleaved teaching and learning units can be of great help to the teacher.

The EoL assessment service activities

A more detailed description of EoL, the experimental assessing tool of SELE, is deserved. EoL was originally designed to evaluate, on the network, the competences acquired by students during an in-company placement on the Leonardo da Vinci Programme (EC, 2009). EoL was later tested on a larger scale for the first intensive course of the theoretical chemistry and computational modelling a Euromaster (www.chemistry-eurolabels.eu). EoL produces individual tests which can be assembled by selecting a set of questions from a bank created by the teacher of a course. This tailors the assessment process to the actual teaching content. The adopted selection algorithm guarantees that the questions are extracted according to specific rules which can be defined or modified by the teacher to provide both a balanced assessment of course content and the required average level of difficulty.

EoL may be accessed using a web browser, though when EoL is used for formal examinations, some restrictions are adopted in order to guarantee the reliability of the evaluation. In particular, a security mechanism is implemented on the server side.

EoL is entirely based on open-source components with the following being the major ones:

· The PHP language parser;
· The Web server Apache, enabled to invoke the PHP language parser;
· The RDBMS Firebird or the RDBMS MySQL.

EoL has been extensively tested and used on Linux Operating System environments. Therefore, its portability to other Unix systems depends only on the availability of the above mentioned software components on the platform used.

In order to enhance the service quality EoL consists of two separated agents: the front office Agent (FOA) and the back office agent (BOA). The FOA is accessed by the web browser allowing the user to perform the assessment test. Before the user can start a test, the teacher has to activate the session for the course of interest by entering the accounting data (login and password) specific for the named test session. The client computers must be able to connect to the EoL server through the Internet. After the EoL system has verified the accounting data specific for the current test session, a check is performed to verify whether the IP address of the client belongs to the set of hosts allowed to connect to the EoL server. Once this check has been satisfactorily completed, the user is asked for identification data and can then start answering the questions sequentially. Each formal assessment test has to be performed in a testing centre under the surveillance of an assistant. The results of the tests and related scores are issued by the teacher after reviewing the answers and having evaluated the performance as a whole. To go into more detail the EoL BOA relies on the implementation of a bank of questions by the teacher. The question bank is articulated in sections, each related to a specific course. The BOA manages each course, analyzes the results on the various tests and manages the clients. Access via the web to the management section of this agent is restricted to approved teachers by a login and password.

BOA consists of the following components:

1. Course management;
2. Test sessions management;
3. Client pools management;
4. Test results management.

Course management involves the administration of the test for the various courses associated with a given teacher. EoL enables two types of test: the *single path* test and the *double path* test. In a single path test all questions are selected from the same bank and have a homogeneous scoring system. Whereas in a double path test, after a preliminary batch of questions selected from a general knowledge (GK) subset, the remaining questions are chosen from a specific knowledge (SK) one.

It is therefore possible to activate two different assessment regimes, each having a different marking scheme. In fact, the level of difficulty for the SK questions can be made dependent on the scores obtained in the first part, the GK phase of a double path test. Less demanding questions can be chosen for the SK phase when the score obtained by the user on the GK section falls below a predetermined threshold T, while more demanding questions will be chosen where the score obtained on the GK phase exceeds this threshold T.

Test sessions management is concerned with the management of tests already performed and the definition of a new test session. When a test session has been completed it can be archived to prevent further modifications. The teacher is also able to activate new test sessions. When opening a session the teacher must choose the name, the date and the time of the session, as well as specify the expected number of attending students, and the location where the test will be performed. Finally, the teacher selects from a menu showing all the possibilities the pool to be used for this test.

Client pools management is concerned with the running of the set of clients enabled to access the EoL system for the test sessions. The agent makes it possible to modify an existing entry or to add a new client pool.

Test results management is concerned with the running of the teacher accesses to the results at the end of the test session in order to review the whole set of tests of the session and to set the final mark for each test.

Data high availability

Data grid

A crucial aspect of modern KM is the volume of data to be handled due to the fact that this may easily amount to the order of tera and peta-bytes since knowledge is increasingly associated with large amounts of data. The communities of researchers need to produce access and analyze large amounts of data (often using sophisticated and computationally expensive techniques). These sets of scientific data are becoming increasingly more numerous and are almost always geographically distributed as are the computing and storage resources that these communities rely upon to carry out their computational activities. Efficient and reliable execution of these tasks may require the appropriate management of terabyte caches, transfer of gigabits of data over wide area networks, coordination of data and supercomputer elaborations, and performance estimations to guide the selection of dataset replicas, as well as other advanced operations collectively optimizing the usage of storage, networking, and computing resources.

Such requirements are not adequately satisfied using traditional Web tools and need ad-hoc hardware and software solutions that only a grid infrastructure can provide. This is, in fact, the objective of data grid applications (Chervenak, Foster, Kesselman, Salisbury, & Tuecke, 1999) which operate in the wide area, multi-institutional and heterogeneous environments, where spatial and temporal uniformity of behaviour or policy cannot typically be assumed.

The main features of data grids are:

- Mechanism neutrality: Substantial independence from the low-level mechanisms is used to transfer and store data and metadata obtained by defining special interfaces which encapsulate peculiarities of specific storage systems, catalogues, data transfer algorithms and the like;
- Policy neutrality: Exposure rather than a black box encapsulated implementation of the decisions is adopted for those using procedures having significant performance implications. Thus, while data transfer is provided as a low-level basic operation, data replication is implemented via higher-level procedures for which defaults are provided (though they can be easily substituted by application-specific codes);
- Compatibility with grid infrastructure: Use is made of the underlying grid infrastructure, e.g. gLite (glite.web.cern.ch/glite/) or Globus (www.globus.org), which provide basic services such as authentication, data and resource management, and information. To perform wide area and multi-institutional operations this data grid architecture is structured so that more specialized data grid (user) tools are compatible with lower-level grid mechanisms;
- Uniformity of information infrastructure: Emphasis is given to uniform and convenient access to information about resource structure as a means for data portability. This means that the same data model and

interfaces are used to access the data grid's metadata and the underlying grid information infrastructure.

In data grids the focus on simple, policy-independent mechanisms encourages and enables broad deployments without limiting the range of applications that can be implemented. To support these activities a first level of components (*core basic services*) is required. We focus, here, in particular, on data access and metadata access, since they refer to two structures of key importance in data grid architecture. As we shall discuss in more detail later the former, in fact, provides mechanisms for accessing, managing, and initiating third-party transfers of data stored in storage systems while the latter provides mechanisms for accessing and managing information on data stored in storage systems. In some circumstances, for example when data is being stored in a distributed database system, as is typical of distributed LMSs, there are advantages in combining metadata and data storage into the same abstraction. Typical of a grid environment, is the fact that data may be stored in different locations and different devices bearing different characteristics. As mentioned above, mechanism neutrality implies that applications should not need to be aware of the specific low-level mechanisms required to access data at a particular location. Instead, applications should be presented with a uniform view of data and with uniform mechanisms of access. These requirements are met by the storage system abstraction (SSA) and the grid storage application program interface (GS-API) which between them constitute the *Data Access Service*.

In the Data Access Service a basic data grid component called *storage system*, which is defined as an entity that can be manipulated with a set of functions for creating, destroying, reading, writing, and altering the attributes of named sequences of bytes called *file instances,* is introduced.

A *storage system* can be implemented using any storage technology that can support the required access functions. Implementations that target Unix file systems, HTTP servers, *hierarchical storage systems* such as (HPSS, www.hpss-collaboration.org/hpss/index.jsp), and network caches such as the *distributed parallel storage system* (DPSS, www-didc.lbl.gov/DPSS/) can certainly be envisaged. In fact, a storage system does not need to map directly on to a single low-level storage device. For example, a distributed file system, that manages files distributed over multiple storage devices or sites, can serve as a storage system, as can a storage resource broker (SRB) system that serves requests by mapping to multiple storage systems of different types.

A storage system holds data, which may actually be stored in a file system, database, or other system. We do not care about how data is stored but specify simply that the basic unit that we deal with corresponds to the requested file instances. The use of the term *file instance* for this basic unit is not intended to imply that the data must live in a conventional file system. For example, a data grid implementation might use a system such as SRB to access data stored within a database management system.

175

The second type of basic machinery that is required is the one concerned with the management of information about the data grid itself, including information about file instances, the contents of file instances, and the various storage systems contained in the data grid. This is, indeed, as already mentioned, what in general we refer to as metadata. The *meta-data service* provides a means for publishing and accessing metadata as a whole, even if various types of metadata can be distinguished. The metadata may describe the information content represented by the file, the circumstances under which the data was obtained, and/or other information useful to applications that process the data. We refer to these as *application metadata*. Such metadata can be viewed as defining the logical structure or semantics that should apply to the uninterpreted bytes that make up a file instance or a set of file instances. They are of vital importance when implementing cooperative activities as could be the synergy between different quantum chemistry codes (Scemama et al., 2008) or quantum chemistry and quantum dynamics codes (Rossi, 2008) for which work is being developed in the new D37 COST action (COST, 2006) or the synergy that could be implemented in this field between research and teaching and learning. A second type of *metadata* is used to describe the fabric of the data grid itself. For example, details about storage systems, such as their capacity and usage policy, as well as information about file instances stored within a given storage system.

Many user communities are now pursuing the use of eXtended Markup Language (XML), or more specifically, in the field of chemical data (CML), and *lightweight directory access protocol* (LDAP, www.faqs.org/ rfcs/rfc1777.html) to represent application metadata and to realize the metadata service as a form of distributed directory service. Finally, the data grid architecture assumes the existence of a number of other basic services, including an authorization and authentication infrastructure, resource reservation and co-allocation mechanisms for both storage systems and other resources such as networks, and instrumentation services which enable the end-to-end instrumentation of storage transfers.

A higher level of components (*higher-level services*) is required in data grid architecture. We focus, here, in particular, on two of them: *Replica management* (identified by replica manager and replica catalogue services) and *replica selection*.

Replica manager is a data grid service whose functionality can be defined in terms of that provided by the storage system and metadata repository services. The role of a replica manager is to create (or delete) copies of file instances, or replicas, within specified storage systems. Typically, a replica is created because the new storage location offers better performance or availability for accesses to or from a particular location. A replica might be deleted because storage space is required for another purpose.

A data grid may, and indeed typically will, contain multiple replica catalogues. For example, a community of teachers interested in a particular topic might maintain a replica catalogue for a collection of data sets or learning units of mutual interest. *Replica catalogue* can thus provide the functionality of logical collections, grouping logical files on related topics. It is possible to create hierarchies of replica catalogues to impose a directory-like structure on related logical collections of resources.

Therefore, a replica manager can perform access control on entire catalogues as well as on individual logical files. By combining the functionality provided by the storage system and metadata repository, the replica manager also can perform a number of basic operations, including creation and deletion of replicas, logical files, and replica catalogues. Note that the existence of a replica manager does not determine when or where replicas are created, or which replicas are to be used by an application, nor does it even require that every file instance be entered into a replica catalogue.

The second representative high-level service provided in the upper level of the data grid is *replica selection*. It is interesting to point out here that it does not build on top of the core services, but rather relies on the functions provided by the replica management component described above. It is the process of choosing a replica that will provide an application with data access characteristics which optimize a desired performance criterion, such as absolute performance (i.e. speed), cost, or security. The selected file instance may be local or accessed remotely. Alternatively, the selection process may initiate the creation of a new replica whose performance will be superior to the existing ones.

Where replicas are to be selected on the base of time or place of access, grid information services can provide information about network performance and the ability to reserve network bandwidth, while the metadata repository can provide information about the size of the file. Based on this, the selector can rank all of the existing replicas to determine which one will be the most convenient to use. Alternatively, the selector can consult the same information sources to determine whether there is a storage system that would result in better performance if a replica was created on it.

The open grid services architecture (OGSA) enables the integration of services and resources across distributed, heterogeneous, dynamic, Virtual Organizations independently of whether this occurs within a single enterprise or is extended to external resource-sharing and service-providing entities (Foster, Kesselman, & Tuecke, 2001).

A multimedia satellite teaching and learning supported experience

As already mentioned a data high availability technology has been exploited by ECTN to administer teaching and learning units on the "Multimedia in the diagnosis and preservation of Mediterranean cultural heritage" project using satellite networks. The project is coordinated by the Department of Chemistry at the Aristotle University of Thessaloniki, Greece, and involves the following institutions: Malta Centre for Restoration (Malta), Rey Juan Carlos University (Madrid, Spain), Avignon University (France), Cà Foscari University (Venice, Italy), Sidi Ben Abdellah University (Fez, Morocco), and Yarmouk University (Irbid, Jordan). It was developed jointly by the ECTN Working Group on Chemistry and Cultural Heritage and the

Euromed project "IKONOS: distance education in cultural heritage" (IKONOS, www.ikonosheritage.org), funded by the European Union to provide cultural heritage preservation courses via satellite supported interactive communication.

The key element of the project, implemented to make the data high availability technology sustainable, was the establishment of a consortium of distance teaching and learning nodes in each partner country. This ensured a common two-way system of communication able to deal with all interoperability related issues such as identification of the hardware and software specifications for functionality purposes.

The consortium identified a bandwidth pool technology, which could be configured and used flexibly by any of the partners simultaneously for video-conferencing, tele-conferencing, tele-monitoring and tele-inspecting as a cost effective networking platform. This was implemented through the creation of a shared cultural heritage cataloguing approach which involved the assemblage of a common catalogue of cultural heritage artefacts, the construction of a powerful distance learning infrastructure, the establishment of a training initiative for trainers on the specific knowledge handling side, the development of solid (long term) distance node links and the build up of expertise on the use of tele-procedures for several activities including risks assessment in remote handling of artefacts on the satellite technology side.

The project was structured to be of an open nature. For the first aspect an open-source CMS was used allowing a joint management of the teaching and learning activities by experts belonging to different partner institutions. In the adopted CMS, as an example, the courses were implemented in a double copy format in which the first copy contains the preparatory material while the second copy is hidden. After the lecture, the first copy disappears while the second one, containing modified and extra materials, shows up. The CMS was combined with a direct dialogue tool and a video web conference browser-based service, which gave the instructor the option not only of offering over-the-Internet presentations, applications and the desktop, but also of conversing directly and using the webcam, without the user needing to install any software.

The project addressed two distinctive and interconnected needs:

1. The difficulty of adequately covering and maintaining all the subjects dealing with conservation science in a single place
2. The need for instructing remote learners on specific topics of interest.

At the same time physical mobility, otherwise essential in a multi-disciplinary subject for both staff and courses, had to be both complemented and replaced by building on the specific potentials of on-line learning and network communication. In this framework the specialized theoretical and practical learning units on conservation science, the seminars aimed at meeting the current demand on diagnostic or safeguarding problems and an open "first aid line" dealing with concrete issues of immediate interest, had to be activated to provide systematic and non-systematic remote adult learners with interactive in-depth instruction delivered by experts belonging to different institutions. Real-time oral communication and simultaneous laboratory training were also offered to all the attendees.

The educational environment was articulated in a three-step sequence: before, during and after each learning unit. In the first step learners get ready for the course by having direct access to all the local and remote didactic material needed. This type of demand has been met in a multifaceted approach, encompassing archived preparatory material of various types, from text files and visual presentations to video presentations and multimedia modules (as well as selected bibliographical references, websites and self-assessment tests at various levels) to fulfil prerequisites requests and access individual evaluation.

In the second step, during the frontal lessons, use was made of video-conferencing and webcasting/archiving. The courses were delivered in a synchronous manner via a video-conferencing and webcasting scheme and the logic of a hybrid environment (e.g. a structured distance-learning setting with definite timetables, fixed audiences and locally organized examination schedules) was followed in which video-conferencing addresses the need for a multidisciplinary trans-national covering and archived material serves private study.

Subsequently, in the third step, the learners benefited from study materials, self-assessment opportunities and opportunities for direct contact with the instructor. The post-course step was mainly based on the parallel activities of study, since the user could connect to the server at a later date and view the archived version of the videoconferences, self-assessment and direct questioning of the lecturer. Learners could use both the direct open line to teaching staff and the distributed infrastructure media on the server.

An open video learning system, implemented for capturing, archiving and webcasting lectures, was adopted to sustain both adult learners and any type of extended self-study. The system was scalable, interactive and able to support live and on-demand broadcasting. In each partner institution a videoconference classroom was set up as a remote node. Each virtual classroom had one or more cameras, microphones, loudspeakers and monitors. The videoconference system was designed to give a feeling of common study, enabling learners to benefit from guest lecturers and collaborative teaching.

Grid virtual organizations

The open nature of data high availability projects increasingly prompts the exploitation of grid technologies and collaborative computing among geographically dispersed scientific laboratories having complementary know-how and interests. This form of cooperative aggregation, originally called *metalaboratory* (COST, 2000), is now known as *Virtual Organization* (VO). In VO a dynamic collection of individuals, institutions and resources are regulated according to shared standards so as to utilize unique authentication, authorization, resource access, resource discovery and other advanced computational challenges. A VO is, in fact, a corporate, not-for-profit, productive organizational entity which uses telecommunication tools to enable, maintain and sustain member relationships in distributed work environments. Critical management dimensions are those applying to the spatial (physical distance between members), temporal (working hours scheduling) and configurational (activity inter-connections) aspects of member relationships in the work environment. A VO comprises a set of independent organizations which share resources and skills to achieve their missions, yet it is not limited to an alliance of for profit enterprises. Actually, the first VOs were originally built around strategy considerations. For this reason VOs needed some adaptations before being applied to science programmes and they are likely to need further adjustment before being used in education.

Education is, indeed, a typical example of activities in which there is a high demand for sharing resources and developing cooperation. In this respect, there is an urgent need to establish active communities able to stimulate the growth of knowledge in a fashion appropriate to economic, cultural and geographic areas. Unfortunately, in the developed areas limited interest and infrastructures are available for this purpose. At the same time, in developing economies, other services are often given a higher priority than education when considering the allocation of limited resources.

However, since knowledge is a commodity that needs mainly brain-ware rather than heavy industrial plants and contemporary society intensively exploits knowledge products for increasing development and deployment of information and communication technologies most of the tools necessary for educational purposes are, in any case, produced by ICT developments in other fields. Moreover, it has been shown in the past, as in the case of the World Wide Web and the Internet (Sherif, 2002), that educational activities have a high capacity for reusing and recycling knowledge technologies designed for other purposes.

The COMPCHEM virtual organistion

At present, progress on the use of the grid for developing molecular sciences knowledge and technologies has mainly concentrated on the assemblage of computational procedures for the a priori determination of complex molecular structures and processes in order to address the need for innovations in many scientific and engineering fields.

In this respect, most of the needs for innovation in chemistry can be met at present by exploiting the grid to carry out ab-initio realistic simulations of molecular processes. To the end of developing collaborative endeavours in science and technology by building a networked community, the chemistry domain of the COST European initiative has implemented the Action D23 *Metachem: Metalaboratories for complex computational applications in chemistry* (COST, 2000). In D23 cooperative research and knowledge handling in chemistry was promoted through the assembly of networks of laboratories, called metalaboratories, through which the ECTN MUTALC Working Group has strongly interacted with COST.

A key outcome of Action D23 was, indeed, the recommendation for structuring the computational chemistry community in a VO. Following this suggestion a VO (COMPCHEM) has been registered and its members have begun to operate on the production Grid of the EGEE project[12]. COMPCHEM is strengthening its links with ECTN in order to implement a range of related teaching and learning activities on the grid. Worthy of mention among these are the administration on the grid of EChemTest sessions, for which appropriate technological and commercial partners are currently being sought, and the distributed management of teaching and learning units where a great deal of design and development work has already been carried out by ECTN members.

Table 1: Levels of membership in COMPCHEM.

Membership level	Short description
User (temporary pre-membership)	*Passive*: Run a program implemented by other members of the VO
	Active: Implement at least one program for personal use
SW Provider	*Passive:* Implement at least one program for use by other members
	Active: Interactive management of the implemented program for cooperative usage
Grid Deployer	*Passive*: Contribute at least a small cluster of nodes to the Grid infrastructure
	Active: Operates above the minimal level as support for the Grid deployment and management
Stakeholder	Take part in the development and management of the VO

Crucial to the growth of a VO is its sustainability (Laganà, Riganelli, & Gervasi, 2006). This is likely to be particularly important in areas such as teaching and learning where funding tends to be scarcer than for example is the case for applied research in the areas of science and technology. For this purpose, COMPCHEM has adopted the policy of offering to its members the possibility of trading their support to the VO activities in exchange for the use of VO resources. Levels of involvement in COMPCHEM are outlined in Table 1. The entry level offers a researcher the possibility of implementing an individual code just for personal use. However, this is thought of as a short-term pre-membership situation useful for screening laboratories on their willingness to seriously operate on a grid platform. Even at this level, in fact, several of the competences necessary for restructuring the code to run in a distributed way by exploiting the

---

[12] COMPCHEM is supported also by the D37 COST Action "GRIDCHEM".

advantages of using a grid platform need to be acquired. In return one acquires the advantages of distributing the code on a much larger platform and more easily interacting with the codes of other users of the VO.

As already mentioned, users can only become actual members of the COMPCHEM VO after committing themselves to open the code implemented on the grid to shared use with other members of the VO. This implies the validation of a stable version of the code and assembly of all necessary GUIs for its friendly use by other researchers. It also implies software maintenance and user support. It may also require the commitment to confer to the grid additional hardware, especially for suites of codes needing special devices after negotiation with the management committee of the VO about the relevance of such a commitment to the strategic choices of the VO.

Obviously, installation of both software and hardware to COMPCHEM will take place gradually due to the time needed to validate new software and to gridify applications. The status of any COMPCHEM member may imply further levels of involvement. VO members, in fact, are welcome to take care of maintaining the local software and segment of grid hardware with particular attention being necessary when installing software, whether commercial or not. However bearing in mind special constraints like payment of fees, commercial, legal and financial aspects are usually better dealt with centrally.

The foundations of such an organization rest, therefore, on the fact that any contributed software needs to be structured following a service-oriented approach, which is the basic concept of the service oriented architecture, which expects that every application has to be designed to support interoperable machine-to-machine interaction over a whole network. In addition, all of the programs defined as web services have to expose one or more interfaces, described in a machine-processable format called *Web Services Description Language* (WSDL, www.w3.org/TR/wsdl/), to interact with other web services. The interaction takes place in a manner prescribed by *Simple Object Access Protocol* (SOAP, www.w3.org/TR/soap/) and its messages are typically conveyed through the HTTP protocol with an XML serialization in conjunction with other web-related standards.

The main purpose of a web service approach is to provide some functionalities implemented by a user, either an individual or an organization, on behalf of all the other users. In particular, the person or the institution providing the appropriate software to implement a particular service is the provider while the person or the institution wishing to make use of a provider's web service is the requester. Consequently, the monitoring activities associated with the application of a Web or a grid service approach allows regulation of the internal and external activities of the VO through a process of credit assignment and redemption. This means that members can receive credits, called "terms of exchange credits" or *toec*, for the resources they make available to COMPCHEM and can redeem them either by acquiring services from the VO or by receiving financial payment.

A key task of COMPCHEM of great value for teaching and learning activities is the design and the implementation of the so called *grid empowered molecular simulator* (GEMS) on the production grid of EGEE. The first prototype version of GEMS (GEMS.0) has been designed and implemented as a demo application in the NA4 work-package (EGEE, egeena4.lal.in2p3.fr) of the EGEE project starting from the molecular dynamics engine of Simulator of Molecular Beam Experiments SIMBEX.

The aim of GEMS is to provide the users with a simulation environment suitable for the study of molecular structures and processes and therefore to offer an innovative tool to generate new knowledge. It is basically articulated in four main steps: The calculation, if needed, of the ab-initio values of the potential energy surface (PES), the fitting, where needed, of the calculated ab-initio values to an appropriate functional form, the integration, when needed, of the nuclei dynamics equations and the final statistical treatment to provide experimental measurable and related microscopic interpretations (Storchi, Taramtelli, & Laganà, 2006).

Various ab-initio approaches can be adopted to calculate accurate potential energy values. Most of them are already embodied into commercial suites of codes, other ready to use packages. Most of these programs follow high level post Hartree Fock approaches and are complemented by sets of tools for further analytical, graphical and statistical treatments of the numerical outcomes. Two types of approach using either classical or quantum mechanics can be followed to integrate the molecular dynamics equations.

The classical mechanics approach is based on the integration over time of the Hamiltonian, or other equivalent sets of equations of motion, for all the atoms of the considered molecular system (trajectories). A large number of trajectories are integrated to provide an appropriate set of initial conditions. From the trajectory outcomes dynamics (like cross sections, rate coefficients and energy, and vector distributions) and thermodynamics (like pressure, enthalpy and entropy) properties can be evaluated. In passing it should be mentioned that for several educational purposes this is the most effective and the most intuitive approach (Baraglia et al., 1992).

The quantum mechanical approach is based on the integration of either the time dependent or the time independent Schrödinger equation. In the former, once determined, the initial form of the wavepacket associated with the reactants, or possibly with a transition state intermediate, for the desired initial, or intermediate, state, a time propagation of the wavepacket is performed by monitoring, if required, at each integration step the coefficients of the wave packet mapping on a reference configuration of reactants (for total) or products (for state to state probabilities). In the latter, because of the elimination of the time variable, the propagation is performed along a suitable spatial continuity variable (the reaction coordinate) on which a set of coupled differential equations averaged over all the other coordinates depend. When rate coefficients instead of probabilities or cross sections are needed one can adopt direct methods and avoid the calculations of detailed state to state or state specific quantities.

GEMS is the computational engine of VMSLab-G and several teaching and learning units concerned with basic concepts of molecular structures, chemical processes, material sciences, environmental modeling and aerothermics simulations.

A vision for the future: The European virtual academy of chemistry

The virtual campus experience

Most of the virtual organization and virtual reality features illustrated in the previous sections of this chapter are also integrated in the virtual campus project coordinated by The University of Helsinki, Finland, carried out in synergy with ECTN for the chemistry curriculum. The University of Helsinki, in fact, leads a consortium managing the Finnish Virtual University (FVU) project which offers selected e-learning products from various member universities (including courses and laboratories) for use by students and teachers.

The consortium supports 20 Finnish universities in their aims to harmonize the information systems, to develop compatible practices, to allow students, teachers, researchers and administrators to share useful products and practices, to provide national support and databases for on-line courses and counselling activities by providing support for these activities on the Web. A first level of shared support provided by the project are the services offered by the "Centre for ICT Education" which acts as a development unit and a coordination engine for the use of advanced ICT in teaching and learning.

The centre has specialized in creating a virtual community among teachers, students and technicians fostering the development of contents, technologies and pedagogical strategies in education. This allows students and teachers to freely use the facilities necessary to produce and use e-learning products. Products include VLEs, LMSs, digital educational material, a videoconferencing support service and training, managerial support and strategic planning. The coordination structure involves dedicated experts from the various campuses who promote local training and technical support activities.

In the particular case of the teaching and learning of chemistry and molecular sciences where ECTN has been very active, significant efforts have been devoted to building a VLE able to support autonomous and personal learning paths in the laboratory through an ad-hoc web interface called NetLab. The interface provides instructions, including animation illustrating molecular processes, on how to carry out organic syntheses, to deal safely with equipment and materials in the laboratory and to write reports. For instance, NetLab provides 3D models to illustrate potential synthesis problems together with electronic feedback.

Other services provided by NetLab include the activation of teaching supports for e-learning processes, personal study plans, motivation of students, visualization of the microscopic processes, interaction between lectures and practical work, illustrations of the laboratory procedures including physical aspects of instrumentation, safety measures and economic implications, planning personal schedules or resources, and searching for chemical information.

A particularly innovative aspect of these services is the use of the IQ (Intelligent Questionnaire, www.virtuaaliyliopisto.fi/iq_etusivu_eng.asp) tools which are intelligent ICT tools for assessing the performances of both individual learners and groups. In particular, *IQ Learn* is the tool for assessing and developing learners' individual qualities and learning skills based on self regulating theory and *IQ Team* is the tool for assessing and developing group processes for collaborative learning and knowledge creation. They are made up of an interactive test bank with three questionnaire sets for students' self-evaluation, a tutoring set with a hypertext structure for each sub-component, tutoring tools for driving the students towards self-regulation with related guidelines for teachers, and a learning diary with a collection of learners' experiences and test profiles. Further details about this project have been published (Virtanen, Niemi, Nevgi, Raehalme, & Launonen, 2003).

Upper layers of virtuality for a teaching and learning virtual organizations in chemistry

The exploitation of the innovative features of grid VOs to develop a specific high level generalized virtual campus, let us call it European Virtual Academy (EVA), for teaching and learning in chemistry open to ECTN activities and members is not only an interesting perspective, it is also a central objective in ECTN's mission. The purpose of EVA for chemistry would be to share the distributed grid platform as an open computing infrastructure among chemistry teachers and students and to share as well manware, the teachers and students themselves, educational tools and contents (e.g. teaching and learning units) which can be based and maintained on any site and computer linked to EVA while being, at the same time, equally well accessible from all the other sites within the organization. In other words in EVA emphasis will be put in generalizing open science approaches in which joint enterprise, mutual engagement and shared repertoires are the common asset.

To proceed with the development of EVA, several aspects such as members/services agreements, usage policies and sustainability have to be considered as well as the restructuring of all applications previously developed in MUTALC to enable them to be accessed on the grid. This means that COMPCHEM itself could act as an incubator for a new teaching and learning dedicated VO that we will call TELCHEM, Teaching and Learning in CHEMistry.

After all, various types of activities bearing different levels of virtuality and already implemented in COMPCHEM can be borrowed for teaching and learning purposes. This is the case for both MVR and HVR tools. The first level of virtuality is, in fact, that of the nano world where *virtual* refers to atoms, molecules and related experiments can be managed as real objects at a macro level. The second level of virtuality is that of laboratories, teaching units and classes, that is the human dimension *virtual* objects. These are sometimes merely based on text documents though, as already mentioned, multimedia technologies are becoming increasingly popular and have made virtual educational objects more and more realistic thanks to hypertexts, videos, audios, animated materials and rendering devices which already involve the synergistic efforts of different experts. The third level of virtuality of key relevance here is that of the organizational dimension, in which *virtual* refers to the organization, that is to geographical and juridical aspects, which at present remains the least developed one.

TELCHEM: Services to start with

The TELCHEM VO will embrace the mission of taking care of the whole process in which knowledge is either imparted from a tutor, a knowledge provider or an expert of any kind to a student or indeed to any to knowledge recipient who at a certain point becomes active and starts a learning process in which he/she defines and perhaps designs and implements the necessary tools. In all cases on-line tutoring may have to satisfy requirements such as broadband Internet access, audio microphone and speaker, a shared screen commonly referred to as a whiteboard on which the student and the tutor can write and a digital pen mouse (for writing, drawing and highlighting text or dealing with mathematical equations), rather than a web-cam or digital video camera for physical demonstrations or high quality visual feedbacks.

Tutoring services typically offered on-line by TELCHEM should be based on the integration of all software components of e-learning (instructional, demonstrative, collaborative and individual research) in which instructions and demonstrations are provided by tutors, collaboration is promoted through on-line discussion or chat group with peers, and individual research is developed through teaching materials made available to the students separately from the on-line instructional components. This also requires a video and audio real time service. Video is essential to provide visual feedback to learning and audio is needed for ease-of-use without incurring additional phone bills and the inconvenience of dealing with two separate devices. Typically on-line audio based on *voice-over-IP* (VOIP), a mature Internet technology, will have to be employed.

Teachers need the ability to understand a subject well enough to convey its essence to each new generation of students: The goal is to establish a sound knowledge base on which students will be able to develop new learning as they are exposed to different life experiences. Some courses will therefore be designed for teachers to provide them with the necessary skills to operate in this environment. Course materials will be certified and archived in a common shared and distributed digital library or database. To this end an intermediate approach between that of the prototype EoL LMS devoted to the development of new technologies for ECTN activities and that chosen for EChemTest devoted to the provision of a professional service through the commercial Question Mark Perception software is better followed. As in the case of the construction of the EChemTest libraries and in the build up of an experimental teaching and learning units' repository a wise choice is the open-source product Moodle (moodle.org).

In particular, Moodle is being used to build the data bank of questions for the intensive course of the European Master in theoretical chemistry and computational modelling in which a large percentage of ECTN members with an interest in computational chemistry are actively involved. The question bank will be used to provide an EchemTest at level 4. Moodle includes facilities for Web publishing, equation typesetting, content management, adaptive pre-labs and lessons, activity locking, parameterized and hierarchical homework banks, flash and shareable content object reference model (SCORM) learning objects, assessment, detailed student tracking, blogging, podcasting, and record-keeping. For this reason it has also been chosen as the production tool by several universities that are members of ECTN. Moreover, the Moodle's chemistry-specific features exploited to carry out assessments and exams are available as third-party plugins. This is the case with JMOL (www.jmol.org) an open-source Java viewer for chemical structures in 3D with features for chemicals, crystals, materials and biomolecules. Molecular structures can easily be inserted into text using a filter that automatically converts a simple link to a .pdb file into an embedded viewer. JMol scripts can be passed to the viewer by typing JMOLSCRIPT{} keyword immediately after the link. Moreover, JMol models can also be offered as standalone resources.

In addition, students can draw molecular structures in exams and homework using the JME (Java Molecule Editor) question type. The question is graded by matching the student and key structures as *Simplified Molecular Input Line Entry System* (SMILES, www.daylight.com/smiles/) strings. SMILES is a simple, yet comprehensive, chemical language in which molecules and reactions can be specified using ASCII characters representing atom and bond symbols. There will still be a requirement for a Coordinating Service to provide linking of e-Learning systems, managing and disseminating of information and best practices and for providing a support mechanism for trainers and users. Such coordination systems could provide trainers and users with uniform access to locally unavailable and prohibitively expensive to duplicate materials.

TELCHEM: Sustainability

In order to be sustainable the TELCHEM VO will need to develop a community economy whose main asset will be research and development in teaching and learning. As a matter of fact, in TELCHEM, research and development in teaching and learning will be considered as a resource in its own right independent of its short term productivity, though not independent of its efficiency and efficacy. For this reason research and development in teaching and learning should not only be treated as a specially protected area for free circulation of ideas and innovations but it should also be supported financially regardless of the revenue it generates.

Contributions to research and development are often evaluated on the basis of regular internal reports and articles in international scientific journals. This will also apply to TELCHEM though particular emphasis should be placed on the stimulation and creation of new ideas in teaching and learning as well as on innovation. To this end the design and development of tools to evaluate the cost of implementing and validating developments that start with existing products will be particularly favoured.

In this respect, *toecs* from a specific budget will be assigned on the basis of the importance that members of the community give to such research and development activities as a key manifestation of community values. This can then be used as an incentive to stimulate and encourage valuable contributions including knowledge gained from failures, failure recovery and retrieval of lost information as research activities. Specific credit will also be given to education, training, dissemination and marketing aimed at making the VO a true knowledge community.

For this reason, in conjunction with a web service approach, also a collaborative service aimed at managing credits will be implemented. Indeed, the goal of this service is that of considering several elements (such as the user's reputation, the quality of the user's activities, the results obtained, the kind and the number of resources managed, the support offered to the VO, the stable and/or innovative services carried out, the use of them and the related feedback) to implement one or more policies concerning the *toecs* assignment for stimulating the user's activity within the VO.

Conclusions

This chapter has attempted to illustrate the evolution of ICT to support teaching and learning by taking as example the activities carried out by ECTN (and in particular by its MUTALC working group) in this field. This has involved an analysis of the efforts made to develop ubiquity and virtuality in teaching and learning activities and to adopt a higher level of abstraction in related contents and methods. From this perspective, the use of knowledge management systems has been promoted and several experiences have been conducted to develop web and integrated systems assisting the users from the beginning to the end of the teaching and learning process.

To this end the use of appropriate ontologies and the integration of the various open operations within a robust security model have been examined. This has led on to a discussion of the introduction of machine understandable metadata in a web environment and in e-learning systems (Berners-Lee & Miller, 2002).

The rapid evolution of new technologies able to provide a complete data management solution for data intensive applications and grid infrastructures for scientific elaborations has led to the possibility of considering teaching and learning as a grid empowered service. The organizational impact of these conceptual and technological evolutions has also prompted the development of virtual organizations gathering geographically dispersed scientists and fostering new research approaches in this information age thus paving the way for a new more global telematic approach to European higher education and encouraging ECTN to refocus its mission towards promoting the development of a European virtual academy.

Acknowledgements

The authors wish to thank the members of the MUTALC (ECTN) and ELCHEM (D23 COST Chemistry Action) Working Groups and, in particular, J. Fröhlich, E. Varella, and K. Wähälä for stimulating discussions and part of the material illustrated in this chapter. Thanks are also due to the EU for financial support (through ECTN and COST grants) and B. Byers for revising the manuscript.

Comments

In May 2007 Stefano Riganelli moved from the University of Perugia to Dow Europe GmbH. His contribution to this chapter represents the personal opinion of the author

References

Ames, A. L., Nadeau, D. R., & Moreland, J. L. (1997). *The VRML 2.0 Sourcebook.* Hoboken: Wiley Computer Publishing.

Baraglia, R., Ferrini, R., Laforenza, D., Perego, R., Laganà, A., & Gervasi, O. (1992). A massively parallel approach to the quasiclassical reactive scattering. *Journal of Mathematical Chemistry, 11*, 1-11.

Barak, M. (2007). Transition from traditional to ICT-enhanced learning environments in undergraduate chemistry courses. *Computers and Education, 48*, 30-43.

Berners-Lee, T., & Miller, E. (2002). The semantic web lifts off. *ERCIM News -W3C, 51.*

Chervenak, A., Foster, I., Kesselman, C., Salisbury, C., & Tuecke, S. (1999). *The data grid: Towards an architecture for the distributed management and analysis of large scientific datasets.* Retrieved January 05, 2009, citeseer.ist.psu.edu/ chervenak99data.html.

COST (2000). *Action D23 - Metachem.* Retrieved January 05, 2009, from www.cost.esf.org/index.php?id=189&action_number=D23.

COST (2006). *Action D37 - Grid computing in chemistry: GRIDCHEM.* Retrieved January 05, 2009, from www.cost.esf.org/index.php?id=189&action_number=D37.

COST (2009). *COST: Chemistry and molecular sciences and technologies.* Retrieved January 05, 2009, from www.cost.esf.org/chemistry/.

Davies, J., Fensel, D., & Van Harmelen, F. (2003). *Towards the semantic web: Ontology-driven knowledge management.* Chicester: Wiley.

Dori, Y. J., & Barak, M. (2001). Virtual and physical molecular modelling: Fostering model perception and spatial understanding. *Educational Technology & Society, 4*, 61-72.

Dori, Y. J., & Barak, M. (2003). A web-based chemistry course as a means to foster freshman learning. *Journal of Chemical Education, 80*, 1084-1092.

Dori, Y. J., Belcher, J., Bessette, M., Danziger, M., McKinney, A., & Hult, E. (2003). Technology for active learning. *Materials today*, 44-49.

EC (2009). *Leonardo da Vinci programme.* Retrieved January 05, 2009, from ec.europa.eu/education/programmes/llp/leonardo/index_en.html.

Edelson, D. C., Gordin, D. N., & Pea, R. D. (1999). Addressing the challenges of inquiry-based learning through technology and curriculum design. *The Journal of the Learning Sciences, 8*, 391-450.

Foster, I., Kesselman, C., & Tuecke, S. (2001). The anatomy of the grid: Enabling scalable virtual organizations. *International Journal of High Performance Computing*

Applications, 15, 200-222.

Gervasi, O., Catanzani, R., Riganelli, A., & Laganà, A. (2005). Integrating learning and assessment using the semantic web. *Lecture Notes in Computer Science, 3480*, 921-927.

Gervasi, O., & Laganà, A. (2004a). EoL: A web-based distance assessment system. *Lecture Notes in Computer Science, 3044*, 854-862.

Gervasi, O., & Laganà, A. (2004b). SIMBEX: A portal for the a priori simulation of crossed beam experiments. *Future Generation Computer Systems, 20*, 703-715.

Gilbert, J. K. (2005a). Visualization: A metacognitive skill in science and science education. In: J. K. Gilbert (Ed.), *Visualization in Science Education* (pp. 9-27). Dordrecht: Springer.

Gilbert, J. K. (Ed.) (2005b). *Visualization in science education*. Dordrecht: Springer.

Habraken, C. L. (1996). Perceptions of chemistry: Why is the common perception of chemistry, the most visual of sciences, so distorted. *Journal of Science Education and Technology, 5*, 193-201.

Hakerem, G., Dobrynina, G., & Shore, L. (1993). The effect of interactive, three dimensional, high speed simulations on high school science students' conceptions of the molecular structure of water. *Paper presented at the Meeting of the National Association of Research in Science Teaching, Atlanta, United States*.

Harasim, L., Hiltz, S., Teles, L., & Turoff, M. (1995). *Learning networks: A field guide to teaching and learning on-line*. Cambridge: MIT Press.

Johnstone, A. H. (1991). Why is science difficult to learn? Things are seldom what they seem. *Journal of Computer Assisted Learning, 7*(7), 75-83.

Jonassen, D. H., Hernandez-Serrano, J., & Choi, I. (2000). Integrating constructivism and learning technologies. In: J. M. Spector & T. M. Anderson (Eds.), *Integrated and holistic perspectives on learning, instruction and technology: Understanding complexity* (pp. 103-128). Dordrecht: Springer.

Kozma, R., & Russell, J. W. (2005). Students becoming chemists: developing representational competence. In: J. K. Gilbert (Ed.), *Visualization in Science Education* (pp. 121-145). Dordrecht: Springer.

Laganà, A. (2007). Tutti in laboratorio (virtuale): Rivisitiamo una esperienza già fatta per capirne a fondo la portata. *GREEN 3*, 12-13.

Laganà, A., Riganelli, A., & Gervasi, O. (2006). On the structuring of the computational chemistry virtual organization COMPCHEM. *Lecture Notes in Computer Science, 3980*, 665-674.

Laganà, A., Riganelli, A., Gervasi, O., Yates, P., Wähälä, K., Salzer, R., Varella, E., & Fröhlich, J. (2005). ELCHEM: A metalaboratory to develop grid e-learning technologies and services for chemistry. *Lecture Notes in Computer Science, 3480*, 938-946.

Linn, M. C. (2003). Technology and science education: Starting points, research programs, and trends. *International Journal of Science Education, 25*, 727-758.

Microsoft (2009). *NET framework developer center*. Retrieved January 05, 2009, from msdn2.microsoft.com/it-it/netframework/default(en-us).aspx.

Mueller, J., Wood, E., Willoughby, T., Ross, C., & Specht, J. (2008). Identifying discriminating variables between teachers who fully integrate computers and teachers with limited integration. *Computers and Education, 51*, 1523-1537.

Riganelli, A., Gervasi, O., Laganà, A., & Fröhlich, J. (2005). Virtual chemical laboratories and their management on the web. *Lecture Notes in Computer Science, 3480*, 905-912.

Rossi, E. (2008). Data archive for material multiscale simulations. *Project submitted to FP7*, INFO-2008-1.2.2.

Russell, J. W., Kozma, R. B., Jones, T., Wykoff, J., Marx, N., & Davis, J. (1997). Use of simultaneous-synchronized macroscopic, microscopic, and symbolic representations to enhance the teaching and learning of chemical concepts. *Journal of Chemical Education, 74*, 330-334.

Scemama, A., Monari, A., Angeli, C., Borini, S., Evangelisti, S., & Rossi, E. (2008). Common format for quantum chemistry interoperability: Q5Cost format and library. *Lecture Notes in Computer Science, 5072*, 1094-1107.

Schellens, T., & Valcke, M. (2006). Fostering knowledge construction in university students through asynchronous discussion groups. *Computers and Education, 46,* 349-370.

Sherif, K. (2002). Virtual learning networks in higher education: The case of Egypt's regional IT institute. *Journal of Global Information Management, 8*(3), 34-41.

Solsona, N., Izquierdo, M., & De Jong, O. (2003). Exploring the development of students' conceptual profiles of chemical change. *International Journal of Science Education, 25,* 3-12.

Storchi, L., Tarantelli, F., & Laganà, A. (2006). Computing molecular energy surfaces on a grid. *Lecture Notes in Computer Science, 3980,* 675-683.

Urhahne, D., Nick, S., & Schanze, S. (in press). The effect of three-dimensional simulations on the understanding of chemical structures and their properties. *Research in Science Education.*

Van Joolingen, W. R., De Jong, T., & Dimitrakopoulout, A. (2007). Issues in computer supported inquiry learning in science. *Journal of Computer Assisted Learning, 23,* 111-119.

Virtanen, P., Niemi, H., Nevgi, A., Raehalme, O., & Launonen, A. (2003). *Towards strategic learning skills through self-assessment and tutoring in web-based environment.* Retrieved January 05, 2009, from www.leeds.ac.uk/educol/ documents/00003227.htm.

Williamson, V. M., & Abraham, M. R. (1995). The effects of computer animation on the particulate mental models of college chemistry students. *Journal of Research in Science Teaching, 32,* 521-534.

Wilson, R. (2004). *The role of ontologies in teaching and learning.* TechWatch report, JISC, Ago.

Wu, H. K., & Shah, P. (2004). Exploring visuospatial thinking in chemistry learning. *Science Education, 88,* 465-492.

Learning from Industry and Employment

KEITH ADAMS
University of Ulster, United Kingdom (retired)

LEO GROS
Hochschule Fresenius, Germany

RAY WALLACE
Nottingham Trent University, United Kingdom

The focus of this chapter is on the learning benefits of activities outside the lecture hall centred on the world of work. In particular we examine the merits of a period of industrial placement and propose a model for its successful integration into the syllabus. Apart from providing practical experience with particular laboratory techniques, industrial placement has considerable potential to develop a broad range of personal skills which are difficult to incorporate into a conventional academic course. Anecdotal evidence presented here indicates that students recognize the value of industrial placement even several years after completing their studies.

Introduction

The needs of learners in Higher Education are changing constantly along with changes in science, the economy and society. However there are some features of acquiring skills and competences in science, and especially in chemistry, which are intrinsic to the subject. These are seen as key to the subject producing a well-rounded graduate.

Among the generic competences learners should acquire for an interdisciplinary scientific and a globalised economic environment (Cooke, Gros, Horz, & Zeller, 2005) we mention:

· Social competences such as working in inter- and multidisciplinary teams, and communication of facts, results and problems in oral and written form.

Chapter consultant: Iwona Maciejowska, Jagiellonian University, Kraków, Poland

I. Eilks and B. Byers (Eds.). Innovative Methods in Teaching and Learning Chemistry in Higher Education, pp. 191-214. © *2009 RSC Publishing.*

- Retrieval and evaluation of information, and transforming facts into knowledge.
- Holistic understanding of processes in research and development, production, marketing and sales related to the field of chemistry, including cost-benefit, project management and quality control issues.

Core competencies which are needed from a student's point of view are:

- Sound knowledge of fundamental facts and of molecular relationships and models that help to classify and organize subject matter knowledge in chemistry.
- A set of reliable and robust problem solving and experimental skills which are transferable to new questions and fields of research and development.
- Intuition and imagination which are indispensable to figure out what happens, what could happen and what could be made possible.

Higher education is not an island. Learners in our universities are no longer a small minority, mainly trained for basic research in a university environment. With increased demand for competent chemists for a wide variety of tasks, the above mentioned generic skills and competences have become more important. Some of these skills and competences are best learned in context, i.e. in situations and at places where they are used in the day to day work of a chemist. Students benefit from this because not only do they acquire generic skills but also their intrinsic motivation is likely to increase as a result of working in an industrial or research and development environment; their practical work is applied in context, they produce useful results, and they work together with experienced colleagues.

Chemistry is and will continue to be a science and a subject that requires sound practical experimental skills. In the majority of cases, university chemistry tuition still employs a 'classical approach' where the focus is on phenomena, their classification and theoretical/model descriptions, including advanced problem solving. Their relevance to the industrial environment is likely to be mentioned only occasionally. As far as theoretical understanding and skills are concerned, one might think this is sufficient. When it comes to using these skills in their applied context and a working environment, university lectures and lab classes can contribute examples and simulation but cannot reproduce the chemistry that would be performed in the industrial context. Getting to know where, how and why chemical experiments are applied to real life situations can inspire students. It gives them a deeper understanding of the rationale, cost-benefit ratio, scope and limitations of experiments and quality assurance aspects. Moreover, many experimental procedures used in industry are not normally performed in university teaching laboratories which often do not have the appropriate equipment to demonstrate the wide variety of research and development methods currently used in the private sector.

Introducing an industrial dimension to on-campus teaching

There are well-established ways of introducing industrial aspects into *on-campus* teaching as well as to expose students to them in an *industrial environment*. Although the main focus of this chapter is on *off-campus* learning strategies, there are a number of 'half-way house' approaches which bring the industrial world into academia, enriching the curriculum.

For example

- Integrating product-specific industrial testing methods into lab courses, borrowing original equipment from companies and using their protocols, such as
    - Working with a patient dialysis apparatus, measurement of the pressure/flow characteristics of dialysis units.
    - Evaluation of the product performance of super absorbers used in hygiene products such as diapers.
    - Devising group mini-projects which centre on certain aspects of commercial processes e.g. waste disposal and pollution, health and safety.
- On-campus in-house companies (e.g. science parks) associated with the university
    - Involving students in research and development work being commercially developed.
    - Allowing students to operate as part of a team alongside permanent employees.
- Industrial site visits
    - Allowing students to come into contact with the equipment that is actually used on an industrial scale.
    - Showing students how the other sciences such as engineering are involved in production processes.
    - Getting students to write reports on industrial visits and to make group presentations.
- Participation of industrial chemists in undergraduate education
    - Involving them in curriculum development and accreditation procedures.
    - Teaching specialised topics related to industry and commerce.
    - Talking to students about graduate employment and the expectations of industry.

Off-campus learning: Industrial placements

Universities and other higher educational institutions offer industrial placements in many different forms. The term *industrial* has connotations of a manufacturing environment but most institutions use the expression to indicate any form of work experience and this is the interpretation used here. Perhaps the term *work-based learning* or *internship* as is commonly used in the United States would be preferable because it does not limit the type of work experience. Participation in work placements (all disciplines) by graduates in Europe is relatively common. In 2000 this averaged around

55% of students but there were quite large differences between individual countries (see Table 1).

Table 1: Graduates who participated in work placements/ internships in year 2000 (Little & Harvey, 2007)

Netherlands	86 %	Austria	45 %
Germany	80 %	Switzerland	43 %
Finland	79 %	Czech Republic	36 %
France	72 %	United Kingdom	29 %
Norway	59 %	Italy	21 %
Spain	56 %		

Industrial placements all have one thing in common – the students spend time away from their academic study to undertake work-based practical experience in a related area. A survey of various programmes of study which include placements in a variety of European countries has been published by Cooke, Gros, Horz, and Zeller, (2005). At one extreme the duration can be as little as a period of two to three months during the summer, in between academic years, while at the other, students spend a whole academic year with an employer. Such academic programmes are often called 'sandwich' courses because the year of employment is preceded and followed by academic study. Some sandwich courses have two shorter periods of work experience each flanked by academic study – so called 'thin' sandwich courses. These are particularly appropriate where the course leads to an award by a professional body which requires 'hands-on' experience but which needs academic input before it can be achieved. For example some courses in the health professions need to integrate academic study closely with practical experience in a hospital. Clearly in this case the placement needs to be an integral and compulsory element of the course. However, in the case of chemistry courses, placement where available, is likely to be optional. We examine below some of the features of the different forms of work placement.

Format of placements (Little & Harvey, 2006)

Where placements are compulsory they are normally fully integrated into the academic programme. This implies that the overseeing quality assurance agencies will require that such placements be monitored and assessed. Sometimes, especially for a year-long placement, a separate qualification such as a Diploma in Industrial Studies is awarded for its successful completion. There may also be a requirement for the university to involve employers formally in the design of the placement programme. For compulsory placements, provision has to be made for those students who are unable to gain a placement. Such provision can simply be the advancement of the student to the next year of the degree without the linked work-based qualification. Another option is for the university itself to resource in-house placements within its research groups. Compulsory placements require substantial commitment by the university to resource academic and clerical staff to underpin their organization. However such commitment can be rewarded by increased funding through student fees and state grants and by increased popularity and student applications for the courses. For example in the United Kingdom the placement year is state-funded at 0.5 of the rate for full-time attending students and students commonly pay 0.5 of tuition fees for the placement year (Wilson, 2004). In recent years there has been a trend for the difference in funding to fall even further so that financially it pays in more ways than one to have a placement year. While the issue of fees is different in the various European countries, at the end of the day education costs normally fall predominantly on the government of that country. While a student is in industry these costs are shifted in the main from the education provider to the employer.

In deciding the duration of a work placement the administrative consequences as well as the educational value need to be considered. It can be difficult to persuade employers to hire students for 3 months or less since it takes significant resources and time to train students before they become productive employees. A further reason for longer placements is that the employer may want to use students to cover holidays and other absences of permanent staff. From an educational standpoint a longer placement is arguably more beneficial than a shorter one. There is also the important pragmatic reason for a year-long placement in that it fits neatly into the academic calendar and is likely to be easier to incorporate into the academic programme than a shorter placement.

Many universities offer non-compulsory or optional placements. The commitment of institutions to such placements is variable. At one extreme there is minimal commitment: The student is provided with a list of companies to approach, there is little or no academic support, the percentage of students gaining placement is small, and successful students essentially take a year out from their studies with little or no academic contact. At the other extreme, the percentage of students on placement is high, support of university staff is substantial and contact is maintained with students during their placement. Some courses have moved from compulsory to non-compulsory placements for various reasons, one of which is the difficulty in obtaining placements due to competition from other institutions (Little & Harvey, 2006). An important consideration for students who pursue optional placements is that their academic progression becomes out of step with that of their non-placement peers and they graduate a year later.

Paid and unpaid placements

The obvious advantage to the student of a paid placement is that there is a welcome source of income to help payment of tuition fees. Other less obvious advantages include a greater commitment by the employer to provide tasks which are meaningful, for which the student is accountable, and which are carried out in a disciplined environment. Although it does not follow that the contrary should apply to unpaid placements, in practice both the student and the employer are likely to be less committed if there is no monetary contract. Where students undertake unpaid placements there is often an arrangement where they can be released for a day or more each week to do paid but unrelated work (Little & Harvey, 2006). In our experience many unpaid placements are in research, at universities, government laboratories and charities.

Type of employer

Employers who take placement students vary considerably both in terms of size and activity and within any particular cohort of placement students, individuals will encounter widely different experiences. The motives of employers for taking placement students are also diverse. For example many of the larger pharmaceutical companies have well defined placement programmes, recruiting significant numbers of students on 12 month contracts each year. The employer trawls internally for suitable research projects for students to undertake and then circulates universities with details. Competition for these places is strong because they are well paid and conditions are excellent. Students are treated as regular employees and commonly given assistance in finding living accommodation, provided with formal staff induction and given access to the company's sport and recreation facilities. In addition students can often avail themselves of staff development courses. Such companies seem to act out of a corporate desire to collaborate with the education sector rather than to add to their productive work force. Many use this scheme as a way of assessing the potential of students as future employees: They have known them for a significant period of time and are able to assess their qualifications as well as their social skills. A further benefit is that students tend to have a refreshing influence within the sections where they are placed.

At the other end of the scale, smaller companies are more likely to take placement students as a way of supplementing their workforce in a cost effective manner. The student is 'an extra pair of hands' and may be required to carry out a variety of tasks, some possibly quite routine and repetitive. The work priorities of the company may change during the year and it may be that students are occasionally required to carry out tasks which bear little relation to their academic studies. Students are therefore more likely to be directly exposed to the competitive business environment when working in a smaller company than for a larger multinational business.

Learning outcomes of industrial placement

Much has been written about the supposed benefits of industrial placement and there seems to be broad consensus (e.g. Little & Harvey, 2006; Ahmed, Brown, Crawford, Haworth, & Holdich, 2006) that the major impact of placement is the development and enhancement of *personal transferable skills*. These are defined as those skills which are acquired in one situation but which are useful when transferred to a different situation e.g. a different career (Fallows & Stevens, 2000). It cannot be assumed that students will gain increased knowledge of their degree subject during their work placement (except in the rather specialized situation of a work placement in a university research group). However, very often students will develop technical expertise in one or more practical techniques. In Table 2 we list the main skills and attributes which are likely to be enhanced and their potential mechanisms of acquisition.

Table 2: Main skills and attributes to be enhanced and their potential mechanisms of acquisition

Skill	Potential work-based mechanisms for development
Oral communication	Frequent discussions with work supervisor and work colleagues, both face to face and by telephone.
Written communication	Written reports often required by employer; university may require reports; written communication by e-mail to work colleagues.
Language skills	In the case of placements abroad: both oral and written communication skills in a foreign language.
Teamwork	Requirement to work collaboratively with others, often from different backgrounds; sensitivity to the needs and feelings of others.
Numeracy	Increasing awareness of the significance of numerical results, of accuracy, source of errors and of units of measurement.
Taking responsibility	Taking 'ownership' of experimental results; being accountable to others; development of authoritative role.
Disciplined working	Need to attend punctually and to meet the demands of the job; need to conform to the rules of the workplace including all aspects of health and safety.
Self organization	Planning of tasks to make best use of time and resources.
Adaptability and flexibility	Making the transition from an academic environment; living away from home; encountering different cultures; being self sufficient.
IT and computing	Word processing; need to process results e.g. with spreadsheets; use of databases; computer control of instruments; computer aided visual presentations; e-mail.
Networking	Seeking out of others in different departments in order to perform tasks and gain information; potential interface with company clients.
Showing initiative	Proposing a better way of doing things; foreseeing tasks that need to be performed; making suggestions for health and safety.
Gaining confidence	Being able to perform to a good standard; receiving praise and encouragement from supervisor.
Career planning	Appraisal of career opportunities within or outside the organization through liaison with others.
Awareness of environmental issues	Critical appraisal of waste disposal and recycling procedures.

Assessment of work-based learning

Universities have devised various schemes for the assessment of work-based learning and there appears to be a fair amount of agreement. As indicated above, a year long placement is usually assessed for a university award such as the Diploma in Industrial Studies (DIS) (Wright, date unknown; Anon, 2005; Armstrong, McMahon-Beattie, & Greenan, 2005; Murray & Wallace, 2003). Bachelor programmes developed in European countries to comply with the Bologna process may designate a degree with compulsory placement, home or abroad, as *Applied Chemistry* (Gros, 2009). Much of the pioneering work on work-based learning has been in the engineering disciplines particularly at the University of Loughborough, United Kingdom. The principles established in that area are now applied to a wide range of subjects. Science students are likely to be placed in a much greater range of work situations than engineering students and the assessment needs to take account of this. The typical features of the assessment for a science-based DIS are outlined below.

Tripartite agreement

Three parties are key stakeholders in any industrial placement: The university, the student and the employer. A document outlining the structure of the placement year, how the DIS is assessed and the roles and responsibilities of the university, the employer and the student should be prepared and agreed before the placement begins. The employer should appoint an *industrial supervisor* and the university an *academic supervisor* who is normally based within the student's academic department. Their roles should be clearly defined as they will be responsible for the student throughout the placement. In the case of LEONARDO or ERASMUS grants for a placement abroad, such tripartite agreements are compulsory.

Visits

The *academic supervisor* visits the student at least once and preferably twice, during the period of placement. The (first) visit should take place early in the placement to ensure a good start. An efficient means of communication needs to be established between all three parties. During the visit the supervisor should informally interview the student which may last up to an hour. The interview should include an assessment of the development of the key skill areas (see Table 2), preferably using a criterion-referenced grid. For example in the area of communication the interviewer may ask the student to describe the tasks he/she is carrying out. The student's response is allocated to one of the following categories: *Communicates clearly without the need for prompting; needs some prompting to aid communication; extensive questioning required to clarify response; barely able to describe tasks.* Such interviews should always be conducted in the spirit of helping students to reflect on the opportunities available for their personal development.

Student's written reports

Students should be required to maintain a logbook or diary of their activities throughout the placement. This is subject to evaluation by the *academic supervisor* during visits and at the end of the placement. In addition the student should prepare two extended reports (up to 5000 words) the first of which might focus on an academic topic directly related to the student's work tasks. The industrial supervisor may well suggest topics. The report is assessed in a similar way to coursework essays and should be available midway through the placement. The second report, produced before return to the university, should ideally cover three areas: An account of the business of the employer, including its operating environment; a description of the tasks/projects carried out during the placement; reflective commentary on the skills enhanced during the placement (see Table 2). All reports which contain potentially commercially sensitive information should be cleared with the employer before release.

Industrial supervisor's report

This should be based on a standardized criterion-referenced grid which focuses mainly on personal skills. Provision should also be made for the employer to make freely structured comments about the student's performance. The report should be 'signed-off' by a senior member of staff. Most universities will allow students to see the report and it is important that the employer is aware of this. The employer needs to complete the report at the end of the placement period and return it to a designated person at the university.

Oral presentations

Students should give a formal oral presentation about their placement experiences, based on the content of the final report, to a panel consisting of two or more academic staff and an employer representative. It is preferable to include a member of staff from a different academic department so that there is some consistency of assessment between the various departments. The presentation should be assessed by the panel using a criterion-referenced grid and will take account of the content of the presentation, particularly of the student's reflective commentary, the effectiveness of the presentation and the use of visual aids. It might be appropriate for the panel to ask questions if clarification of a particular issue is needed.

Assessing overall performance

The weighting of each of these assessment components should reflect student effort. For example a reasonable weighting of the components might be:

Supervisors' reports	20%
Student's written reports	55%
Student logbook	10%
Oral presentation	15%

The overall mark for the award of DIS might be set at 50%, while a simple pass mark (needed for progression to the next stage of the course) might be 40%. In addition a condition might be set that the Industrial Supervisor's mark should be at least 40% for the award of DIS.

e-Portfolios (Duffy, Anthony, & Vickers, 2008)

It is self evident that a period of industrial placement can provide the student with a very potent learning experience. If we can encourage the student to continuously *reflect* on that experience it is likely that more meaning will be made of it and the learning will be enriched. An electronic portfolio (see Brouwer & McDonnell in this book) is a computer-based template that provides a framework for recording experiences and achievements. The template tools are designed to stimulate the student's reflective practice i.e. to understand what and how they are learning. As the portfolio is developed, both the student and the tutor can track student progress. Since e-portfolios are an online resource they have much potential to contribute to the placement situation where learning takes place at a distance. E-portfolio's can be incorporated into virtual learning environments (VLE's) such as *WebCT* and *Blackboard* and there are also custom-built packages such as *Profile* (see Brouwer & McDonnell in this book).

Does industrial placement improve degree performance?

According to Wallace (2002), "*.....the rigours and discipline of a work placement can do much to focus the mind, sharpen the organizational skills and improve the work ethos of the individual for return to the university.*" Wallace compared the final results of 195 students who had completed a BSc Chemistry optional sandwich degree at Nottingham Trent University, United Kingdom, for the academic years 1997/1998 through to 2000/2001. While the majority (131) of the students had not pursued the sandwich option, the remaining 64 had undertaken an industrial placement year. It was apparent that the performance of students who had pursued the sandwich option was substantially higher than those who had not; this resulted in a much greater percentage of placement students achieving first and upper second class honours degrees compared to their non-placement counterparts. Wallace also examined the results of students on optional sandwich chemistry degrees from 11 UK universities during the period 1995 – 1998. He concluded that a sandwich student "*...is on average three times more likely to gain a first class honours degree as compared to his/her full-time counterpart.*" While these studies provide compelling evidence of better performance by placement students, they do not shed light on the reasons for the difference in performance. In the absence of further study it cannot necessarily be assumed that the placement year has a beneficial effect on performance. For example the placement process may simply be selecting the better students, either through self selection by the students themselves or by the application procedures applied by the employer. If there is a causal relationship between placement and improved performance and especially if this is linked to the acquisition of generic *personal* skills then this should be evident from studies carried out in other subject areas.

Mandilaras (2004) conducted a statistical study on the performance of students of Economics and Business Economics with Computing, who graduated in 2001 and 2002 at the University of Surrey, United Kingdom. 60% of the students did an industrial placement. He investigated the effect of a number of the students' characteristics on their final results. His results indicated that students who had done the placement increased their chances of getting an upper second class honours degree (i.e. a mark of 60% or over) by 30%. Furthermore a student who had done no placement had a 69% probability of attaining a lower second class honours degree (i.e. a mark of 50 – 59%) compared to a 39% probability for a placement student. Among the reasons he suggested for this improved performance were that industrial placement brought about an increase in maturity, a realization that academic performance is related to professional development, an increase in ambition, reliability and focus, and a greater awareness of the relevance of their academic studies.

Gomez, Lush, and Clements (2004) carried out a study into the performance of 164 undergraduates enrolled in a bioscience degree which had a full-time option of 3 years' duration and a sandwich option (containing a placement year) of 4 years' duration. This group of students graduated in 2001 and 2002. 75% of the group did the placement year and 25% did the full-time option. The authors investigated possible associations between the final degree mark and factors such as (i) the entry qualifications of the student, (ii) performance in earlier years of the course (at the end level 1 and level 2), (iii) gender, and (iv) whether or not the student had undertaken the placement year. The authors were able to demonstrate that there was a strong correlation between the final degree mark and the placement year. There was a nearly 4% advantage in the overall degree mark for students who had carried out placement compared to those who hadn't. The study showed that this improvement was independent of gender. In this particular degree the final year contributed 75% toward the overall mark for the degree. For those degrees where the degree mark is based exclusively on performance in the final year we might expect the beneficial effect of placement to be even greater. In attempting to investigate whether the explanation for the improvement was due to better students (i) selecting the placement option and (ii) gaining more from placement, the authors found that students opting for placement had significantly higher entry qualifications for the degree than those who didn't. However, how well or badly the students performed at level 2 had no significant bearing on the beneficial effect of the placement on the final marks. The authors speculated that the improved laboratory skills of placement students might be one reason for their better results, especially since practical projects contribute substantially to the final mark of bioscience and chemistry degrees. In addition they suggested that the transferable skills gained during placement could be applied to academic studies.

Mendez (2008) studied the performance of 80 engineering students who graduated in the years 2005, 2006 and 2007 at the University of Leicester, United Kingdom. 40 had taken the year of industrial placement and 40 had not. The students were selected by 'structured random sampling'. Based on marks gained in the 1st year, students were randomly selected from three groups in the mark ranges <50%, 60-69% and 70% and over. For each individual student in the sample the difference between the percentage 1st year mark and the percentage final year mark was calculated. This difference was then expressed as a percentage of the student's 1st year mark. The overall percentage increase for non-placement students was nearly 73%, whereas the figure for placement students was 112% indicating a clear causal relationship between industrial placement and academic performance. This was reinforced by the fact that 8 out of the 10 best performing students had undertaken the placement year. Mendez also noted that students who had "underperformed" in the 1st year, benefitted most from placement in terms of their final degree mark. In speculating on the reasons for this effect of placement he drew attention to the work of Raelin (2000) who identified *metacognition* (learning to learn) as a value-added component of work based learning. Students were able to apply these acquired learning skills to their final year of study. He also hypothesized that other transferable skills such as time management and an increase in confidence and maturity gained as a result of industrial placement, translated into an improved performance in the final year.

Industrial placement and employability

The Bologna declaration for higher education clearly states that the first degree, i.e. the Bachelor degree, shall be "relevant to the European labour market". This means that a first degree should offer reasonable prospects of employment to its holder. In the United Kingdom in February 2000 the Secretary of State for Education declared that all higher education students should have a minimum of work experience.

In the United Kingdom employability of graduates is monitored. Every university is required to submit a return of the first destination activities of their graduates six months after graduation to the Higher Education Statistics Agency (HESA). Students' responses are allocated to the broad categories: *employed, unemployed, further study, unknown.* An analysis (Bowes & Harvey, 1999) indicated that graduates from thick and thin sandwich chemistry and physics programmes had higher employment rates (i.e. were in full-time paid employment) compared to counterparts on full-time courses. However their data suggested that the differences were not huge. For example for graduates with biology, chemistry and physics degrees, 46.1 % of thick sandwich students compared to 43.4 % of full-time students were in full-time paid employment six months after graduation. With regard to students classified as *unemployed* (within six months of graduation), there were fewer physics and biology sandwich graduates in this category compared to their full-time counterparts; however, surprisingly, the percentage (9.5%) of thick-sandwich chemistry graduates in this category was higher than their full-time counterparts and higher than for graduates in the other science subjects. Possible reasons for this were not considered but clearly merit further analysis.

A report into employability and work-based learning (Little, 2003) suggested that while there was a strong link between work-based learning and employability for newly qualified graduates, the effect of such learning diminished rapidly as the graduates progressed with their careers. Three years into their careers there was no evidence that graduates' performance was linked to previous work-based learning at university. Furthermore it was suggested that full-time students who have had no work experience rapidly make up the ground after gaining employment.

Unpublished results obtained by Gros at Hochschule Fresenius, a German University of Applied Sciences, showed that of 301 graduates from a 4 year course with a five month period of compulsory placement and a final year project in industry, for the period 1997-2007, 22.5 % went on to further studies (Masters, PhD). Of the remaining students, 90% had found employment in the first six months after graduation.

Organization of placement

In this section we document some of the practical issues connected with the organization of a successful placement programme. This is taken mainly from our own experience but a comprehensive account is given by Murray and Wallace (2003).

Finding placement employers

A successful and sustainable placement programme requires a significant amount of management and it is desirable to appoint a *placement administrator* to carry out the administrative and clerical tasks. The first task of the administrator is to establish a database of potential placement employers. If starting from scratch the process needs to be commenced several months before students enter their pre-placement year. Potential employers can be identified from a variety of sources: The university's career office should possess a comprehensive portfolio of employers; leads may be obtained from job adverts in scientific publications; for small local employers, job adverts in the local press can provide useful leads; business information directories such as *Kompass* provide an enormous amount of well-organized information on a wide range of companies nationally and internationally; the use of web search engines may also be productive. Contact with employers can be made by letter, e-mail and telephone. An information pack giving details of the academic programme, the organization of the placement year and the responsibilities of the placement employer, needs to be sent to potential employers. This should be accompanied by a covering letter outlining the potential benefits to the employer. Examples of such benefits are the cost effectiveness of employing students; the possibility of undertaking projects for which resources are not otherwise available; the opportunity to evaluate students as possible future employees; the addition of a young enthusiastic person to an established team. It is essential that the employer can easily contact the placement administrator through all available channels during the working day and outside normal working hours. Positive responses from employers are commonly achieved from only 10 – 20% of those contacted. This can be improved by ensuring that the correct person within the employing organization is identified and contacted. This is best achieved by telephone.

If industrial placement is carried out on a recurring annual basis, the university will develop a network with enduring contacts in a number of companies over time. This network will facilitate the allocation of students but needs "maintenance" through regular contacts and visits. The European network *University Network with Industry in Chemistry* (UNIC) with eight universities and a core group of some 20 companies across Europe is such an example (Cooke et al., 2005, p. 14).

Health and safety issues

Normally if the employers have studied the University's information pack they will be able to judge if they can offer suitable employment. However, given the fact that the university is responsible for the student, the university should establish a protocol to verify the suitability of the employer. In most cases and especially for larger companies and government organizations the verification is quite straightforward. However for smaller, less well-known companies care should be taken to ensure that they meet statutory health and safety requirements as well as the academic needs of the student. In such cases it is often necessary to visit the employer to assess discretely the suitability of the workplace. The shortcomings of unsuitable employers are often obvious to the visiting placement tutor e.g.:

> *"I visited a prospective placement employer based in a former textile mill. The 'laboratory' consisted of kitchen units. There didn't appear to be any protective wear since the workers hands were covered in dyestuffs. The dye vats were unprotected, and some of the walkways around the production areas were 2-3 metres above ground level. There were no guard rails. Furthermore the stone walkways appeared to be damp and possibly slippery. I subsequently discovered that effluent was being discharged into a small stream next to the premises....."*

Clearly such an environment would pose a serious risk to the students' health and safety. Universities must take such issues very seriously, not least because there are important legal considerations which could prove extremely costly. The legal position stems from a 'duty of care' concept. The employer, the university, the student and the visiting placement tutor all share a responsibility to ensure that both the work environment and the working practices are safe. It is necessary for the university to carry out a risk assessment on potential employers prior to the commencement of a placement. As indicated the extent of the risk assessment is likely to vary according to the employer. In all cases a 'paper trail' or audit needs to be maintained to show that risks have been assessed. Additionally the student should be provided with a checklist of safety issues which needs to be completed by the student and returned to the university soon after the placement has commenced. The ASET website (www.asetonline.org) gives an excellent account of relevant safety issues.

Managing student applications to employers

The aim should be to provide all students with an industrial placement. However students should be aware that seeking a placement is a competitive process with the involvement of many other universities. Students should be encouraged to make multiple applications to different employers. This can be facilitated by providing copies of application forms or alerting students to online procedures of the various employers. The tendency in recent years, in the United Kingdom in particular, has been for such applications to be made directly 'online'. This leaves the onus very much in the hands of the student and makes it more difficult for the placement administrator to ensure that students do not fall foul of avoidable application errors. Larger companies (e.g. multinationals) tend to seek applications from students at least ten months in advance of the placement whereas smaller companies tend to work to a much shorter timescale. Ideally a calendar spanning the twelve months prior to placement indicating the times when different employers require applications should be prepared. The placement administrator needs to establish a good working relationship with employers. Care has to be taken to ensure that students do not accept multiple offers of placements since this will sour the university's relationship with employers. Thus some ground rules need to be established; once students have accepted an offer they should normally be expected to withdraw their other placement applications. Students should have a moral obligation to other members of their course to 'free up' placement opportunities. The placement administrator needs to be aware of the students' placement situations at all times. In some cases the employer will contact the university for copies of students' *curriculum vitae* (CV) and in others the placement administrator may dispatch CV's to potential employers.

Preparing students for placement

It is essential that some preparation for the placement year is undertaken by students. Students need to know something about their potential future placement employer. Some universities prepare files with employers' brochures and application forms. It is a good practice to get previous placement students to make a short presentation to pre-placement students followed by a question and answer session. They may also provide a short written description of their placement experience.

Students need to be given advice on preparing a CV, on completing application forms and on interview techniques. Most universities have a career services department, and they will almost certainly have abundant resources to inform students in these areas. It may be possible to engage careers staff in classes with the students during the pre-placement year. All students need to prepare a short CV (e.g. two pages) which contains their personal and contact details, details of their academic record, a description of any previous work experiences, their hobbies and interests and a personal statement which might describe their achievements and aspirations. Such CV's may need to differ slightly from the normal graduate CV in that the students should point out the laboratory skills that they have acquired to-date and also highlight other transferable skills they have. The use of the official CEDEFOP 'Europass CV' forms (europass.cedefop.europa.eu) should be encouraged especially where students are applying for a placement abroad. Most employers will require an academic reference and this should be prepared well in advance and kept on record with the administrator. Ideally a *placement tutor* in the academic department should be appointed to oversee all aspects of placement preparation.

At the end of the academic year preceding placement it is good policy to set aside a day for placement induction. This should aim to reinforce the requirements and responsibilities of placement students. An information pack should be issued to students. A workshop format allows students to talk about their aspirations and fears. It is a good idea to involve an employer. Students should be encouraged to undertake reflection and self evaluation while on placement. There is usually an air of excitement on the induction day and it provides an excellent launch pad for the placement year. Universities may consider combining this day with presentations by students reporting about their placement experience. This gives the aspirants a chance of getting first-hand information about possible placement companies.

During placement

The importance of good communication between the student, the university's placement tutor and the student's employing supervisor cannot be overemphasized. Telephone and e-mail contact are essential. When the placement tutor visits the employer it is quite likely that the employing supervisor (to whom the student reports) will not be adequately briefed about the university course and the assessment requirements and some time should be set aside to cover this. The placement logbook also needs to be examined. Some telephone contact should occur before the visit to establish a programme for the visit. It is likely that a tour of the facilities will be provided but time needs to be allowed for interviewing the student and discussions with the supervisor. Around an hour and a half should be sufficient. Preferably two visits should be made – one at the beginning and one midway through the placement. The student should have completed the first written report prior to the second visit. In case of placements abroad of up to six months, the first or second visit may be replaced by telephone interviews, e-mail communication, or video conferencing.

Return to university

Post-placement student interviews are best carried out immediately before the start of the next academic year. A timetable of interviews needs to be drawn up and a suitable room for presentations needs to be available. The assessment panel, which should ideally include an employer, needs to be organized well in advance. One or two days need to be set aside for student interviews. Normally a satisfactory result from the placement year will ensure progress to the final academic year. This represents good practice and can be regarded as the ideal. At the very least each student should receive some form of debriefing which provides an opportunity for reflection on returning to the university.

The Hochschule Fresenius, Idstein, Germany, has a tradition of offering a seminar over 5-6 sessions during the summer term. Placements are normally carried out in the 5th semester (a winter term). Returning students are required to give a 20 minute oral report which is followed by a period for questions and discussion. The seminars are also compulsory for the 4th semester students who have the opportunity to obtain first hand information about their future placement companies and also about a wide range of tasks carried out by their fellow students both in Germany and in 50-80 % of the cases abroad.

What do industrialists think about placements?

Anecdotal feedback from placement employers

SBS Specialist Bioanalytical Services, Egham, United Kingdom

"For a SME, the relative impact of placement students is high."

My company is a very small SME, consisting just of myself and another half-time person. Additionally, I have contract personnel, e.g. one person two days a week in King's College, London, United Kingdom, and one post doctoral fellow on demand. The turnover of my business varies a lot, and I can never be sure of next year's projects. So I keep expenses low, have literally no overheads. I must be and I am very flexible. I can make my own decisions, do not have to sit in board meetings, but, on the other hand, I am fully responsible for success and failure.

A placement means real life experience in a real company, and combined with the academic education it provides an excellent preparation for the work life. When I was a student myself, I used to work in companies informally during the summer. A semester or year of placement is more structured.....

I give the students a basic chromatography and mass spectrometry training and some safety training. Then I assign them to tasks, usually half routine, and half research project work. They have hands-on-experience with my highly sophisticated equipment. I still have contact with some of my former students. They have all found excellent jobs, and in some cases it was their thorough and practical introduction to a modern analytical technique that required experience to yield reliable results, that proved to be a key factor for their employability.

Chemetall Frankfurt, Germany

"Social Duty, Investment, Clear Benefits"

The analytical laboratory of Chemetall has 18 staff. Seven staff members are Fachhochschule graduates; eight are technical assistants or technicians and two laborants. The daily work in the analytical laboratory is to solve technical process and product related problems of internal and external customers, mainly using modern analytical techniques:

What will my placement students learn, what do we expect from them and what are we prepared to invest in their training?

Our "investment" starts when I go to universities and present my department and possible projects to students. We provide the students we employ with a sound training of skills and knowledge in all analytical procedures that we use. This training is practically oriented and relevant for their future job, since it is part of our daily work. They learn in the context of real tasks. My staff supervise the placement semester students. With the final year project students I have a weekly meeting to supervise their work.

We expect students to join in with our daily work and to comply with the rules for safe, exact and neat analytical practice. They must produce meaningful profitable results that we can sell to our customers, compensating for the time that we invest to train them. They must be able to work in a team and be diligent and punctual.

A placement semester student must have sound basic knowledge, especially in Analytical Chemistry. They must be trained to work methodically. A final year project student should have more profound knowledge and be able to do scientific work with a level of independence, including the writing up of reports and conducting literature searches which include accessing books and original papers as well as the internet! The students acquire these competences through learning by doing. In the end, students get an individual assessment for their personal record, plus a standardised evaluation form ...."

What do former students think about their placement experiences?

Anecdotal feedback from placement students

Students who had undertaken industrial placement as part of their degree were invited to give feedback a number of years after graduation. We believe such feedback is valuable because they are able to reflect on their placement in a broader sense as a result of experiencing other types of employment post graduation. Graduates from two degree courses were surveyed. The first set of responses is from graduates from a four year combined chemistry course which contained a twelve month period of compulsory placement. The placement was assessed for an award of a DIS. All students were paid by their employers which were located in Northern Ireland, England and Missouri, USA. Placements were mainly from the following sectors: Pharmaceutical, contract research, analytical, diagnostics and government laboratories.

Graduated in 1996, currently a university lecturer in biomaterials and tissue engineering:

> *"Having had a year of industrial experience gained before graduating, I found it very easy to obtain interviews for jobs (in science). At the end of my degree I had applied for a PhD (in the area of biomaterials), and jobs with two other local companies. I received offers for all of these and in the case of the two job offers the employers specifically mentioned that I had prior*

experience and would be capable of settling into a post with them very quickly."

Graduated in 1997, currently leader of a group of analytical scientists at a medium sized contract pharmaceutical company:

"The skills and analytical techniques I used during my placement year played a huge part in helping me to get a job as soon as my finals were completed. The friends and contacts I made during placement have provided me with a large network of people in the industry and have proved beneficial to my current position working closely with large pharmaceutical companies."

Graduated in 1997, currently study director for genetic toxicology in a large contract research pharmaceutical company:

"Following my placement year it was definitely easier to understand practical applications for some of the topics we were studying (e.g. mass spec in analytical chemistry and drug development). I ended up with a job at my placement company straight after qualifying and am still there 10 years later. I got a higher starting salary and a job right away due to my previous experience."

Graduated in 1999, currently key account manager Northern and Western Ireland for manufacturer of chromatography equipment:

"I first started in [my current company] as the Chemistry technical specialist which dealt with column/chemistry chromatography issues. Without having experience in HPLC I wouldn't have got the job. In my current role I sell both HPLC and MS, so the knowledge I gained in [my placement at] Covance about this was beneficial. Working with Covance also gave me an insight into lab practices and the need to be compliant to various regulatory bodies. I still draw on this knowledge regularly when dealing with pharmaceutical companies."

Graduated in 2000, currently a government scientist:

"My placement year provided me with an opportunity to work within a leading pharmaceutical organization for 1 year, and allowed me to gain a wide range of interdisciplinary research and development activities, all skills which have been transferable throughout my career to date. ... ... not only was I allowed to develop my scientific skills but also to develop skills such as use of IT systems, team working, written and oral communication, planning and organizing work loads and looking after resources, all skills which have been transferable."

Graduated in 2002, currently research and development manager for a bioscience company:

"During my placement at ABC Labs [in the USA], I was treated like any other employee and I had the same duties and responsibilities as anyone else who would have been employed in my position on a permanent contract. This in itself spurred me on to work harder and I really felt like I was making an active contribution to the company and the service we provided. The training I also received was exceptional.... After 3 months I was given my own projects to work on as I showed an interest in taking on more responsibility, so I was rewarded accordingly for my enthusiasm."

Graduated in 2002, currently study coordinator in a large contract research pharmaceutical company:

"I think the placement experience was very advantageous and gave me a very good insight into the type of work I would be involved in for my future career. I truly believe that putting the theory learned over the first two years of the degree into practice gives a much greater understanding of how processes work and how the analytical instrumentation operates..... I am still working in the same scientific environment seven years on from my degree and I am continuously learning and enjoying the work I am doing."

Graduated in 2003, currently a government scientist, formerly chemical analyst with Almac Sciences:

"My placement experience provided an insight into how laboratory work is performed, from Quality Assurance, to Health and Safety, to calibration of equipment and all that this entailed, to reporting structures and methods, to customer confidentiality, support and satisfaction, amongst many others... I have now moved into a different field (Dept of Health) and still find I use many of the skills learned when on placement."

Graduated in 2004, currently postdoctoral research:

"[Placement] was one of the main factors that helped me to decide to do a PhD. I realized during my placement that I really enjoyed scientific research. ....and I chose a PhD project that was also sponsored by Pfizer, as it meant the subject had clinical relevance... Although I have now decided to pursue an academic career rather than working in industry, I do believe that my placement year was key in my development..."

Graduated in 2005, currently studying for a professional qualification in dietetics having completed PhD:

"Although my placement year was not directly related to the field of work that I am entering into, the life skills that were obtained have proved to be valuable. Working in a company like Unilever gave me a sense of what it was like to work as a part of a team. I developed other important transferable skills such as

communication and time management skills, skills which are paramount in all areas of employment including within the NHS. Moving [to another country] gave me independence and the confidence to realize that I could succeed on my own."

Two graduates of Hochschule Fresenius, University of Applied Sciences in Idstein, Germany.
Graduated in 1996, currently environmental consultant in a multinational consulting company in the U.K.

"...I could apply my theoretical knowledge in practice [...] I did my work placement in a Research Centre located....in the French speaking part of Belgium. I learnt to work in a research team and contribute to the output of the research group, and I improved my French language skills. I added one semester ......studying... in the USA, I could improve my English to a high degree, which allowed me to find a job more easily, but I also learned to work in a team to realise project aims. The practical experience I have gained during my studies was and is a key element in my professional development and success...."

Graduated in 2003, currently quality and risk manager in a multinational pharmaceutical company in Germany:

"... understand foreign structures and habits [...] I did my work placement at Specialist Bioanalytical Services in the UK..... Naturally, it is difficult to understand foreign structures and habits, but this is the ingredient which makes a stay abroad interesting, makes you sensitive and broadens your horizons. A work placement abroad should be obligatory. Besides the scientific work, a talent to get yourself organized, to succeed in a team and to cooperate with your team mates plus tolerance is of importance....."

Two graduates of Institut Químic de Sarrià , Barcelona, Spain.
Graduated in 2007 with a PhD, currently working in an SME in Spain:

"...practical work experience abroad of 3 to 6 months duration should be available for all students [...] I did my placement with a LEONARDO grant..... My most important experience during the placement time abroad was that I got to know a different culture during and after work time. Language and work habits are equally important. Although work experience in a company is good to get in contact with, work life going abroad is an even more rewarding experience, since you are in a completely unknown place where you have to adapt quickly.....planning, organization and presentation of the results is impossible without speaking the language. For problem solving during the project, you must make yourself understood."

Graduated in 1998, currently working as an R&D-manager in a multinational company in Spain:

"...one key factor for a multinational company to offer me a job [...] I want to stress that all the work during my placement was done using a foreign European language, German. This placement experience proved to be a key factor when I was offered a job by a multinational company. In the interviews ..., my five month placement in Germany was regarded as highly positive. Later, the usual personal and telephone contact with clients, suppliers and the German branch of my company reminded me of this foreign placement period."

Conclusions

The focus of this chapter has been on industrial placement and the learning experience that this provides. There is overwhelming evidence that the main benefit to students is development of their personal skills. These skills are not easily incorporated into the academic curriculum, within the lecture hall so to speak. However we should not forget the opportunities to develop personal skills through *extra-curricula* activities such as involvement in student societies, social networking and participation in the various sports available. Of course such activities are not usually monitored or assessed; they are rather a 'by-product', albeit a very important by-product, of a university education. It is unfortunately the case that many students, either through lack of opportunity or inclination to participate, will not benefit from the personal development that such *extra-curricula* activities can offer. In contrast a compulsory period of industrial placement which is at the core of the curriculum and which is monitored, structured and assessed provides *all* students with valuable opportunities for personal development. The importance of reflection on personal development can be formally emphasised.

Some students mention the acquisition of practical, technical and subject specific skills as an important feature of their industrial placements. While this may be valuable, there are considerable difficulties in securing industrial placements designed to meet specific technical training requirements and even greater difficulty to match these with suitable students. Usually then the challenge becomes one of providing the opportunity for relevant work experience with a scientific employer to all the students.

There seems to be significant evidence that industrial placement correlates with an improved performance in academic study in the final year. This appears to vindicate the practice of sandwiching industrial placement between years of academic study. The reasons for the improvement may be better time-management, greater maturity and responsibility as well as greater motivation and a clearer sense of direction. While this is to be welcomed, it has to be recognized that placement students have undertaken an extra year of "study". This is why students should be awarded credits for their assessed placement periods (whether compulsory or optional), expressed in ECTS or comparable credits and duly described in their 'Diploma Supplement'. Universities adopting these aspects of best practice will encourage their students to opt for a placement. An important non-academic benefit of industrial placement is the financial contribution it makes to the student's welfare. This may lessen the need to undertake part-time paid employment in the final year.

In terms of employability and career development, placement students enjoy an initial advantage over their non-placement counterparts; they are likely to be more proficient in the job interview and to have an employer's reference based on twelve month's experience. They are also likely to have clearer preferences and to be more selective with regard to their future employment. However there is evidence (Mason, Williams, Cranmer, & Guile, 2003) to suggest that these advantages diminish rapidly as their careers develop such that after around three years post-graduation there is no discernable difference in the performance of students with and without industrial placement. Nonetheless, the personal experience gained during a placement, especially when done abroad, is rewarding in itself as amply witnessed in much of the feedback received.

References

Ahmed, Y., Brown, G., Crawford, A., Haworth, B., & Holdich, R. (2006). The impact of work placements on the development of transferable skills in engineering. ASET Conference Proceedings 2006. Retrieved February 01, 2009 from www.engcetl.ac.uk/downloads/research/students/yussuf/yussuf_ahmed_2006_aset.pdf.

Armstrong, G., McMahon-Beattie, U., & Greenan, K. (2005). *Work-based learning in the University of Ulster: Embedding employability in business studies.* Higher Education Academy Report. Retrieved May 01, 2009, from www.heacademy.ac.uk/assets/bmaf/documents/Resources/Employability_case_studies/Employability_Gillian_Armstrong.pdf.

Bowes, L., & Harvey, L. (1999). *The impact of sandwich education on the activities of graduates six months post-graduation.* Birmingham: Centre for Research into Quality, University of Central England. Retrieved May 01, 2009, from asetonline.org/documents/The_Impact_of_Sandwich_Education_on_the_activities_of_graduates_6_months_after.pdf.

Cooke, M., Gros, L., Horz, M., & Zeller, W. (Eds.) (2005). *Chemical education for a competitive and dynamic Europe. Components of a European house of chemical education: Situation – good practice – recommendations.* Impuls Nr. 16. Bonn: Nationale Agentur Bildung für Europa beim Bundesinstitut für Berufsbildung. Retrieved May 01, 2009, from face.hs-fresenius.de/whitebook.pdf.

Duffy, K., Anthony D., & Vickers F. (2008). *Are e-portfolios an asset to learning and placement?.* Research report from De Montfort University and ASET. Retrieved May 01, 2009, from www.asetonline.org/documents/AreE-PortfoliosAnAssetToLearningand Placement-ASETandDMUReport-March2008_001.pdf.

Fallows, S., & Stevens, C. (2000). Building employability skills into the higher education curriculum: A university wide initiative. *Education and Training*, 42 (2), 75-83.

Gomez, S., Lush D., & Clements, M. (2004). Work placements enhance the academic performance of bioscience undergraduates. *Journal of Vocational Education and Training, 56,* 373–385.

Gros, L. (2009). A flexible life long learning toolbox for chemists. Vocational and university education with mobility elements. 38th IGIP Symposium, Graz, Austria.

Higher Education Academy (Ed.) (2005). *Engineering subject centre guide: Industrial placements.* Retrieved May 01, 2009, from www.engsc.ac.uk/ downloads/resources/placements.pdf.

Little, B. (2003). *Employability and work-based learning.* A report of the Higher Education Academy, York, United Kingdom. Retrieved May 01, 2009, from www.palatine.ac.uk/files/emp/1244.pdf.

Little, B., & Harvey, L. (2006). *Learning through work placements and beyond.* A report for HECSU and the Higher Education Academy's Work Placement Organisation Forum. Retrieved February 01, 2009, from www.asetonline.org/documents/Work _based_learning_LH_BL.pdf.

Mandilaras A. (2004). Industrial placement and degree performance: Evidence from a British higher institution. *International Review of Economics Education, 3*, 39-51.

Mason, G., Williams, G., Cranmer, S., & Guile, D. (2003). *How much does higher education enhance the employability of graduates?*. Retrieved May 01, 2009, from www.hefce.ac.uk/pubs/rdreports/2003/rd13_03/.

Murray, R., & Wallace, R. (2003). *LTSN physical sciences practice guide: Good practice in industrial work placement*. Retrieved May 01, 2009, from www.heacademy.ac.uk/ assets/ps/documents/practice_guides/practice_guides/ps0077_good_practice_in_industri al_work_palcement_sept_2003.pdf.

Mendez, R. (2008). *Correlation between industrial placements and final degree results: A study of engineering placement students*. ASET Research project. Retrieved May 01, 2009, from www.asetonline.org/documents/TheCorrelationBetweenIndustrial PlacementsandFinalDegreeResults.pdf.

Raelin, J. (2000). *Work-based learning: The new frontier of management development*. New Jersey: Prentice Hall.

Wallace, R. G. (2002). A sandwich year can seriously damage your chances of obtaining a poor degree. Paper presented at ASET European conference, Cambridge, United Kingdom. Retrieved May 01, 2009, from www.asetonline.org/PDFs/ A%20Sandwich%20Year%20Paper.pdf.

Wilson, J. (2004). *Student fees and the placement year of sandwich courses*. Retrieved February 01, 2009, from www.asetonline.org/PDFs/Student%20fees%20 and%20the%20placement%20year.pdf.

Wright, B. (n. d.). *Case study higher education academy: The diploma in industrial studies*. Retrieved May 1, 2009 from www.cebe.heacademy.ac.uk/BPBN/casestudy/ lough_cdc6ii.htm.

Assessment in Higher Level Chemistry Education

STUART W. BENNETT
The Open University, Milton Keynes, United Kingdom

IAIN WILSON
Manchester Metropolitan University, United Kingdom

Assessment represents a significant part of the workload of the teacher and much student activity (and concern) is motivated by assessment. There are good reasons for having assessment but the assessment is not always designed to promote effective learning. This chapter hinges on the essential mapping of learning outcomes and assessment and offers a critical view of the strengths and limitations of a range of assessment methods. Different modes of assessment can measure different attributes and it is important to take this into account when combining scores or grades.

What is assessment for?

Teachers in higher education are increasingly aware that, for many students, assessment is a major driver for learning. If a concept, skill or knowledge package is seen to be assessable, in the sense that it counts towards the overall goal of the student (degree, diploma etc), it assumes a high priority in the learning strategy of the student. This is not perhaps what the teachers would wish but nonetheless it needs to be recognized. For this reason alone, assessment should be given a central role in course design and not regarded merely as an 'add on' to be considered only after the work of developing a course has been completed.

Assessment is responsible for much work (and distress) by both students and teachers so why is it done? Assessment has to fulfil a range of sometimes conflicting functions. It is there to classify students for the 'benefit' of the institution, potential employers and even the students themselves. It can provide valuable feedback for teachers with respect to the effectiveness of learning as well as a means of diagnosing faults and misconceptions. Prompt feedback is a powerful aid to improving student

Chapter consultants: Bill Byers, University of Ulster, United Kingdom, and Ingo Eilks, University of Bremen, Germany

I. Eilks and B. Byers (Eds.). Innovative Methods in Teaching and Learning Chemistry in Higher Education, pp. 215-228. © 2009 RSC Publishing.

learning and has been identified by Chickering and Gameson (1987) as one of their seven principles of good practice in undergraduate education.

Learning outcomes and assessment

As assessment can powerfully modify the learning strategy of the student, it is essential that the design of assessment should embody this responsibility. Both students and teachers should be clear on what is to be assessed and how it is to be assessed as this is the basis of openness and a contract between students and teachers. The key is the set of learning outcomes for the module, course or programme of study. Learning outcomes can be defined as statements that predict what students have gained as a result of learning and the achievement of which a student should be able to demonstrate. Providing that we are able to write good learning outcomes, the student should be clear on what is to be assessed and how it is to be assessed. So how can we write quality, unambiguous and clear learning outcomes?

The key is to focus on what the students are expected to be able to *do* on completion of their studies. It is tempting (and easy) to write that 'students should have an understanding of ligand field theory' or an 'appreciation of the scope and basis of retrosynthetic analysis' under the heading of learning outcomes. Whilst these statements give some idea of what might be included in the course in terms of topics, they are of little value in indicating to the students exactly what will be expected of them. There is no indication of what the student is expected to *do* to demonstrate the understanding of ligand field theory. For this reason, terms such as 'understand', 'have an appreciation of', 'have knowledge of' and 'know' should not appear as learning outcomes. They may well be in the teacher's mind amongst the aims of the course but the role of learning outcomes is to articulate such aims as concrete, demonstrable actions. A useful document from the UK's Higher Education Academy Physical Sciences Centre (2005) suggests that learning outcomes should be couched in terms such as analyse, appraise, apply, calculate, choose, compare, contrast, create, criticize, demonstrate, derive, describe, design, develop, differentiate, discuss, explain, evaluate, extrapolate, formulate, identify, list, measure, name, plan, plot, postulate, predict, present, propose, recall, recognize, use, utilize. All these terms give a much clearer idea of what is expected of the student and, in many ways, are the tangible actions that demonstrate understanding.

There are no guidelines on how many learning outcomes there should be for a particular course, module or activity. It may be that several simple (in terms of the structure of the) learning outcomes are appropriate in some cases while in others fewer, more complex, learning outcomes may be preferable.

The reason for introducing learning outcomes at this stage is that writing the learning outcomes is the first thing that should be done in the design of any new course or module. This necessarily means that the assessment is designed at this early stage. The 'material' in the course is then selected for its role as a vehicle for delivering the stated learning outcomes. This is not to say that there should be no iteration between the learning outcomes, assessment and the material of the course: indeed such a process is essential to produce a well designed course. The key point is the order of initial development of these three areas.

Learning outcomes then map directly onto assessment (or assessment is an integral part of learning outcomes). The next questions are 'Do all learning outcomes have to be assessed?' and 'Should students have to achieve all learning outcomes?'. There are two kinds of assessment. One can be described as a threshold assessment in which a particular standard must be achieved in a range of outcomes. An airline pilot not only has to pass a set of health checks but must achieve a threshold standard in navigation and weather, ground operation, take-off, climbing, cruise, descent and landing (and probably several others). Failure in any key area in the regular testing programme would have the effect of barring the pilot from flying until all the appropriate threshold competencies had been achieved. Surgeons would also come into this category where the consequences of on-duty failure might cause danger to the public. In contrast, the consequence of failure to reach a threshold standard in organic reaction mechanisms by an undergraduate chemistry student is unlikely to have life or death consequences. For this reason, it is very unusual in chemistry (and most other university subject areas) for examiners to demand competence in each and every learning outcome. So the norm is that not all learning outcomes are assessed and students do not have to achieve all learning outcomes. Furthermore, with the development of modular courses and the growing importance of continuous assessment, the student 'assembles' competency achievement over a period of time unlike the 'in-car' part of a driving test when demonstration of all the relevant competencies is required in the same session. However, what is essential is that there is no assessment item that does not relate directly to a stated learning outcome and that there is no attempt to write learning outcomes that cannot be assessed.

Assessment strategy

Before looking at individual assessment methods, it is worth while taking an overview of assessment. Closed book, time limited, formal examinations were the mainstay of university assessment until the 1980s when continuous, open book, assessment began to gain a level of credibility (Eilertsen & Valdermo, 2000). (An aside here is that the term continuous assessment can mean regular assessment of a closed-book nature although the term is generally used for open book, non time-limited, on-going, assessment. It is important to be clear to which the term refers.)

Both formal, examination-based assessment and open book, non time-limited assessments have particular attributes (Table 1) which should be considered when selecting the most appropriate form of assessment with regard to linking to the specific learning outcomes to be tested.

Table 1:   Attributes of formal (closed-book) examinations and of open-book continuous assessment.

Formal examinations (closed-book)	Open-book continuous assessment
Allows for verification of students' work	Can be less certain that it is students' own work
Limited time (time management)	Time is only student limited
Skills and knowledge tested at the same time	Skills and knowledge tested over a longer period time but wider range of skills tested
Relatively easy to administer and grade consistently	Can be more difficult to administer and grade consistently
Good discriminator on many criteria	Reasonable discrimination but tendency to low standard deviation
Unable to test transferable skills well	Better at testing transferable skills
Memory tested	Not so memory dependent
Disadvantages some students ('exam nerves' etc)	Less pressure on students
Tests at particular point (and can encourage shallow learning)	Tests over longer period (and can encourage deeper learning)
Choice of questions in examination can result in important learning outcomes being omitted	Can be designed to include all relevant learning outcomes

These two forms of assessment can be regarded as being at either end of a spectrum which encompasses open-book, time-limited, formal examinations and open-book informal examinations with time limits of a few days. These intermediate points have some of the attributes of both systems. Any meaningful and fair assessment strategy is likely to include more than one of the general methods in this spectrum.

A particular challenge for assessment strategy (to which we have already alluded) is related to the development of modular programmes of study. Larger modules in a programme can be of 20 ECTS points (European Credit Transfer and Accumulation System) with smaller ones being as small as 5 points representing between 100 and 150 hours of study-time. Given the 180 ECTS points required for a three year bachelor degree, the result is often a multiplicity of individually assessed modules. There is a tendency in the minds of many students to dismiss a module once the assessment is complete. Indeed, there is sometimes resentment when a skill from a previous module is retested (in a different context) in a new module. The modular system does not encourage synoptic learning with knowledge and skills being compartmentalized. Although it is clearly easier to allow students to be assessed in individual modules separately, the challenge is to devise a synoptic assessment system for a modular programme.

Assessment methods

The UK Chemistry Benchmark Statement (QAA, 2007) suggests that the assessment of degree level chemistry should be based on formal examinations, including a significant proportion of 'unseen' examinations, laboratory reports and skills, problem solving exercises, oral presentations and the planning, conduct and reporting of project work. It goes on to say that 'additional evidence' for the assessment of student achievement may include essay assignments, portfolios on chemical activities undertaken, literature surveys and evaluations, collaborative project work, preparation and displays of posters reporting project work and reports on external placements where appropriate. There are other assessment methods too (Race, 2009) but the aim of this Section is to try to identify the strengths and limitations of some of the more widely used assessment methods.

The importance of tying learning outcomes to assessment cannot be over stressed in the context of the use of a range of assessment methods. It is essential that a synoptic mapping grid be created which can then indicate the learning outcomes that have been tested, those that have been over-tested and those that have not been tested at all (Bennett, 2004). There is a tendency to use questions that are easy to set and easy to mark but this does not necessarily create a balanced assessment of achievement of learning outcomes. It is useful to keep the learning outcomes at one's side when writing questions for the assessment.

Formal, time-limited examinations

This assessment method ensures that all students are set the same tasks, to be completed under the same conditions at the same time. In many ways, this can be seen to be a fair method but it does not take into account the general 'health' of the student on the day of the examination. It is certainly a stressful experience for many students to the extent that performance may be inhibited and it provides only a picture of that student on that particular day. It would be interesting to give students a follow-up examination (without warning) a week or a month later. For fairly obvious reasons, such a large scale study has never been carried out, but there are indications that performance on the follow-up test would be likely to be significantly worse. Formal examinations can lead to shallow learning in the period leading up to the examination with retention being transient.

Setting good questions is not easy. It is important to be clear exactly what the question is testing both in terms of knowledge and of process. Use simple, short sentences, make it very clear what the student is expected to do (maybe through structuring the question) and where, appropriate, give an indication of the length of the answer expected. Write an answer to your own questions, preferably in long-hand just as students are expected to do. How long did it take you? If you have taken longer than half the time allowed for a student to complete a question, then the question is certainly too long. Next, involve colleagues and get at least one person to write an answer to the question. Ask a colleague what is being tested in the question. It may be that there is a valid approach that you had not thought of. Even with what seems to be the clearest of questions, someone in a group of examinees may well find ambiguity, but by then it is too late.

Now you are in a position to write a marking scheme. In general, marking schemes should be tight and the marks for each part of a question indicated on the examination paper. There is no place for a question such as 'Write an essay on the oxidation states of hydrogen (25 marks)' without more structure to the question and an indication of the priorities for mark allocation. It should be possible for a colleague using your marking scheme to mark your question in a very similar manner to yourself.

Having written good draft questions and marking schemes which have been considered by at least two people, the paper can then be put together. The paper will follow a pre-determined structure which may involve a section of short questions that should be within the ability of most students, there may be longer questions that are individually designed to test a range of student abilities and there may be a choice of questions. No matter what the structure of the paper, this is the stage when the paper itself should be checked against the learning outcomes that it was designed to assess. Ensure that all learning outcomes that you want to assess are there, that some learning outcomes are not being repeatedly assessed and that there are no questions that assess things that are not part of the set of learning outcomes. This process is particularly important when the questions have been written by several academics. You may need to replace some questions which might upset colleagues. Explain to them why you are making the change. It is far more important to ensure that the examination paper is fair to the students and assesses what it purports to assess than worrying about the demeanour of colleagues. Now check that the paper can be completed in the time allotted by a moderate student. Look at the times taken for the long-hand answers to be written by yourself and colleagues for each question and ensure that the total time is no more than half the time allotted for the examination.

Marking of examinations is not regarded as the highlight of the year by many academics. You might have many scripts to mark but each one represents a student for whom the outcome may be vital. The hundredth script is every bit as important as the first one. Whether one marks an individual script in its entirety before moving on to the next one or marks say Question 1 on all scripts before returning to the first script to embark on Question 2 is a matter for the individual and depends on the length and complexity of the examination paper. Whichever approach to marking is to be taken, it is well worthwhile starting by marking ten or fifteen scripts (in pencil) and then looking again at the marking scheme. There should be some provision for double marking and the observations of the second marker from this initial sample of scripts should be considered alongside your own. Are there variations from the answers that were expected and are any of these different answers valid in the context of the wording of the question? If so feel confident in adapting the marking scheme to accommodate this answer range but make a note so that this observation can be used in the future to set a less ambiguous question. You need to decide at this stage whether you are going to provide individualized feedback for students or more generic feedback. The effort put in by students in the whole examination process certainly deserves some level of feedback.

Now the main marking task can be undertaken. Refer to the marking scheme frequently. It is easy to deviate or subconsciously get involved with mark 'creep'. The objective is to be fair to all students so try not to mark when you are tired. Once the examination is marked and any negotiations with a second marker resolved, write feedback which should be addressed both to students and involved colleagues. What did you think that the questions were going to test, what did they actually test, what were the common errors or misconceptions, what has the examination indicated about how the course should be modified?

Formal, time-limited examinations are not confined to the 'closed book' category where there is necessarily significant reliance on memory. Students can be allowed to take books and other resource materials into the examination. Access to these resources relieves some of the 'memory' pressure and can test retrieval skills. The potential unfairness of some students having more and better resources than others can be removed by prescribing exactly what can be brought into the exam.

With access to resources, the nature of the examination is changed. Questions can be set that are more concerned with selection of relevant information and with process. Time should be allowed for the fact that searching for information makes inroads into the time for writing. There is some merit in being very generous with the allotted examination time as this will remove the potential disadvantage suffered by slow writers.

Short answer and multiple choice examinations

This method of assessment may form part (or even all) of a major examination or be linked to shorter tests as part of a continuous assessment programme. The question paper is highly structured with short questions requiring only a few sentences as an answer or a simple calculation. Short answer questions represent a trade-off compared with longer questions. Using longer questions it is possible to address the deeper learning that students have acquired, process skills and the organization of information but with the limitation that with fewer questions a smaller proportion of the knowledge part of the syllabus can be tested. Short questions (in greater number) can cover a larger proportion of the syllabus but these questions are not generally able to explore the deeper range of process skills. This style of test is also useful in a diagnostic sense in identifying gaps in knowledge which can be addressed before a student starts a course and can be useful in formative assessment.

An alternative to questions that demand short, written answers is the multiple choice question. Such questions have the potential of being computer marked opening up opportunities for the teacher and the student. But good multiple choice questions are not easy to write and take time (e.g. Schmidt & Beine, 1992). There are several types of question structure. One is a simple choice of one response from a key that might have up to six alternatives. If the answer is numerical, it is useful to phrase the rubric with 'select from the key the response that is *closest* to your answer' thereby avoiding problems with small variations from 'rounding up' errors. Next one can have several correct responses from a key to be used with a question such as 'Which of the following elements exhibit oxidations states smaller than -2 in compounds stable under normal conditions'. Note that with multiple choice questions it is particularly important to ensure that there is no ambiguity as the student is unable to qualify a response. In the above example if one of the expected responses is 'nitrogen', will the student read the question as -3 being smaller than -2 as intended or will some students focus on the modulus so that (-)1 is considered smaller than (-)2? In this question, it is chemistry that is the subject of the test and not semantics. A more extensive key can be developed using a multi-line grid and often the same grid can be used for several questions. Another variation is to have linked questions although care is needed here. One needs to minimize problems arising from an incorrect answer to the first of two linked questions being responsible for an incorrect response to the second question. Cautionary factors associated with multiple choice questions are identified by Tamir (1990) and by Ambusaidi and Johnstone (2000).

If questions are to be answered on line (rather than using a photoreader of response forms), additional possibilities are available. The answer to a question could involve the identification of relevant parts of a picture or diagram through 'hotspots'. An initial, incorrect response could be followed with an indication of what the error might be. This could go through say two cycles with a proportion of the marks being lost for each additional cycle and advice. Immediate feedback in this manner can contribute to learning.

One problem with multiple choice questions is that it is generally possible to gain marks by guessing. For a test comprising questions each of which has five possible responses, guessing should on average produce an overall mark of 20 per cent. If the 'distracter' incorrect responses are poor (so likely that they can be ruled out on the basis of minimum knowledge), the odds of getting the correct answer are much improved. Ruling out just two of a possible five responses, improves the 'guessing' odds to 33 per cent of obtaining the correct answer, beginning to approach a pass mark with very little knowledge of the subject matter being tested. Some teachers favour a system of negative marking which removes marks for incorrect responses. An interesting variation suggested by Dressel and Schmid (1953) is to ask how certain the student is that they have selected the correct answer. More marks are available for selecting the correct answer and being sure that it is right than for selecting the correct answer with a lower degree of certainty. The downside (for the student) is that an incorrect response coupled with a high degree of confidence that it was the correct option results in the loss of even more marks.

Whatever, system is being used, it is essential (and fair to the student) that this information is made clear *before* the test and is indicated at the beginning of the test.

Computer marking of tests has a number of significant advantages. The quality of the distracters in the key can be easily assessed. If very few students are choosing a distracter, it is not doing its job properly. Similarly, if a very high proportion of students are getting the correct answer, the question is not very discriminating. Good distracters are difficult to write and this, coupled with the need for clarity and a complete absence of ambiguity makes the design of quality multiple choice questions very time consuming. A range of considerations in the writing of multiple choice questions is clearly expounded by Johnstone (2004). Considerable investment in time and effort for the pre-testing of questions (by students and colleagues) is needed. However, once a data bank of questions has been assembled, student assessment through computer-mediated, multiple choice tests requires very little time on behalf of the teacher. Tests can be put together automatically from questions tagged with learning outcomes. Over- and under-testing of particular learning outcomes is avoided and individual student question sets can be generated though care still needs to be taken in ensuring the validity of the tests (Johnstone, 2004). Question Banks in the physical sciences have been catalogued by Bacon (2009) and the *EChemTest* (www.echemtest.net) features questions across all branches of chemistry although they are arranged as a test rather than in a form ideal to plunder for one's own question bank.

Assessment should be seen as an opportunity for learning and computer-mediated tests readily provide such an opportunity. If each question in the question bank is tagged with staged feedback, as soon as a student has completed the test feedback specific to that student can be generated and the more rapid the feedback is received, the more use it is likely to be to the student.

In addition to the above, advantages of computer-mediated assessment are that the marking is automatic, individual student progress can be monitored and class data are available.

Essays

The use of essays both for continuous assessment and for examinations is much more common in the arts and social sciences than it is in science. Essays allow the writer to qualify statements, put forward supported views, opinion and interpretation and construct arguments. Use in chemistry has been quite limited but this is probably as a result of the way the subject has been taught. A new undergraduate in literature for example is likely to be encouraged to become involved in discussion and interpretation and expressing his or her own ideas and opinions from the start. The culture of selecting and retrieving information from many sources with which to construct an argument or case is a skill that is developed progressively throughout an undergraduate career by many arts students. In contrast, the traditional science teaching model has been for the undergraduate to assemble a portfolio of knowledge and skills which are really often only brought to bear on an issue or problem that demands a creative approach during project work towards the end of an undergraduate programme. But is science really intrinsically so different from the arts? Recent advances in problem- and context-based learning and their introduction in the early stages of undergraduate study have brought the chemistry undergraduate face-to-face with the information selection and argument construction skills familiar to the arts undergraduate. There is certainly room for the essay in an assessment portfolio for chemistry.

The best way to find out about setting and marking essay questions is to stroll over to your arts and social science faculties and ask questions. Here people have huge experience with essays. Students should not be set an essay for summative assessment without having had some experience beforehand. The essay topic should provide an opportunity for the student to express the depth and application of learning yet the question should indicate how the marks are to be divided. Even a simple scheme with marks allocated to categories such as selection of relevant information and data, organization of information, argument and thesis construction, meaningful conclusions, engaging writing style can make the task of writing the essay much easier for the student and the marking much easier for the marker. Marking of essays is time consuming so essays should be used sparingly as an assessment method.

Group work

Group work probably comes closer than any other single activity in the undergraduate curriculum to preparing students for employment (see Eilks, Markic, Bäumer, & Schanze in this book). Whether the student goes on to employment in a chemistry-related or other area, it is likely that there will be the need to work in teams focused on a common objective. Many teachers are still wary of group work partly as a result of not being confident in assessing individual members of a team fairly (Boud, 2001).

As with all assessment but particularly for group work, it is essential that the student is told just how assessment is to be carried out and what the criteria are *before* beginning the activity. A key decision is whether each member of the group gains the same mark which is based solely on the overall group performance, whether each member has an individual mark reflecting the quality and quantity of input to the group task or whether a combination of individual and group marks is used (Byers & Wilkins, 2005) The behaviour of team members can be materially affected by the collective or individual marking regime. With a collective score, there is the tendency for one or more team members to leave the work to others and this is a situation that has to be monitored. Marking in this regime can be relatively easy with the project report for each group being assessed by the teacher and the same mark awarded to each member of the group. However, it is perceived to be fairer if an individual mark is assigned to each member of the team.

Clearly, it is impossible for the teacher to monitor the inputs of each member of every team but it is possible for each member of a team to monitor the input from the other members of the team. Peer assessment suffers from possible problems of personality clashes, pacts and relationships but these are quite rare and can often be identified. Whilst peer assessment should not be the totality of group assessment, it is useful for it to be a component part. A proportion of the remaining marks should be reserved for the teacher's assessment of contribution based on observation of the team members at work and perhaps interview, poster or presentation. The remaining marks would go to the quality of the team task report, either written collectively or with each member submitting their own report. The balance between these components can be quite flexible, but serious thought should be give to any assessment package that includes more than about 40 per cent of peer assessment. Chin and Overton (2005) provide examples of assessment packages for group assessment.

Presentations and posters

The need to make a short presentation can be a particularly good way of forcing students to organize and prioritize their work and making a presentation is a skill that is likely to be useful in employment. A clear set of assessment criteria should be available and the involvement of student colleagues in assessment is helpful. A brief question and answer session allows the student to 'defend' their work. This can also be achieved using the poster as part of the assessment with the teacher (and perhaps even students) asking pertinent questions. Assessment should consider both the quality of the poster and the response to questioning.

Reports and dissertations

These are useful methods of testing the skill of the student in the organization and presentation of work in a logical manner. However, reports and dissertations take up much time by the students and are very time consuming for the teacher to grade. They should be used sparingly.

Oral examinations

For some students the trauma of making a presentation to an audience is only surpassed by the oral examination or *viva voce*. One can do everything possible to make this process less threatening (not conducting the session across a table, discussing with the student the format of the process beforehand, explaining just what it is the you want to find out) but there will be some students who will still not perform to their potential. The oral examination is probably best for answering questions in the mind of the teacher. If a student has a poor examination score but a good continuous assessment score, the oral examination can relatively easily determine which better reflects the student's true ability. Oral examinations are good for exploring process, logical thinking and reasoning and for identifying limitations of applications of ideas and theories.

Practical work

Valid assessment of practical work is difficult and it is particularly important for both the teacher and the student to be clear what the learning outcomes are and how they are to be assessed. Issues associated with practical work are discussed in the assessment section of the practical work chapter (see Bennett, Seery, & Sövegjarto-Wigbers in this book).

Quality of assessment

Race (2009) identifies a number of essential attributes of good assessment which can apply to individual questions in a test and to the overall assessment regime.

Validity has a specific meaning in the context of assessment and it is that the test measures what it sets out to measure. This might seem to be a fairly obvious criterion but it is not uncommon for a test to claim something that it does not achieve. As mentioned, commonly practical work is assessed by grading the write-up or report of a laboratory activity. Students who score well are regarded as being good at practical work which is often translated as being good at the bench. The report may measure several things (such as organized writing, processing of data, reaching conclusions and communication of those conclusions) but it does not measure the quality of the student's bench working. To do this, the student would have to be observed and assessed when at the bench. The report is a valid assessment of some qualities but it is an invalid method for assessing bench performance.

Assessment should be *reliable*. A test should give similar results when used on the same students or with a similar group of students on the same course (Johnstone 2004). In practice, it is easier to test for reliability with large groups of students where the variation in performance of individual students on different testing occasions can be minimized.

Transparency of assessment is essential. Students should be clear where the goalposts are. Not only should the learning outcomes be available to all students, there should be some guidance from the teacher as to what the learning outcomes actually mean in terms of student performance. Students should have some exposure to questions that test particular learning outcomes before being subjected to summative assessment. There should be no tricks or surprises in assessment.

Having taken care to produce high quality assessment, what should be done with the resulting data from student performance? A module will likely have a number of assessment types which contribute to the overall assessment with different weightings. For example, the end of module examination may represent 50 per cent of the overall score, essays during the semester 35 per cent and group work 15 per cent. The usual way of producing the overall assessment is to take each method (marked out of 100), weight them accordingly, add together to yield the overall assessment per cent score. But is this a justifiable way to treat the data? Lets us assume that each assessment method produces a normal distribution (and this is a big assumption). It is almost certain that the means and standard deviations for each method will be different; after all, each method is measuring different attributes. Typically examination scores result in higher standard deviations that do essay scores. To be able to combine scores from different assessment methods, the means and standard deviations should first be normalized. Johnstone (2004) outlines methods for doing just this.

An increasing problem in assessment is plagiarism. Ready access to the Internet has enabled students to excise information and, in too many cases, incorporate significant copied material into work of their own. Paradoxically, the electronic submission of work has enabled the teacher to identify plagiarism by using plagiarism detecting software, available online and offline (e.g. www.scanmyessay.com; www.checkforplagiarism.net) Most institutions have checking systems in place. Students should be made aware that plagiarism checks will be made; they should be taught what constitutes plagiarism and appropriate ways of referencing and quoting the work of others.

Assessment has the specific function of producing a measure of the student's achievement of the set of learning outcomes but it can do so much more. Such is the desire of many students to achieve a high grade or good degree classification; assessment can be a major driver and director for learning. To maximize the benefits, students need feedback on their performance. Feedback is useful for diagnosing weaknesses and for improving a range of skills. Feedback needs to be encouraging and constructive and certainly should not embody any level of sarcasm or insult. Feedback should be constructed with the aim of improving the performance of the student in time for the next assessment. Above all, for feedback to be useful to the student, it should be timely. A student is less likely to study and act on feedback if there is a long time interval between the assessment and the receipt of feedback. This, of course, puts pressure on the teacher to turn marking round quickly. Computer marked tests, as discussed above, can provide instant feedback to the student.

Resources

For further information the reader should consult the respective chapter on assessment and evaluation within the *International Handbook of Science Education* (Tamir, 1998a), i.e. the contributions of Tamir (1998b) and Gitomer and Duschl (1998). A more recent overview is given by Bell (2008).

References

Ambusaidi, A., & Johnstone, A. H. (2000). Fixed response – what are we testing. *Chemistry Education Research and Practice, 1*, 323-328.

Bacon, R. A. (2009). *Physical sciences question bank*. Hull: Higher Education Academy Physical Science Centre. Retrieved June 05, 2009, from secure.eps.surrey.ac.uk/pssqb/spad/psqbank.php.

Bell, B. (2008). Classroom assessment of science learning. In: S. Abell & N. Lederman (Ed.), *Handbook of Research on Science Education* (pp. 965-1005). Mahwah: Lawrence Erlbaum.

Bennett, S. W. (2004). Assessment in chemistry and the role of examinations. *University Chemistry Education, 8*, 52-57.

Boud, D., Cohen, R., & Sampson, J. (Eds.) (2001). *Peer learning in higher education*. London: Kogan Page.

Byers, W., &. Wilkins, H. (2005). The Midwich Cuckoos revisited: Promoting learning through peer group work. Proceedings of the Science Learning and Teaching

Conference (University of Warwick, United Kingdom), 90-95.

Chin, P., & Overton, T. L. (2005). *Assessing group work.* Hull: Higher Education Academy Physical Sciences Centre. Retrieved June 07, 2009, from www.heacademy.ac.uk/ assets/ps/documents/primers/primers/ps0083_assessing_group_work_mar_2005_1.pdf.

Chickering, A. W., & Gameson, Z. F. (1987). Seven principles for good practice in undergraduate education. *AAHE Bulletin,* 39(7), 3-7.

Dressel, P. L., & Schmid, J. (1953). Some modifications of the multiple choice item. *Educational and Psychological Measurement, 13,* 574-579.

Eilertsen, T. V., & Valdermo, O. (2000). Open-book assessment: A contribution to improved learning?. *Studies in Educational Evaluation, 26,* 91-103.

Gitomer, D. H., & Duschl, R. A. (1998). Emerging issues and practices in assessment. In: B. J. Fraser & K. G. Tobin (Eds.), *International Handbook of Science Education* (pp. 791-810). Dordrecht: Kluwer.

Higher Education Academy Physical Sciences Subject Centre (2005). *Writing learning outcomes.* Hull: Higher Education Academy Physical Sciences Centre. Retrieved June 07, 2009, from www.heacademy.ac.uk/assets/ps/documents/primers/primers/ ps0091_writing_learning_outcomes_mar_2005.pdf.

Johnstone, A. H. (2004). *Effective practice in objective assessment, LTSN physical science practice guide.* Hull: Higher Education Academy Physical Sciences Centre. Retrieved June 07, 2009, from www.heacademy.ac.uk/assets/ps/documents/practice_guides/ practice_guides/ps0072_effective_practice_in_objective_assessment_mar_2004.pdf.

QAA (2007). *Chemistry benchmark statement.* Gloucester: Quality Assurance Agency. Retrieved June 07, 2009, from www.qaa.ac.uk/academicinfrastructure/benchmark/ honours/chemistryfinal.pdf.

Race, P. (2009). *Designing assessment to improve learning.* Hull: Higher Education Academy Physical Sciences Centre. Retrieved June 07, 2009, from www.heacademy.ac.uk/assets/ps/documents/practice_guides/practice_guides/ps0069_de signing_assessment_to_improve_physical_sciences_learning_march_2009.pdf.

Schmidt, H.-J., & Beine, M. (1992). Setting multiple-choice tests. *Education in Chemistry, 29,* 19-21.

Tamir, P. (1990). Justifying the selection of answers in multiple choice tests. *International Journal of Science Education, 12,* 563-573.

Tamir, P. (1998a). Section 7 – Assessment and Evaluation. In: B. J. Fraser & K. G. Tobin (Eds.), *International Handbook of Science Education* (pp. 761-868). Dordrecht: Kluwer.

Tamir, P. (1998b). Assessment and evaluation in science Education: Opportunities to learn and outcomes. In: B. J. Fraser & K. G. Tobin (Eds.), *International Handbook of Science Education* (pp. 761-790). Dordrecht: Kluwer.

Training Programmes for Newly Appointed University Chemistry Teaching Staff

PAUL C. YATES
University of Keele, United Kingdom

IWONA MACIEJOWSKA
Jagiellonian University, Krakow, Poland

It is increasingly recognized that newly appointed university teaching staff, in both chemistry and other disciplines, require training in order to teach effectively and promote student learning. This chapter considers the requirements of such training in order for it to be effective, and describes some of the programmes which are running in individual countries and across Europe, to provide this. Training is provided at the level of the institution, faculty and discipline representing considerable variation in practice. We also highlight a number of resources which may be helpful to the new chemistry lecturer; these include, books, journal articles, and electronic resources.

Introduction

An early proposal for the training of university lecturers identified classroom teaching, tutoring, empowering students to conduct individual study, empowering students to conduct co-operative study with their peers, and practical work projects as a basis for training activities (Martínez, Gros, & Romañ, 1998). To these were subsequently added the design of curricular materials (including study guides, web based material and interactive tutorials), the orientation and tutoring of students throughout their studies, and the evaluation of learning activities developed by students. It was suggested that lecturers' own experiences should be taken into account when delivering training, and that it could begin with participants reporting in which classroom teaching situations they felt at ease or not. Finally, there was a proposal that such training should be led by experts in the teaching of the discipline who would have "sufficient moral authority" to perform this function.

Chapter consultant: Natasa Brouwer, University of Amsterdam, The Netherlands

I. Eilks and B. Byers (Eds.). Innovative Methods in Teaching and Learning Chemistry in Higher Education, pp. 229-256. © 2009 RSC Publishing.

Bamber (2002) has given a useful discussion of the development of training courses for new lecturers in the United Kingdom. She noted that they were first suggested in the Robbins' review of higher education in 1963, but have only become widespread following the recommendation of their introduction by the Dearing Committee (National Committee of Inquiry into Higher Education, 1997).This was appointed to make recommendations on how higher education in the UK should develop over the next 20 years. Bamber's research (Bamber, 2002) showed that such courses were a probationary requirement in 42% of UK universities and compulsory in a further 26%. Senior managers were generally seen to be supportive of such courses although this was often not backed up by the provision of sufficient resources. Heads of Department, on the other hand, seemed to be well aware of the resource implications which meant that their new staff would have less time to spend on teaching and research. This meant that they were often less enthusiastic and supportive of the training.

A study of new lecturers' experience of formal and informal induction processes (Hodkinson & Taylor, 2002) identified mentoring and supervision, appraisal, peer review of teaching and informal contact with colleagues as some characteristics of the process. Participants in the study saw generic training as complementary to subject based mentoring and supervision. The role of such generic programmes in facilitating lecturers to understand themselves as learners was seen as critical for developing their understanding of students. Such programmes should also provide opportunities for interaction with their peers both within and across disciplines. Finally, the study noted that new lecturers from overseas or outside the university sector had even greater need of such development opportunities.

While most of the literature in this area is UK based, there are some studies which attempt to draw comparisons with other countries. One of these studies (Trowler & Bamber, 2005) contains a summary of the training of university lecturers in seven countries: In the Netherlands, Australia and New Zealand it is at the discretion of individual universities, in Finland and Norway it is compulsory while in Sweden and the UK an intermediate state exists. This paper notes that such training was introduced in Sweden because of the increase in student diversity and lack of student preparedness. The authors also state that there is no established relationship between the training of lecturers and student outcomes.

An international group of medical educators has reviewed the evidence of effectiveness of faculty development within their discipline, as described in 53 published papers describing work in the United States, Canada, Egypt, Israel, Malta, Nigeria, the United Kingdom, Switzerland and South Africa (Steinert et al., 2006). Some of the findings were that microteaching and the opportunity to practice were very well received, there was no evidence for any change in student examination performance, several participants took on new educational responsibilities, and that interventions can have both negative and positive effects. There were reports of faculty development interventions which were of greatest benefit to both experienced and inexperienced staff. The paper concludes with a number of implications for practice, including the need to make more use of theory and principles in the design of programmes, to acknowledge the importance of context, to develop more programmes that extend over time, and to develop programmes that encourage reflection and learning among participants.

A study within a single United Kingdom university noted that efforts are required to establish new academic staff since many of the former informal means of doing so are now not available (Barlow & Antoniou, 2007). New staff valued the chance to interact with staff from other disciplines at formal training courses, as well as appreciating the broader perspective such courses provided on the academic role. This work has led to recommendations that the teaching development needs of new staff may be better met if university managers better understand the role of such courses, and the time required for attendance at these courses is built into staff timetables.

It has been noted (Coffey & Gibbs, 2000) that there is little evidence that initial training programmes for new university teachers have any impact with which to guide policy decisions, the choice of rationale, or the pattern of provision. The Student Evaluation of Educational Quality (SEEQ) (Marsh, 2002) was administered to 20 randomly selected students of 20 teachers undertaking such training programmes at each of ten United Kingdom universities at three points in time. The findings indicated that training had a positive effect on some aspects of teaching: Student learning, teacher enthusiasm, clarity of teacher explanation, teacher rapport with students, and breadth of explanation. However, the authors note that these results should be treated with caution because the sample of teachers was self selected, the improvements could have been a consequence of additional teaching experience, the students were a self-selected sub-set of a randomly selected sample, and the students might be more favourably disposed to their teachers after longer experience of their teaching or closer to final assessment.

These authors subsequently undertook a more extensive study of training across 22 universities in eight countries (Gibbs & Coffey, 2004), which also incorporated inclusion of a control group. This was based on the premise that student focused teachers are more likely to have students who take a deep approach to learning, and that such students demonstrate superior learning outcomes. Thus changing the teachers' approach should improve both student learning processes and outcomes. The data obtained supported three conclusions.

· Training can increase the extent to which teachers adopt a student focus.
· It can improve a number of aspects of teaching as judged by students.
· Finally it can change teachers so that their students' learning is improved.

A further benefit noted was that a training programme can help to check the negative influence of departments, where an interest in teaching may be positively discouraged.

An approach to continuing professional development of academics through problem based learning has been described (Stefani & Elton, 2002). It is asserted that this is at the intellectual level of experienced research active members of staff who are interested in the improvement of learning and teaching. Five aspects of the course were particularly praised in external assessments:

· Flexible assessment criteria were determined by negotiated learning agreements.
· The standard of work produced by course members consistently exceeded that that would reasonably be expected.
· The relationship between tutor and course member from teacher via facilitator to colleague, as is the case in research supervision.
· Course members were supported by a local mentor.
· There were particular advantages to running the course in a distance format, and it is stated that it could not have been run face to face.

Given the intellectual rigour of the course as being equivalent to that of research, it is interesting that the authors note the United Kingdom's research assessment exercise discourages staff from putting additional time and work into activities connected with teaching, such as the course described.

Overview of lecturer training within Europe

The first activity of the ECTN's working group for newly appointed university chemistry staff was to gain an overview of the status of training within European universities. This was done through the administration of a questionnaire (Figure 1) at the ECTN plenary meeting in 2004. The nature and number of responses was such that it is not possible to give a detailed breakdown of the situation in each country; however, we hope that that the following descriptions give a flavour of what training might have been offered in each country at that time. It is important to remember that these descriptions apply to individual institutions within the countries mentioned and may not be representative of the country as a whole. It must also be emphasized that we are aware that in a number of these countries the situation has changed within the last five years.

Austria: Informal and optional training is available to postgraduate research students and postdoctoral research staff. No training is available for faculty lecturing staff. Informal training is available through discussions with other colleagues.

Bulgaria: Both formal and informal training is available to all staff who teach. Formal training is provided through organized courses within the department and at institutional level, while informal training is provided through individual consultations, books and journals.

Czech Republic: No training is available for any categories of staff who teach.

Finland: Optional training is available to faculty lecturing staff only. This is delivered at the institutional level; the university provides courses on didactics and e-learning.

France: Informal and optional training is available to postgraduate research students and faculty lecturing staff, but not to postdoctoral research staff. The training for research students is provided by volunteers from an organization within the Ministry of Education.

Italy: Informal training is offered to postgraduate research students and postdoctoral research staff; this may consist of discussions between course professors and their laboratory assistants. No training is available to faculty lecturing staff.

Questions:

1. For each category of staff, please indicate the type of teaching performed:

   a. Doctoral research students: laboratory tutorial/seminar lecture

   b. Postdoctoral research staff: laboratory tutorial/seminar lecture

   c. Faculty lecturing staff: laboratory tutorial/seminar lecture

   Please also indicate the type of teaching performed by other categories of staff, and any other type of teaching which hasn't been mentioned.

2. Please indicate whether any training is offered to each category of staff who teach in your institution, and whether this is formal (e.g. courses) or informal (e.g. guidance from experienced colleagues). Please also indicate whether any formal training is optional or compulsory.

   a. Postgraduate research students training
      No Formal Informal Compulsory Optional

   b. Postdoctoral research staff
      No Formal Informal Compulsory Optional

   c. Faculty lecturing staff
      No Formal Informal Compulsory Optional

   d. Other (specify):_____
      No Formal Informal Compulsory Optional

3. If appropriate, please indicate who delivers this training:

   a. Formal: Department Institution External trainer

   b. If Institution or External Trainer please give brief details

   c. Informal: Please give details

4. Please indicate any problems or make any comments relating to the training of newly appointed staff in your institution

Figure 1. Survey on training new teaching staff.

Latvia: Training for postgraduate research students and postdoctoral research staff is informal but compulsory. This may consist of seminars and discussions with visiting professors.

Netherlands: Formal courses are compulsory for postgraduate research students and postdoctoral research staff, and optional for faculty lecturing staff. Such training is delivered by departments such as the Institute of Science Didactics, and consists of a course lasting five days.

Poland: Research students receive both formal and informal training, while no training is available to postdoctoral research staff or lecturers. Training is provided within the department.

Spain: Formal training is compulsory for postdoctoral research staff, while informal training is optional for postgraduate research students and faculty lecturing staff.

United Kingdom: Training is compulsory for faculty lecturing staff, while informal training is available for postgraduate research students and postdoctoral research staff. Training is delivered principally at the institutional level, and so does not contain subject specific material.

We will subsequently examine the training provided in four countries in more detail.

Design of Training

Target groups

The training needs of teaching staff naturally vary according to their responsibilities, the country, and their specific university. This is mirrored to some extent by the training opportunities offered in each case. Some of the teaching activities which are undertaken by such staff can be characterised as:

- Lectures
- Laboratory classes (including pre- and post-lab activities)
- Seminars (presentation of papers prepared independently by students followed by a discussion)
- Proseminars (extension of the content of lectures in the form of a discussion guided by the teacher)
- Problem classes (solving computational tasks)
- Mini-projects
- Preparation of bachelor's and master's theses (research work, literature study, writing the thesis)

It is worth noting that different categories of staff may undertake a different set of such activities in different countries. For example, in some countries doctoral students only assist in the running of laboratory classes, while in Poland, for example, such students may lead proseminars and seminars independently. Consequently the training needs of this group in different countries may be quite different.

In some countries, lectures may be given by anyone with a doctorate, as long as they are employed as an academic teacher or postdoctoral research fellow. In central and eastern Europe, lectures may be given only by "independent academics with outstanding academic achievements", usually with several years of experience. Such staff often do not feel that they need to improve their teaching skills. Technical staff and postgraduates (both masters and doctoral students) often also have teaching responsibilities, such as demonstrating an experiment during the course of a lecture. Lectures or seminars may also be given by visiting teaching staff, most usually from industry or external scientific institution.

While most training activities have been directed towards new teaching staff, other factors which may lead to a need for training include:

·   Staff moving to a new position
·   New pedagogical developments
·   Changes in national educational policy
·   Changes in law (e.g. the Bologna declaration, new curriculum standards, new safety regulations)

Although different employers will also have individual training needs, some universal requirements of teaching staff can be identified:

·   Good demonstration skills.
·   Ability to select an appropriate experiment for a given objective.
·   Ability to select appropriate lecture content.
·   Ability to motivate students to think and study.
·   Ability to adjust language and content to an appropriate level.
·   Ability to deal with a multicultural student environment and students with different levels of knowledge.
·   Ability to introduce students to the rules, regulations, customs and traditions of the particular university.

Timing

There are several possibilities for the timing of this training. At some American universities an academic teacher is not allowed to teach until they have undergone basic "didactic" training. This is typically delivered in the form of an intensive course in the month preceding the start of semester in a pre-service orientation programme. This has the advantage of making staff aware of the safety aspects of working with students in laboratories, and the appropriate rules and regulations applicable to academic study. However, the lack of experience in teaching may impede such training; the participants are more likely to experience passive receipt of knowledge rather than participating in active discussions about their teaching. It may well be more advantageous to organise such training in the form of an in-service or apprenticeship programme after the participants have taught for at least one semester. In this case it is likely to be easier to achieve active participation in training sessions, as the participants will have their own experiences and precise expectations as they already know where they encounter difficulties. The course may also be better adjusted to individual needs.

Other universities run less intensive courses, typically in the form of one or two hour meetings organised once a week throughout a semester or academic year. This allows the trainer to observe the development of the participants and to react to didactic problems on an ongoing basis.

There is also a need to improve the skills of established teaching staff. This may be done through in-service workshops (typically consisting of a lecture followed by discussion, often at lunchtime) led by specialists from other universities or countries, or workshops on specific subjects run by specialists from staff development units, where such units exist.

Another possibility, as yet less developed, is to offer training in the form of "awaydays" or summer schools remote from the workplace. Potential problems with this form of delivery include:

- The need for a higher level of financial support than would be needed with other forms of training.
- Problems related to absence from the workplace.
- Problems related to absence from home for those with caring responsibilities.
- The need for a very intense programme.

On the other hand, the advantages of this form of training are that:

- The participants focus on the course since there are no work distractions.
- The precise timings can be adjusted to the needs of the participants.
- There are opportunities for the participants to interact during informal settings (such as meals, excursions and when travelling) which leads to better integration and networking.

Mode of delivery

Training academic staff constitutes a form of educating adults (Armitage et al., 1999), and as such it has to comply with the following principles:

- Make references to existing knowledge and previous experiences.
- Emphasise the significance and value of included content.
- Allow the learner to ask questions, make mistakes and express doubts.
- Take place in an atmosphere conducive to open expression of opinions.
- Actively involve the learner in the process.

The following methods are typically used in the training of teaching staff:

- Lectures
- Workshops
- Online methods
- Directed reading tutorials.

The mutual exchange of experiences is particularly valuable, as well as sharing problems with other course participants and the joint search for solutions to these problems. Lectures on subjects with which chemistry teachers are not usually familiar, such as pedagogy and psychology, have to be taught in the same way as students are taught new material in everyday teaching. Participants would also typically be expected to obtain information from sources of knowledge which they discover independently of the course leader. They will also need to develop a familiarity with specialist educational terminology in order to understand this material in some cases. The mutual evaluation of course activities by course participants often produces better results than that provided by the trainer.

An effective method for improving presentation skills is for course participants to present a short talk to the group which is recorded and then discussed. This can be analysed further by using the technology to separate out the visual and audio elements of the presentation.

It is, of course, possible to use a variety of methods for the online delivery of training. This can have the advantage of reducing the time that busy academics need to spend on this activity, and allow access when they are away from their home institution. However, the benefits of the interactions resulting from face to face training cannot be overestimated, and these are inevitably lost to some extent. Academics have also noted that timetabled sessions during working time are far more likely to be protected, whereas with online delivery the training is more likely to have to take place in their spare time.

Generic versus discipline specific

As we have seen, much of the training that has been developed is at the institutional level. From an economic viewpoint, this is efficient as the numbers of staff from each discipline may be relatively small. However, this does then mean that such training is unable to address discipline specific aspects of learning and teaching; one that comes to mind in the case of chemistry is that of laboratory classes. Neumann (2001) notes that studies of university teaching and learning have also focused on generic aspects, despite the fact that academics identify most strongly with their own discipline.

It is obviously desirable to provide discipline specific training wherever possible, and some ways in which this has been done are noted below. Separate sessions for a group of scientists have been run within a generic course, and a summer school for new chemistry lecturers within Europe has been run. In the second case expanding the geographical area has allowed a critical mass of participants to be reached. An intermediate stage is represented in the UK by the New Lecturers' Workshop run by the Physical Sciences Centre of the Higher Education Academy (2007). However, this is open to both chemists and physicists.

Content

In order to effectively train teaching staff, it is important to identify the "hard" and "soft" competencies which are required. Most training tends to concentrate on the generic skills such as effective communication, presentation of knowledge, building authority, motivating students and conflict management. While the contents of individual courses do vary, the contents of typical programmes are well represented by the material covered in any of the many relevant textbooks now available (Light & Cox, 2001; Newble & Cannon, 1989; Race, 2001).

It will be apparent from the previous discussion that not every topic will be relevant to every target group; in the following table we suggest a mapping of training topics to groups. This is based on our own personal views, and others would no doubt recommend slightly modified schemes:

Table 1: Mapping of training topics to target groups

Topic	Target Group				
	New lecturer	Lecturer	Teaching assistant	Lab assistant	Demonstrator
Pedagogy, adult learning, elements of andragogy		●	●		
Presentation skills		●			●
E-learning, blended learning		●			
Pre-labs and practical classes				●	
Methods of teaching, context and problem based learning		●	●		
Assessment		●			
Disability issues	●	●	●	●	●
Evaluation	●	●	●	●	●
Group work		●	●	●	
Supervision		●			
Portfolios	●	●	●	●	●
Survival for new lecturers	●				
Didactics: curriculum / organization and forms of classes in university education / principles of teaching / preparation of teacher for classes		●	●		
Social communication	●	●	●	●	●

Here we are assuming that a teaching assistant takes problem classes and tutorials, and that a demonstrator takes charge of a laboratory session with the aid of an appropriate number of laboratory assistants. It will be no surprise that the greatest number of topics is required by established lecturers, who are involved with curriculum development and quality improvement.

Examples of Training

A case study from Poland

The training provided within the Faculty of Chemistry at Jagiellonian University in Krakow, Poland, is intended to meet the teaching quality guidelines set for the European Higher Education Area (EHEA) by the European Network for Quality Assurance (ENQA). These stipulate that *"teaching staff should be given opportunities to develop and extend their teaching capacity"* and that *"institutions should provide poor teachers with opportunities to improve their skills to an acceptable level"* (European Association for Quality Assurance in Higher Education, 2005).

Academic staff and PhD students within this faculty have traditionally been able to extend their didactic experience in the following ways:

- By participating in full-time courses or events organised as part of the series *Selected Problems of Chemistry Didactics in Tertiary Education*, which have been run since 2001 and in a residential form since 2005
- By participating in courses *Ars Docendi* organised by the university's teaching department for all the university's employees since 2004 (www.uj.edu.pl/dydaktyka/dydaktyka.php?id=26)
- By participating in open sessions of the didactic commission of the faculty council
- By attending lectures about the teaching of students given by external experts
- By participating in national and international conferences organised by the faculty
- By becoming acquainted with other educational systems through participation in staff exchange programmes such as the EU's Socrates-Erasmus.

In 2001 the faculty began a course for PhD students and new teaching staff entitled *Selected Problems of Chemistry Didactics in Tertiary Education*. Here we will describe the course in the form in which it was delivered in the academic year 2007-2008. The course consists of classes on general subjects, conducted by a psychologist or pedagogue, and on discipline specific issues, conducted by a member of the Department of Chemical Education. In both cases they are supplemented by material provided by academic chemistry teachers.

There are three components to the residential course:

- Preparation for the event, consisting of two or three meetings covering course organization, the environment (consisting of the principal teacher's aids such as posters, models, overheads, literature, computer programs, internet resources, items which may cause problems in transportation, etc.), and discussions with deans and curriculum developers.
- The three day residential course itself.
- One or two follow up meetings, which include presentations of proposed teaching activities for students, discussion of the impact of the

residential course on teaching methods subsequently, and any ideas arising which may be presented at conferences (Wietecha, Mania, Woźniakiewicz, Madej, & Maciejowska, 2003).

During the course there is also the opportunity to consider the broader perspective of the requirements of a potential employer. The job prospects of students are affected by what professional experience they have as well as how and what they are taught. The pharmaceutical industry is a major employer of chemistry graduates in this case, and such involvement emphasised the importance of proper documentation of experiments, since *"anything not documented properly has not been done"* (Organisation for Economic Co-operation and Development, OECD, 2006). Since contemporary industry is governed by the rules of Good Manufacturing Practice (GMP), it follows that modern chemistry laboratories are obliged to follow Good Laboratory Practice (GLP) (Brindell, Maciejowska, Mania, Wietecha-Posluszny, & Yates, 2007).

The following assessments are set in order to judge whether participants have successfully completed the course:

- Preparation of a correct course description, including a statement of learning outcomes.
- Preparation of an evaluation questionnaire for one's course.
- Presentation of one didactic problem which has posed difficulties for the participant, together with its solution.
- Presentation of a scenario of new or revised classes, where teaching methods are used which promote active learning.

The materials developed as part of these assessments are typically presented at national and international conferences, where they often stimulate discussion and require the presenters to defend their proposals.

Contributions to the *Ars Docendi* course are predominantly from scholars and authorities recognized in Poland. Participants benefit from the teaching of outstanding lecturers and from becoming acquainted with the experiences of academic staff in other faculties. Although the course has a positive effect on the personal development of participants and their views of teaching, it may have only a limited effect on the quality of teaching to chemistry students through the lack of direct applicability of some of the techniques proposed and the restricted number of specific examples.

A case study from the United Kingdom

The Teaching and Learning in Higher Education Programme (www.keele.ac.uk/depts/aa/landt/ma/tlhep.htm) began at Keele University, United Kingdom, in 1993. It was consequently one of the early examples of such a programme in the United Kingdom, although virtually all universities now provide such programmes for new teaching staff. As might be expected, the course has evolved since its inception, and here we describe the course as it is running in 2007-2008. It is offered at two levels: Associate and Postgraduate Certificate.

The course handbook states that *"teaching is viewed as an aspect of academic work that, just like research, demands both practical competencies and a theoretically informed and critical approach"*. It goes on to state that participants are encouraged to develop knowledge about how students learn, collegiality, an understanding of contexts, competence in a range of pedagogic skills and techniques, a reflexive and experimental approach, personal professional values, theoretical rationales, and an awareness of the scholarship of learning and teaching.

The course is accredited by the Higher Education Academy (HEA). This is the national body in the United Kingdom which provides the framework of support and standards for teaching and learning in higher education. It has a set of national standards (Higher Education Academy, 2007), onto which the two levels of TLHEP have been mapped. Those who complete the Associate module are eligible to become HEA Associate Fellows, while those who complete the Postgraduate Certificate are eligible for admission as HEA Fellows.

For a number of university staff, successful completion of the TLHEP is a contractual requirement before an appointment is confirmed at the end of probation. This includes academic staff with less than four years experience of teaching, and Graduate Teaching Assistants. The course has also been taken by other staff when space has been available. The advantage of HEA accreditation is that the course will be recognized in other institutions within the United Kingdom, thus assisting staff mobility.

The course is structured into three components:

1. Structured input consists of two introductory days which provide a common starting point with a practical bias. These are followed by weekly sessions which cover core themes relevant to all candidates, and optional sessions which will be more relevant to some participants than others. Candidates are expected to attend ten of the latter according to their own requirements. They are also invited to lead workshops in disciplinary areas related to issues arising out of their own teaching. The list of topics covered in these sessions is given in Table 2.

2. Practical activities include a requirement to engage in peer observation of teaching, through both observing and being observed. They are also required to read material related to the areas covered, focusing on areas of particular interest. A conscious decision has been taken not to provide a definitive reading list, so that candidates are encouraged to direct their own reading in consultation with course tutors. Participants are also required to build productive professional support networks, and to engage in discussion with colleagues on aspects of teaching and learning. They should keep a reflective diary, which includes reflection on critical incidents which have caused them to re-think their understandings, expectations and assumptions.

3. Candidates are expected to attend and reflect on other meetings related to learning and teaching, as appropriate. These include talks by invited speakers, and workshops provided by the Centre for Professional Staff Development.

At both levels the course is assessed by means of a portfolio. Candidates are asked to provide a critical commentary, with illustrative examples, on planning, preparation and presentation of teaching sessions, challenges encountered and overcome, how their thinking about teaching has evolved, evaluation of their teaching, the relationship between learning, teaching and assessment, additional professional development undertaken, discussions with colleagues and administrative tasks undertaken. It should also include evidence of teaching and a mix of self, peer and student evaluation. Portfolios are marked by a programme tutor and a second marker, followed by moderation by an external examiner. The criteria for success are that a candidate has critically reflected on learning, teaching and assessment, has drawn upon theoretical models of learning, teaching and assessment to inform practice, and has monitored and evaluated practice, making changes where necessary.

Table 2: Core and optional sessions in the Keele University Teaching and Learning in Higher Education Programme.

Core Sessions	Optional Sessions
Introductory days	Group teaching techniques
Understanding student learning	Lecturing
Promoting student centred learning	Session planning
Assessment	Marking and feedback
Evaluation	Dealing with plagiarism
Catering for diversity	Helping your students make the best use of ICT
Reflective writing and completing a portfolio	Problem-based learning
	Personal development planning
	Designing modules and courses
	Designing ICT into modules and courses
	Balancing teaching and research
	Candidate-led workshops

The course is taken by eligible staff from all disciplines across the university. Consequently, the formal part of the programme is unable to address discipline specific issues. To address this, in the current academic year a group of science lecturers on the programme has been set up under the guidance of a programme tutor who has a science background. This group meets to discuss aspects of science teaching which are unique and to examine previous successful TLHEP portfolios in the sciences. A particular area of concern for this group has been how to develop their reflective writing skills, which has been addressed through discussion and with reference to the literature (Kreber, 2005). The opportunity has also been taken to introduce relevant literature both within science education and specific disciplines, supported by material on WebCT.

A case study from Finland

The strategic plan for the University of Helsinki, Finland, stipulates that every new university teacher should have access to relevant training (Postareff, Lindblom-Ylänne, & Nevgi, 2007). This is on a voluntary basis, but members of staff are usually highly motivated to attend in order to enhance their careers.

Three short courses, lasting between four and six months, provide staff with the basic skills to plan, instruct and assess their courses. A subsequent one year course, organized by the Centre for Research and Development of Higher Education, seeks to deepen their understanding including the opportunity to reflect on their teaching and development. The final training component lasts for two years, and gives teachers the opportunity to carry out a research project in teaching in higher education.

Given the voluntary nature of these programmes, teaching staff can engage with the process up to whatever level they feel is most appropriate.

A case study from the Netherlands

All new members of staff at the Universiteit van Amsterdam, The Netherlands, are required to successfully complete the learning and teaching in higher education certificate (LTHEP, in Dutch BKO) (Universiteit van Amsterdam Faculty of Science, 2007). This is provided in the Faculty of Science for natural science and mathematics education.

The aims of the programme are to

- Promote the professional development of new lecturers.
- Ensure that each new lecturer is familiar with the university's education vision, faculty organization, quality assurance and the curriculum.
- Ensure that new lecturers are competent to perform independently all the functions expected of a member of academic staff in a research university.
- The components of the programme are summarised in Table 3, which also shows the activities associated with each and the average time required to complete each one.

Table 3:   The Learning and Teaching in Higher Education certificate in the Faculty of Science at the Universiteit van Amsterdam

Component	Activities	Time /h
Orientation to Education at the faculty	Getting acquainted with the education practice and organization at the Faculty	10
Lectureship	Active participation in departmental meetings	8
Hands-on workshops	7 day-meetings	49
Teaching practice	Design and provision of teaching, developing of teaching materials and quality control	162
Supervision, feedback, peer review	Mentor, peer feedback, coaching by LTHEP coordinator	30
Assessment (portfolio)	Preparation of the portfolio	16
TOTAL		275

The programme is assessed by means of a portfolio submission which is evaluated according to:

- Design of teaching
- Provision of teaching
- Supporting the learning process
- Organizing education and quality control
- Professional attitude
- Evaluations by students.

The LTHEP matrix (see: www.science.uva.nl/amstel/dws/lthe/index.php?page_id=1171) is used to monitor and assess participants. Other faculties at the Universiteit van Amsterdam have a different programme but with the same overall list of competencies. In all cases assessment is by means of a portfolio.

Case study of international training within Europe

The second, and major, activity, of the Newly Appointed University Chemistry Teaching Staff (NAUCTS) working group of the ECTN was "*to plan the organization and content of a summer school to provide teacher training, to provide a forum for the exchange of ideas and good practices, and to provide European networking opportunities for new staff*". The aim was to provide such a summer school for around thirty staff addressing a range of topics taught by experts in their fields from across Europe.

The summer school ran over five days and consisted of workshops on portfolios for students and staff, peer group work, practical classes, presentation skills, assessment, evaluation, context and problem based learning, online resources, and supervision. In addition to these interactive workshops there were shorter information giving lectures on European developments in chemical education, European funding and widening participation, and evening discussion sessions on the European image of chemistry and the many roles of the teacher. The summer school began with a highly interactive icebreaker activity and ended with a session looking at how participants could continue to network.

Prior to the summer school a message board was set up with one of the international web services. This allowed information about the summer school to be posted, and participants to introduce themselves. As can be seen from Table 4, 27 lecturers from 12 European countries attended. Detailed feedback was collected during and at the end of the summer school; this was overwhelmingly positive and showed that this was regarded as a highly valuable event.

This led the ECTN Management Committee to apply for funding for a second summer school to run in 2007. This application was successful, and the number of applicants increased quite considerably. The summer school ran with 30 participants, the distribution of countries being shown in Table 4.

A number of changes to the programme were made in the light of experience. There was far more emphasis on interactive workshop sessions, no formal lectures, and only one evening discussion session. The emphasis was thus very much on practical teaching techniques. The feedback was again very positive, leading the organizers to hope that it will be possible to run further events of this type.

In both cases the participants were required to contribute to the proceedings of the summer school (European Chemistry Thematic Network, 2005, 2007). Different pairs of lecturers, from different countries, were assigned to report on each individual session. It was also hoped that this might foster longer term collaborations. There is some evidence that this has happened.

Table 4 shows that during the course of the two summer schools, 57 lecturers from 18 European countries have been trained. It is noteworthy that not all of the countries have been represented on each occasion. As far as the authors are aware, this remains the unique example of a Europe wide training event for teachers in higher education within a single discipline.

Table 4: Number of participants at the ECTN summer schools by country

Country	2005	2007
Austria		1
Bulgaria	4	3
Czech Republic		4
Finland	1	
France		1
Germany	3	
Greece	1	
Hungary	1	
Ireland	5	2
Italy	1	
Lithuania		1
Malta	1	
Netherlands		1
Poland	3	5
Portugal		1
Slovakia	1	
Spain	1	3
United Kingdom	5	8

Comparing the examples

Consideration of these five examples highlights three factors which are fundamental to such training activity:

- The difference between compulsory courses and those which participants attend out of a desire to improve their skills. One would obviously prefer staff to adopt the latter course of action, but it is likely that compulsion does result in such training being provided to a larger group of staff.
- The difference between generic courses, those offered at science faculty level, and those offered specifically within chemistry. This is generally related to the likely size of cohort, with only larger institutions being able to offer courses at the level of the discipline. There may, therefore, be some merit in continuing to develop chemistry specific training at the international level.
- The level of experience of the participants. All the examples of training here are aimed at relatively new lecturers, but some continue to offer support over a longer period of time than others. There is considerable provision for new staff, but far less for the continuing professional development of experienced staff.

The relationship with other training activities

The majority of training that has been developed for academic staff is focused on support for learning and teaching in traditional undergraduate and taught postgraduate courses. However, recent developments in the United Kingdom have concentrated on training for academics who will be supervising research students for the first time. The outline of such a programme is given in Table 5. The course is supported by a textbook (Taylor & Beasley, 2005), and papers from the research literature on topics such as management styles (Gatfield & Alpert. 2002) and the examination process (Mullins & Kiley, 2002). Each session is facilitated by an experienced trainer in this area, with input from an academic who is an experienced supervisor. This allows input to the generic course from a range of disciplines.

Table 5: Research supervisor training programme at Keele University, United Kingdom.

Session	Details
1	*Introduction to Programme* • Experiences of supervision - group activities based on the article "Delaying Higher Degree Completion". • The multiple roles of the supervisor • Adult learning – reactions to statements
2	*Codes of Practice* • Supervision as a regulated process • Introduction to national and international contexts. • Quiz containing 20 questions on the Keele Code of Practice. Feedback with discussion.
3	*Expectations in research supervision* • Discussion of the "Expectations in Research Supervision" questionnaire • Common features and disciplinary differences • Support for supervision – the role of mentors
4	*Managing and monitoring student performance* • Project management • Learning plans • Managing student performance (case study)
5	*Managing relationships with students* • Discussion of "Meeting of Minds" article from the Guardian. Development of an equivalent checklist for supervisors. • Some views from experienced supervisors • Personal vs. professional, advisor vs. regulator • Consideration of the needs of diverse students using the list in Phillips and Pugh (2005, pp131-134).
6	*Submission and Examination – the supervisor's role* • Discussion of the paper "It's a PhD, not a Nobel prize" (Mullins & Kiley, 2002). • Case study "Under Pressure from the Start" (Tinkler & Jackson, 2004, p187).

Evaluating Training

General Considerations

It is important when evaluating training not to rely too heavily on a single source of information. The main sources are likely to be self evaluation, evaluation by the participants, evaluation by peers and evaluation by an external party (Kozyra, 2009). Some useful information on procedures relating to the evaluation of teaching can be found in the final report of the ECTN working group which considered this topic (European Chemistry Thematic Network, 2006).

Evaluation by Participants

The views of participants in training activities may be sought using questionnaires, a metaplan, an open discussion, or by introducing a researcher to the group. It is possible to use technology in the feedback process, in the form of a website or "*book of complaints*" (Kozyra, 2009).

The questions posed may relate to issues such as the course and programme, the learning environment (for example access to literature, the range of teaching aids used by the leader and participants, conditions of studying during classes), and the effectiveness of the trainer. They may be very basic (such as "were difficult issues explained clearly and precisely?" or "did classes take place according to the schedule?"), have a general character (such as "to what extent do you agree with the statement that 'I am satisfied with the course as a whole'?") or more detailed (such as "the trainer paid more attention to the things I memorized than to the things I understood").

It is important that there are sufficient questions in order to fully characterise the behaviour and didactic skills of individual teachers. On the other hand, too many questions may result in the submission of questionnaires which have been incompletely answered. It is also important that questionnaires are tailored to specific courses, depending on the information which is required.

Analysis of the results provides an opportunity for reflection and the consideration of introducing changes suggested by the participants. However, it is important to be aware of the limitations of this process and to avoid over-interpretation of the results and being too self critical. Some of the most common problems with the process are (Kozyra, 2009):

- Submission of an insufficient number of questionnaires to be statistically valid. Individual evaluations are largely subjective.
- If completion of the questionnaire is not mandatory, they may be completed only by enthusiasts and sceptics. The absence of indifferent responses may need to be taken into account.
- If completion of the questionnaire is mandatory, some respondents may select random answers.
- Participants may negatively evaluate sessions at which they were absent, relying on the views of others.

Longer term

While it is far less common to evaluate the longer term effects of training, it is important that methods for doing this are developed. It is desirable to ascertain the effect of training on teacher variables (knowledge, attitudes, behaviour) and student variables (achievements, attitudes, rating of instructions) (Gregory, 1980). Teaching staff and students could be randomly assigned to either a training or control group, and pre-test and post-test measurements carried out. This could be done using questionnaires, interviews, observations and video recording. True experimental studies tend to concentrate on a narrow range of topics.

Resources

The emphasis in this section will be on resources which could be accessed by someone wishing to set up a training programme, or which an individual member of staff could be directed to.

Needless to say most of the discussed aspects are considered further from different foci in the various chapters of this book.

Books on teaching and learning in higher education

There are many titles which could have been included in this section. However, most books in this area are predominantly generic, so we have tried to select those which have specific chapters of most use to chemists. This will often relate to teaching in the sciences generally, or laboratory work. However, before doing that it is worth noting the volume by Barrett (1996) in the *"Interesting Ways to Teach"* series. This covers assessment, evaluation, industry and community links, laboratories, new technologies, presentation of information, and writing. It would provide a useful starting point to anyone starting to teach chemistry at the tertiary level who required an introduction with some subject specific material.

An earlier book in this series, by Gibbs and Habeshaw (1989) contains chapters on supervising project work and teaching labs and practicals. Exley (1999) has written on the *"key aspects of teaching and learning in science and engineering"*. This chapter includes a case study on a team based approach to practical work in chemistry, a planning matrix for laboratory and practical work, and a section on assessing practical work with large numbers of students. Brown and Atkins (1988) include a chapter on effective laboratory teaching. This discusses some alternatives to conventional methods, the design of a laboratory manual, and the evaluation of laboratory teaching. There is also a section on ways in which one can study the process of learning within the laboratory setting.

There are fewer relevant books available in languages other than English. However, one which may be of use to those in Slavonic countries has been published in Polish (Maciejowska, 2008).

Journals on teaching and learning in higher education

Chemistry Education Research and Practice (www.rsc.org/Publishing/ Journals/RP/Index.asp) is described as *"the journal for teachers, researchers and other practitioners in chemistry education"*. It is published free of charge, electronically, four times a year and covers:

- Research, and reviews of research in chemistry education.
- Effective practice in the teaching of chemistry.
- In depth analyses of issues of direct relevance to chemistry education.

Recent articles have included "Contextualizing nanotechnology in chemistry education" (O'Connor & Hayden, 2008) and "Students' perceptions of when conceptual development occurs during laboratory instruction" (Domin, 2007). It is worth noting that this journal was formed by combining two journals in 2005, so that articles referenced in University Chemistry Education may also be accessed from the journal website.

In the US, the *Journal of Chemical Education* (jchemed.chem.wisc.edu/Journal/Issues/index.html) is the principal journal which will be of interest to new lecturing staff in chemistry. This is largely concerned with practical suggestions for teaching, although other areas are also covered. Recent articles to have appeared in the journal include "Strategies to simplify service-learning efforts in chemistry" (Sutheimer, 2008) and "Using oral examination as a technique to assess student understanding and teaching effectiveness" (Roecker, 2007).

While these two journals are likely to be the principal sources of material for new chemistry lecturers, others may also be worth consulting. Education in Chemistry (Royal Society of Chemistry, www.rsc.org/Education/EiC/index.asp) does carry articles relevant to tertiary education, and more general journals devoted to this level of education do carry relevant articles and occasionally ones that are specific to chemistry.

Although not strictly a journal, Educational Reviews (Higher Education Academy Physical Sciences Centre, www.heacademy.ac.uk/physsci/publications/journals) commissions reviews of teaching, learning and assessment resources in physical sciences, many of which refer to materials which can be invaluable to teaching staff.

Significant journal articles

The starting point for a new chemistry lecturer who wants to know more about the pedagogy of chemistry teaching in an accessible way must be the review by Bailey and Garratt (Bailey & Garratt, 2002). This references all the essential literature that might be required, including generic pedagogy and that which is more specific to chemistry. An invaluable section of the paper summarizes the principles which the authors gain from educational theory:

- The starting point for constructivist theory is "what do the students already know or understand.
- Tutors need to take account of the fact that the way in which students study depends on their motivation, ability and character.
- Feedback, participation, constructivism and environment drive the learning process.
- Over assessment can encourage students to rote learn, and reduce their motivation.
- Tutors should provide students with the opportunity to influence learning.
- Curriculum overload should be avoided to allow time for students to reflect.

An earlier more generic overview of science education at tertiary level (Laws, 1996) is now somewhat dated, but nevertheless still gives a useful overview of some of the important literature. This is divided into sections on teaching, learning and students. Teaching covers funding and quality, tutorials, the culture of science teaching, pedagogy, lecturing, laboratory work, project work, course content, structure and assessment, and educational technology. Learning addresses models, study techniques and student conceptions. The section on students covers statistics, access, attitudes, and gender issues. Although there has not been a recent update of this work, DeHaan (2005) has provided a useful extension to the review of the literature in this area.

Laboratory work has been addressed at the tertiary level (Johnstone & Al-Shuaili, 2001). Although this paper is apparently generic it does appear in a chemistry journal and is biased towards the subject. The authors note that much of the literature has been generated by researchers at secondary school level, but that their findings can be applied at university level. The paper also defines four laboratory instruction styles based on the outcome, approach and procedure of a particular experiment.

Online resources

There are obviously many websites which contain information that may potentially be of use to the new chemistry instructor. In this section we highlight a small number which are of particular value, and which come from trusted sources.

The *Oxford Centre for Staff and Learning Development* (OCSLD) describes itself as "*one of the UK's largest provider of staff and educational development for higher education, with a reputation for innovation in learning and teaching*". Part of its website (www.brookes.ac.uk/ services/ocsd/2_learntch/index.html) contains a number of links relevant to learning and teaching; these include materials on independent learning, theories of learning, small group teaching, course design, and the purposes and principles of assessment.

The *Physical Sciences Centre* of the UK's *Higher Education Academy* (www.heacademy.ac.uk) maintains a database of collected resources on learning and teaching. These consist of descriptions of materials, downloadable resources, descriptions of activities, and summaries of effective approaches and strategies. The Journal of Chemical Education has a Chemical Education Resource Shelf (jchemed.chem.wisc.edu/JCEWWW/ Features/CERS/index.html) which contains links to details of printed and electronic resources, listed under specific categories.

Finally, the *Division of Chemistry Education at Purdue University* (chemed.chem.purdue.edu/chemed/bodnergroup/index.html) has a large number of lecture demonstrations and problem solving strategies and other materials on general and organic chemistry. A test bank of exam questions may also be accessed by arrangement with the author. It is worth noting that these resources have been developed by a group which is active in chemical education research.

Benefits of training

The evaluation of the *Selected Problems of Chemistry Didactics in Tertiary Education* produced a number of interesting comments (Brindell et al, 2007). Participants appreciated the opportunity to share experiences and ideas. They also found the constructive criticism of the oral presentations and learning and teaching of chemistry beneficial in a wider context. They also listed as useful, valuable and important:

· Adjusting the programme to the needs of participants.
· Introduction of formal regulations.
· Increased self awareness.
· New knowledge, such as the Bologna declaration.

Following the ECTN summer schools (European Chemistry Thematic Network, 2005, 2007) one of the authors observed that presentation skills of participants had improved. It is important to remember that such skills are likely to be determined by a number of factors so that a direct relationship cannot be established. On the other hand, networking activities are easier to relate directly to such events. The laboratory regulations at Jagiellonian University were modified by people conducting the classes as a result of discussions initiated during the summer school. Collaboration has also developed between Strathclyde University (UK) and Dublin Institute of Technology (Ireland), which successfully obtained external funding, as a result of a partnership developed at the summer school. The authors intend to continue to evaluate the impact of this programme over the longer term. This is likely to include interviewing a sample of the participants. Suggested questions include:

· What were your expectations of the training?
· Have you fulfilled them?
· What were the direct benefits of the training?
· What were the indirect benefits of the training?
· Has your knowledge changed as a result of the training? How?
· Have your attitudes changed as a result of the training? How?
· Has your behaviour changed as a result of the training? In what way?
· What future plans have you made as a result of the training?

Conclusions

We have outlined a number of training programmes which are available to new chemistry lecturers both within specific European countries and also internationally. However, it is important to remember that in many countries such training is not available or even seen as being needed. Consequently we believe that there is a useful role for the provision of international activities which expose participants to best practice in other countries.

Many resources are available to assist the new chemistry lecturer, and here as in training it is important to make use of both generic and chemistry specific materials as appropriate.

Acknowledgements

The authors would like to thank Natasa Brouwer, University of Amsterdam, The Netherlands and Sari Lindblom-Ylänne, University of Helsinki, Finland for providing details of the programmes running in their institutions.

References

Armitage, A., Bryant, R., Dunnill, R., Hammersley, M., Hayes, D., Hudson, A., & Lawes, S. (1999). *Teaching and training in post-compulsory education.* Buckingham: Open University Press.

Bailey, P. D., & Garratt, J. (2002). Chemical education: Theory and practice. *University Chemistry Education, 6*, 39-57.

Bamber, V. (2002). To what extent has the Dearing policy recommendation on training new lecturers met acceptance? Where Dearing went that Robbins didn't dare. *Teacher Development, 6*, 433-457.

Barlow, J., & Antoniou, M. (2007). Room for improvement: The experiences of new lecturers in higher education. *Innovations in Education and Training International, 44*, 67-77.

Barrett, J. (1996). *Teaching university students chemistry.* Bristol: Technical and Educational Services.

Brindell, M., Maciejowska, I., Mania, J., Wietecha-Posluszny, J., & Yates, P. (2007). *Residential course – New proposal for academic teachers training.* Retrieved April 01, 2009, from www.pg.gda.pl/chem/InneJednostki/PTChem/Roczniki_2007/all_annals.pdf.

Brown, G., & Atkins, M. (1988). *Effective teaching in higher education.* London: Routledge.

Coffey, M., & Gibbs, G. (2000). Can academics benefit from training? Some preliminary evidence. *Teaching in Higher Education, 5*, 385-389.

DeHaan, R. L. (2005). The impending revolution in undergraduate science education. *Journal of Science Education and Technology, 14*, 253-269.

Domin, D. S. (2007). Students' perceptions of when conceptual development occurs during laboratory instruction. *Chemistry Education Research and Practice, 8*, 140-152.

European Association for quality assurance in higher education (2005). *Standards and guidelines for quality assurance in the European higher education area.* Retrieved April 01, 2009, from www.bologna-bergen2005.no/Docs/00-Main_doc/050221_ENQA_report.pdf.

ECTN (2005). *Newly Appointed University Chemistry Teaching Staff Summer School, Malta, 22-27 June 2005, Proceedings.* Retrieved April 01, 2009, from www.cpe.fr/ectn-assoc/archives/lib/2005/N04/200504_NAUCTS_SumSch_Proceedings_v21.pdf.

ECTN (2006). *Final report working group on teacher/teaching evaluation by students.* Retrieved April 01, 2009, from www.cpe.fr/ectn-ssoc//archives/lib/2006/N05/200612_TeachTeachEvalByStudents.pdf.

ECTN (2007). *Newly Appointed University Chemistry Teaching Staff Second Summer School, Malta, 12-16 June 2007 Proceedings.* Retrieved April 01, 2009, from www.ectn-assoc.cpe.fr/archives/lib/2008/200805_NAUCTS_SumSch2_Proceedings.pdf.

Exley, K. (1999). Key aspects of teaching and learning in science and engineering. In: H. Fry, S. Ketteridge & S. Marshall (Eds.), *A handbook for teaching and learning in higher education* (pp. 265-288). London: Kogan Page.

Gatfield, T., & Alpert, F. (2002). The supervisory management styles model. In: A. Goody, J. Herrington & M. Northcote (Eds), *Proceedings of the 2002 Annual International Conference of Higher Education Research and Development Society of Australasia* (pp. 263-273). Perth: Higher Education Research and Development Society of Australasia.

Gibbs, G., & Coffey, M. (2004). The impact of training of university teachers on their teaching skills, their approach to teaching and the approach to learning of their students. *Active Learning in Higher Education, 5*, 87-100.

Gibbs, G., & Habeshaw, T. (1989). *Preparing to teach.* Bristol: Technical and Educational

Services.

Gregory, C. J. (1980). Effects of training programs for university teaching assistants: A review of empirical research. *The Journal of Higher Education, 51*, 167-183.

Higher Education Academy (2007). *The UK professional standards framework for teaching and supporting learning in higher education.* Retrieved April 01, 2009, from www.heacademy.ac.uk/assets/York/documents/ourwork/professional/ProfessionalStand ardsFramework.pdf.

Hodkinson, S., & Taylor, A. (2002). Initiation rites: The case of new university lecturers. *Innovations in Education and Teaching International, 39*, 256-264.

Johnstone, A. H., & Al-Shuaili, A. (2001). Learning in the laboratory: Some thoughts from the literature. *University Chemistry Education, 5*, 42-50.

Kozyra, P. (2009). *Od ewaluacji nie uciekniesz!.* Retrieved April 01, 2009, from www.chemia.uj.edu.pl/maciejow/skrypt/pdf/1.6_od_ewaluacji_nie_uciekniesz.pdf.

Kreber, C. (2005). Reflection on teaching and the scholarship of teaching: Focus on science instructors. *Higher Education, 50*, 323-359.

Laws, P. M. (1996). Undergraduate science education: A review of research. *Studies in Science Education, 28*, 1-85.

Light, G., & Cox, R. (2001). *Learning and teaching in higher education. The reflective professional.* London: Paul Chapman.

Maciejowska, I. (2008). *Jak kształcić studentów chemii i kierunków pokrewnych? Podręcznik nauczyciela akademickiego.* Kraków: Wydział Chemii Jagiellonian University.

Marsh, H. W. (2002). *Student evaluation of educational quality (SEEQ).* Retrieved April 01, 2009, from cbt.uts.psu.edu/Protected/TestPilot/SEEQ/seeqdemo.tp3? USER_ID=test.

Martínez, M., Gros, B., & Romaňa, T. (1998). The problem of training in higher education. *Higher Education in Europe, 23*, 483-495.

Mullins, G., & Kiley, M. (2002). It's a PhD, not a Nobel Prize': How experienced examiners assess research theses. *Studies in Higher Education, 27*, 369-386.

National Committee of Inquiry into Higher Education (1997). *Higher education in the learning society.* Retrieved April 01, 2009, from www.leeds.ac.uk/educol/ncihe/.

Neumann, R. (2001). Disciplinary differences and university teaching. *Studies in Higher Education, 26*, 135-146.

Newble, D., & Cannon, R. (1989). *A handbook for teachers in universities and colleges.* London: Kogan Page.

O'Connor, C., & Hayden, H. (2008). Contextualising nanotechnology in chemistry education. *Chemistry Education Research and Practice, 9*, 35-42.

OECD (2006). *Good Laboratory Practice. OECD Principles and Guidance for Compliance Monitoring*, Paris: OECD Publishing.

Phillips, E., & Pugh, D. S. (2005). *How to get a PhD. A handbook for students and their supervisors (eth ed.).* Buckingham: Open University Press.

Postareff, L., Lindblom-Ylänne, S., & Nevgi, A. (2007). The effect of pedagogical training on teaching in higher education. *Teaching and Teacher Education, 23*, 557-571.

Race, P. (2001). *The lecturer's toolkit. A practical guide to learning, teaching and assessment.* London: Kogan Page.

Roecker, L. (2007). Using oral examination as a technique to assess student understanding and teaching effectiveness. *Journal of Chemical Education, 84*, 1663-1666.

Stefani, L., & Elton, L. (2002).Continuing professional development of academic teachers through self-initiated learning. *Assessment and Evaluation in Higher Education, 27*, 117-129.

Steinert, Y., Mann, K., Centeno, A., Dolmans D., Spencer, J., Gelula, M., & Prideaux, D. (2006). A systematic review of faculty development initiatives designed to improve teaching effectiveness in medical education: BEME Guide No.8. *Medical Teacher, 28*, 497-526.

Sutheimer, S. (2008). Strategies to simplify service-learning efforts in chemistry. *Journal of Chemical Education, 85*, 231-233.

Taylor, S., & Beasley, N. (2005). *A handbook for doctoral supervisors.* Abingdon:

Routledge.

Tinkler, P. & Jackson, C. (2004). *The doctoral examination process. A handbook for students, examiners and supervisors.* Maidenhead: Open University Press.

Trowler, P., & Bamber, R. (2005). Compulsory higher education teacher training: Joined-up policies, institutional architectures and enhancement. *International Journal for Academic Development, 10*, 79-93.

Universiteit van Amsterdam, Faculty of Science (2007). *Certificate programme in learning and teaching in higher education (BKO).*

Wietecha, R., Mania, J., Woźniakiewicz, M., Madej, K., & Maciejowska, I. (2003). Is this last will fraudulent? - An experiment for the forensic chemistry course for undergraduate students. *Forensic Science International, 136,* Suppl.1, 181-182.

258

Authors

Dr. Keith Adams recently retired from a senior lectureship in Chemistry at the University of Ulster (United Kingdom). As well as teaching chemistry at a range of levels on a wide variety of courses, he was strongly committed to course development and particularly to the incorporation of industrial placement. To this end he undertook significant roles on university committees dealing with student placement and developed strong links with the business community. During his career he has published research and secured grants for his main research interests which have been in the acquisition of personal transferable skills by students and in the computer-aided assessment of chemistry. The University recognized his contributions through the award of a distinguished teaching fellowship in 2003.

Dr. Gustavo Avitabile is Professor of Macromolecular Chemistry at the University Federico II of Naples (Italy). He has taught Chemistry for over 40 years, ranging from introductory courses for Chemistry and Biology majors to advanced courses in polymer science. His research fields have been X-ray crystallography and polymer phase structure. His current interests include the use of computers in learning, University - High school interactions and the public awareness of science. He has worked on ECTN projects to develop EchemTests at pre-university level and to produce a website "What is Chemistry" for the general public.

Dr. Marcus Bäumer is professor of Physical Chemistry and Materials Science at the University of Bremen (Germany). His research focus is surface science and catalysis. As a dean of studies, he was intensively involved in the implementation of a new bachelor curriculum in chemistry in 2005. Together with Ingo Eilks, he received the University of Bremen award for excellence in teaching and its innovation in 2006 for the development of a new lab course in general chemistry with elements of cooperative learning. With a strong inclination to teaching, he is particularly interested in new forms of teaching and learning as a means to improve education at the university level.

Dr. Stuart W. Bennett is a senior lecturer at The Open University (United Kingdom). After gaining BSc and DPhil degrees at the University of Sussex, he taught and carried out research at universities in New Zealand and the USA. His earlier research in nitrogen fixation and organometallic chemistry has now given way to research in science education which parallels his work in innovative approaches to teaching. In recognition, he gained the Royal Society of Chemistry Higher Education Teaching Award in 2000 and Galen Education Award in 2001. He has chaired the editorial board of the journal *University Chemistry Education,* the Royal Society of Chemistry Tertiary Education Group and recently completed a three year term as President of the Education Division of the Royal Society of Chemistry. He is now chair of the editorial board of *Chemistry Education Research and Practice.*

Dr. Natasa Brouwer is a senior consultant in university science teaching at the University of Amsterdam (The Netherlands). Her background is in organic photochemistry. After completing her PhD she focused on chemistry education and later on science education. Her special interest is the use of ICT in science education. She coordinates the training programme of newly appointed lecturers at the Faculty of Science at the University of Amsterdam. She was previously a member of the ECTN working group on developing independent learners in chemistry.

Dr. Bill Byers is a senior lecturer in Chemistry at the University of Ulster (United Kingdom). He has taught chemistry on a variety of courses from sub-degree to postgraduate level to a wide range of students studying many disciplines for over 30 years. His initial research interests in bioinorganic and environmental chemistry have given way to an interest in improving pedagogy. He has been head of different working groups within ECTN, e.g., dealing with developing independent learners in chemistry. He has received a number of awards for his teaching including the 2002 Royal Society of Chemistry tertiary education award.

Dr. Stefano Crocchianti received his PhD in Chemistry in 1997 working on accurate quantum calculations of observable properties for reactive atom diatom systems and is at present research scientist at the University of Perugia (Italy) where he teaches General Chemistry, Informatics and Chemistry on Computers. His research activity focuses on the theoretical and computational study of chemical reactions and on the production of innovative algorithms for the solution of molecular problems on serial, massively parallel and distributed platforms. He works also on the development of models for the simulation of the production of secondary pollutants in the atmosphere and in laboratory experiments as part of his ECTN activity.

Dr. Ingo Eilks is a professor in Chemical Education at the University of Bremen (Germany). Following a period as a grammar school teacher of chemistry and mathematics, he became involved in the field of chemistry teacher education and commenced research in the didactics of chemistry. His main research interests are in cooperative learning, the promotion of process oriented skills, and studies about science teachers' and science student teachers' beliefs and knowledge. He was actively involved in redesigning and restructuring the Chemistry study programmes at the University of Bremen to comply with the Bologna Process. He has received a number of awards for his research and teaching including the University of Bremen award for excellence in teaching and its innovation jointly with Marcus Bäumer in 2006. He has been head of different activities within ECTN, e.g., a working group on the link between secondary schools and universities.

Dr. Noelia Faginas Lago is research assistant in Theoretical and Computational Chemistry at the University of Perugia (Italy). She graduated from Salamanca in July 1998 and worked as a research assistant in Bielefeld (Germany) in 1999. Her research interests are in the field of

theory and computations on molecular dynamics and gas phase reactive scattering in collaboration with the University of Barcelona (Spain). She is currently a member of the ad hoc EChemTest Committee of ECTNA for level 4 tests.

Dr. Odilla Finlayson is a senior lecturer of Science Education at the CASTeL, School of Chemical Sciences, Dublin City University, (Ireland). She teaches courses e.g. in Chemistry for in-service and pre-service second-level teachers and physical chemistry to undergraduate chemistry students. Her research interests include effective teaching methodologies to engage students (at all educational levels) in conceptual understanding of science, particularly chemistry. This includes inquiry methods, problem-based and research-based learning, effective assessment of curricula, teacher education - both pre- and in-service, sustaining science across school level to university transitions.

Dr. Michele A. Floriano is a professor of Physical Chemistry at the University of Palermo (Italy). He teaches undergraduate and graduate level courses in basic physical chemistry as well as statistical mechanics and computational chemistry. He also teaches courses in didactics of chemistry for prospective school teachers. He is currently coordinator of the Image of Chemistry working group of ECTN, vice President of the Italian Chemical Society, a member of the management committee of its didactics division and coordinator of the Italian agency for the award of the Eurobachelor and Euromaster labels.

Dr. Osvaldo Gervasi is a researcher in Computer Science at the University of Perugia (Italy). He teaches architecture of computer networks, virtual reality languages and the related laboratories to computer science students. His research activity is concerned with the development of virtual reality tools and middleware instruments for computing grids. He has also been engaged in producing tools for learning management systems some of which have been used for ECTN activities.

Dr. Martin J. Goedhart is currently professor in Mathematics and Science Education at the University of Groningen (The Netherlands). He is head of the Department of Education in the Faculty of

Mathematics and Natural Science. He is also affiliated to the University Centre for Learning and Teaching and the Institute for Teacher Training at the University of Groningen. His research interests include the relationship between research and teaching, the teaching of academic skills in universities, and the role of language in science teaching at secondary and tertiary level.

Dr. Leo Gros is professor of Chemistry at the Hochschule Fresenius, University of Applied Sciences, Idstein (Germany). He has taught chemistry since 1981 with emphasis on Analytical and Polymer Chemistry. He is vice-president for international affairs at his university and placement officer for the department of Chemistry and Biology. Leo Gros has been head or member of various international working groups in ECTN and IGIP and serves as a Bologna expert of DAAD (German Academic Research Exchange Council). Over the past 15 years he has contributed to the development of an international placement network for chemistry students (UNIC) and a series of EU-funded projects to foster chemistry teaching, placements and mobility in a European context.

Dr. Antonio Laganà is professor of General and Inorganic Chemistry at the University of Perugia (Italy) where he teaches Computational Chemistry, Informatics, Chemistry on Computers for Chemistry students and Computing and Networked Applications and Elements of Atomic and Molecular Structure for Computer Science students. His research activity is concerned with the development of ICT tools for handling and producing chemical knowledge. He is at present director of the Chemistry Department of the University of Perugia where he has also directed the Computer Centre. He has been Chairman of the Italian Computational Chemistry Group, the Technical Committee of the COST Chemistry European initiative and its Action D23 (METACHEM). He is at present a member of the board of the European Division of the Computational Chemistry of EuCheMS, a member of the Domain Committee of the Chemistry and Molecular Science and Technology domain of COST and a member of the international committee of the Theoretical Chemistry and

Computational Modelling Euromaster. He has also served as a member of the Administrative Council, vice-president and president of the European Chemistry Thematic Network Association (ECTNA) as well as chairman of its "Multimedia for teaching and learning chemistry" working group.

Dr. Sari Lindblom-Ylänne is professor of Higher Education and director of the Centre for Research and Development of Higher Education (YTY) at the University of Helsinki (Finland). Among other functions she is currently president-elect of the European Association for Research on Learning and Instruction (EARLI).

Dr. Iwona Maciejowska is an assistant professor in the Department of Chemical Education, Faculty of Chemistry, Jagiellonian University in Kraków (Poland). Her research interests focused on chemistry, photochemistry and kinetics of coordination compounds; nowadays she is also involved with chemical and environmental education. She is the author of many educational materials, designed for chemistry teachers at both secondary and tertiary levels of education. Since 2000 she has been running educational training courses for newly appointed university teaching staff. She is currently the Vice-Chair of the Division of Chemical Education in EuCheMS.

Carlo Manuali is the head of the Scientific Computing Services Office and Security Manager in the Department of Mathematics and Informatics, University of Perugia (Italy). At present he is also studying for a PhD in Computer Science. He has worked in the past in the Computer Centre of the University as a network and systems manager. He is a senior professional licensed engineer in information science and collaborates with a specialized Informatics magazine in the field of Operating Systems. He is member of the ad hoc ECTN EChemTest Committee and bears responsibility for its IT Services Management.

Dr. Silvija Markic is a secondary school teacher in chemistry and will become a lecturer in science education at the University of Bremen (Germany) from summer 2009. After training to become a grammar school teacher of chemistry and mathematics, she decided to follow a career in the field of chemistry teacher education and commenced research on the didactics of chemistry. Her research interests include science teachers' beliefs and pedagogical content knowledge, linguistic issues in chemistry education, cooperative learning and alternative teaching methods.

Dr. Claire McDonnell is a lecturer in organic chemistry at the Dublin Institute of Technology (Ireland) where she has taught since 2000. She completed a Postgraduate Diploma in Third Level Learning and Teaching there in 2006 which included a module on designing online learning. Her research interests relate to analysis of organic reaction mechanisms and to implementation of effective methods to support learners in chemistry. Pedagogic methods used include online support and assessment, project-based learning and community-based learning. Claire Mc Donnell previously worked with an ECTN working group on developing independent learners and was awarded a DIT President's Commendation for Excellence in Teaching in 2005.

Dr. Tina L. Overton is professor of Chemistry Education at the University of Hull (United Kingdom) and Director of the Higher Education Academy Physical Sciences Centre. She worked in industry and the NHS before entering academia. She has published on the topics of critical thinking, context and problem-based learning and on the development of problem solving skills and has co-authored several textbooks in chemistry. She has been awarded the Royal Society of Chemistry's Higher Education Teaching Award and Tertiary Education Award and is a National Teaching Fellow.

Dr. Christiane S. Reiners is professor of Chemistry and Chemistry Education at the University of Cologne (Germany). She has taught chemistry as well as the didactics of chemistry on a variety of courses from sub-degree to postgraduate level to a wide range of chemistry student teachers. Her initial research interests focused on epistemological aspects of science and the question of how teacher education can be improved by authentic learning practices. She has been vice-rector of the University of Cologne and is currently serving as the National Representative for Germany on the IUPAC CCE committee.

Dr. Antonio Riganelli is at present Senior EH&S Specialist at Dow Europe in Zurich (Switzerland). He previously worked as a research associate at the University of Perugia (Italy) where he taught a course on multimedia to computer science students. His research interests have been concerned with the development of multimedia tools for supporting the teaching and learning of natural sciences and he has developed multivariate software for the optimization of industrial food components. He has also been engaged in developing libraries for the EChemTest of ECTN.

Dr. Sascha Schanze is a professor of Chemistry Education at the Leibniz University, Hannover (Germany). He previously taught mathematics and chemistry at secondary school. His principle research interest focuses on collaborative inquiry learning and in particular on the use of computer-based learning environments. Further research has involved the use of cognitive tools like computer-based concept mapping as a reflective tool in learning processes.

Dr. Michael K. Seery is a lecturer in Physical Chemistry at the Dublin Institute of Technology (Ireland). He teaches students from first to final year degree level. His research interests are in the area of semi-conductor photocatalysis. His pedagogic interests include implementation of problem-based learning in a laboratory setting using context-based scenarios and the use of e-learning for teaching chemistry. In addition, he is currently completing a masters degree in third level learning and teaching, examining the role of prior chemistry learning on subsequent performance at undergraduate level. He was involved, e.g. in the Newly Appointed University Chemistry Teachers and the Innovations in Chemistry Teaching working groups of ECTN.

Dr. Anthony K. Smith is a Professor of Chemistry and Director of International Relations at the Lyon School of Chemistry, Physics and Electronics (CPE Lyon), Lyon, (France). After having worked in the United Kingdom, Australia and France with a research focus in the area of organometallic chemistry and catalysis he shifted his interest towards the European dimension of higher education in chemistry. Since 1997 he has been the co-ordinator of the European Chemistry Thematic Network (ECTN), a network of over 160 European University Chemistry Departments and National Chemical Societies concerned with all aspects of higher education in chemistry. This has involved a number of different Thematic Network projects since this network has been successful in attracting funding since the inception of the Thematic Network action. He has participated in many Socrates-Erasmus and Leonardo da Vinci projects concerning higher education in chemistry. He was a member of the management committee and Chemistry Subject Area Group of the project 'Tuning Educational Structures in Europe' and from 2002 – 2004 President of the European Chemistry Thematic Network Association (ECTNA). In 1996 he received the UK Erasmus prize for the development of a degree programme for chemistry with languages and a student exchange network with 18 European chemistry departments.

Dr. Doris Sövegjarto-Wigbers is a scientific assistant in the Centre for Environmental Research and Sustainable Technology at the University of Bremen (Germany). Her research interests involve toxicology and environmental chemistry, particularly in relation to occupational health. She is the coordinator of the environmental management system (EMAS) and author of the sustainability report of the University of Bremen. She coordinates a sixth form course "green chemistry" at the University of Bremen and further courses in chemistry for pupils and teachers. She was appointed to the German Committee on Hazardous Substances (AGS) by the Federal Ministry of Work and Social Affairs in 2005.

Dr. Ray Wallace is professional placements manager for the School of Science & Technology at Nottingham Trent University (United Kingdom). Additionally he is a principal lecturer in the Department of Chemistry where he has taught and researched for almost 30 years. His initial research interests in heterocyclic chemistry have given way to student focused activities aimed at enhancing their potential as graduate scientists. His interests range widely from good practice in industrial work placements, curriculum development, presentation skills through to designing icebreakers to encourage networking! In 1999 he was honoured by the Royal Society of Chemistry Education Division by the presentation of their Higher Education Teaching Award for 'establishing the Diploma in Industrial Studies which gives formal recognition to the value of a period of sandwich training in industry and for subsequently promoting, at national level, the benefits of this aspect of learning.'

Iain Wilson worked as a member of the Advanced Materials Research Group at Manchester Metropolitan University (United Kingdom) until recently. He was involved in basic skills education before obtaining his BSc degree at Manchester Metropolitan University. Later, he spent a period in industry before returning to continue research. His research interests are in the fields of zeolite adsorption of pollutants and mesoporous silica oxides' uses as templates for crystalline nanorod growth. He has now moved into secondary education Chemistry teaching.

Dr. Paul C. Yates is academic staff developer in the Centre for Professional Staff Development at Keele University (United Kingdom). He is involved in providing training to new lecturing staff and research student supervisors. Prior to this he worked for thirteen years as a lecturer in Physical Chemistry. He is currently chair of the Tertiary Education Group of the Royal Society of Chemistry and Vice-Chair for Western Europe of the Division of Chemical Education of EuCheMS. Since 2003 he has been leader of the ECTN working group on Newly Appointed University Chemistry Teaching Staff, which has held two successful summer schools.

Index

Breinigsville, PA USA
04 January 2010
230092BV00012B/1/P